DAN MURPHY

Australian
Wine
THE COMPLETE GUIDE

Sun Books · Melbourne

Sun Books Pty Ltd
South Melbourne, Victoria 3205, Australia

First published as
The Australian Wine Guide 1966
Reprinted 1967, 1968 (twice)
Revised edition published as
Australian Wine: The Complete Guide 1970
Reprinted 1974
Copyright © D.F. Murphy 1966, 1970
National Library of Australia
card number & ISBN 0 7251 0114 8

Set in Intertype Times

Printed in Hong Kong

PROLOGUE

In my introduction I mention the
fact that a wine book rapidly becomes out of date. In the
four years since this book was first published Australian
winemaking has developed rapidly. Some of the things I
suggested in the book have been adopted, not I feel because
I suggested them, but simply because the natural development of wine in Australia made them inevitable.

Probably the greatest difference I have noticed in the
last four years is the intense interest taken by people who
are not even remotely connected with the wine trade. This
is expressed in more startling terms by those amateurs who
have set up their own vineyards and plan to make their

own wine. Since this is a most hazardous business which could cost such adventurers an enormous amount of money in losses, I can only assume that it is the relentless urge created by love of wine which is the cause. Obviously hope of profit has nothing to do with it. The same love of wine has caused thousands of Australians to put down small fortunes in the way of vintage clarets and ports. In some cases the person who does this must be aware that the fruit of all his endeavours can only be enjoyed by his heirs.

Thus encouraged, I have endeavoured once again to produce a book, the sole purpose of which is to give people a basic knowledge of wine and Australian wine in particular.

I wish to acknowledge with gratitude the frequent instruction, the helpful advice and the useful information I have received over the years from John Brown, John Davoren, Colin Haselgrove, Cyril Henschke, George Kolarovich, the Morris family, Colin Preece, Eric Purbrick, Max Schubert, Tom Seabrook, George and David Sutherland Smith, and Eric Thomson. The illustrations have been kindly supplied by the Department of Trade & Industry, Wine Information Bureau, and S. Wynn & Co. Maps are by M. S. Godfrey.

I extend my heartfelt thanks to my wife, Beryl, who never flagged in the wearying task of perusing and assessing every line.

INTRODUCTION

I SHOULD hate to think that anyone who reads this book should believe that I am endeavouring to set myself up as a final authority.

Admittedly, I use the first person and quote my own opinions extensively. My reason for this is that I do not wish my thoughts and ideas to be expressed as though they were truths agreed upon by all.

In Australia there is no fixed body of opinion on wine and its uses. It ill becomes anyone to lay down categorical laws and to define terms as if he were quoting from accepted authorities.

This may be fine in books on European wines. In Australia, we have not yet built up an acceptable tradition on the types, qualities and use of Australian wines. No doubt, at some time in the future we shall have such a tradition. However, the intense interest shown in wine as a cultural occupation has been a phenomenon only of recent years.

It is, therefore, obnoxious for any person to set himself up as a sole authority and to pontificate on such things as to the wine one should have with particular foods and where the best wine comes from in Australia. One is entitled only to have an opinion on these things and to back it with reasons.

The Australian Wine Board, it is true, does issue quite a deal of propaganda on these and other questions, all designed to promote the sale of wine. The prevalent tag for example, 'Drink what you like with what you like', is definitely slanted so as to induce people to drink more wine. Whether it will is extremely doubtful, but an author of a book on wine is not concerned with whether his effort sells more wine or not.

Any man who writes on wine in Australia must only be expressing his own ideas. We are only in the process of building up an independent culture in Australia whether it be in the field of art, music, literature or social habits such as the drinking of wine. Our culture, though modelled on that of Europe, must be so tempered by our environment, economic conditions, racial mixture and a host of other factors as to be completely different from that of Europe.

Should anyone disagree with me, he will not be able to say that I claim to be speaking with the voice of authority. The only authority I shall use will be that of experience. I have studied the subject intensively all my life, listened attentively to the opinions of others with many years in the trade and drunk a lot of wine thoughtfully. It is inevitable that I should give my opinions from a winemerchant's point of view.

In the final analysis, only men in the trade can speak with any degree of knowledge about wine. There are many fine amateurs of wine, with much experience and good minds; but you must be at wine all day and every day to know it thoroughly. For the amateur, time is the limiting factor.

A book on a subject such as wine is only as up to date as the day of its publishing. Winemakers die or retire and a wine company's products begin to deteriorate; or a small firm goes out of production. Another company will suddenly improve its products. An area might quickly come into prominence because of a variety of factors as Coonawarra did in 1950 when Wynn's took over and set it up as a wine producing area of importance.

Therefore I have to face one of the most discouraging aspects of writing a book on culture in a rapidly developing country. That is, that barely has my book been printed than some of the facts are outdated, some of the opinions discredited and many of the axes I have had to grind have been ground, or some of the improvements I have suggested have already been put into practice.

For example, the policy of having the vintage year on bottles of claret was opposed for many years by all major wine companies for very sound reasons. Even ten years ago practically no wine firm used the procedure. Journalists advocated the practice for a long time. Suddenly, almost overnight, it became common. Any book that deplored this gap in our wine labelling is out of date.

Wine books often laud the practice of copious daily drinking of less than average quality red or white wines – or what the French call, 'vin ordinaire'. I disagree with the philosophy implied. To my mind wine drinking is part of civilized life. The Italian, French and Spanish peasants might find that their daily bread would be quite insufficient if it were not bolstered up by the intake of cheap wine which is in itself a food. This is not so in Australia where we have plenty of food much cheaper than wine. There is, therefore, no excuse for the drinking of poor wine at all, and hardly any for drinking wine in copious quantities. If we are to put anything into our stomachs let it be pleasing to the palate on the way through.

Wine drinking is a product of leisure.

More than that, it is at the basis of our civilization. It is part of our culture. It is conceivable that other cultures can exist without wine; but not so the European culture which we have inherited with European laws and language, and European philosophy and religion.

The vine was present at the birth of European civilization. It forced the nomad to become an agrarian because it rooted him to one spot. This established the community and the community was the core of social life. Once fixed in a community the early European built himself an abiding dwelling. In his leisure time he studied methods of improving his dwelling and making it more decorative. And so we had the beginning of European architecture and art.

With the growth of the community were developed social entertainments – folk songs and folk dancing, the telling of stories by poets and the acting of scenes of war and heroics by groups of histrionically minded villagers.

And with this, all the time, was the drinking of wine. There were the leisured hours after the day's work when the community sat down to its evening meal and sipped at the beverage that promoted peace and relaxation and stimulated conversation and prompted ideas that produced paintings and sculptures and theatre and literature.

The early Europeans invented for themselves gods of wine and fertility. Later the tendrils of the vine decorated their paintings. Grapes were carved in the stone of their cathedrals; wine became an integral part of their culture. They could not think of life being lived pleasantly without it.

Wine, too, was a major topic of conversation at the long end-of-the-day meal. Its colour was appreciated. Its bouquet praised. Its variances of flavour remarked upon.

And so through the ages up to the present time wine drinking has held a unique place in the culture of the European.

This is a natural development. The innate urge for the soothing influence of alcohol is a characteristic of the human race. It has found expression in all temperate climates in the making of wine. Where the climate was so cold that grapes could not ripen, man made cider and beer. Naturally, wine is the first alcoholic beverage known to man, because it is the simplest to make.

Wine is more wholesome than any other alcoholic beverage. It has a high nutritive value, can carry no germs and is the perfect accompaniment to a meal. Beer, indubitably, is nourishing but in the form in which we drink it in Australia as an aerated beverage it is not suitable for use with meals and in some conditions has an irritating action on the alimentary canal.

Wine is meat and drink to the average Frenchman and Italian. There is no doubt that were it not an alcoholic stimulant as well as a food it would lose its place with them as the primary beverage. It cannot be denied that alcohol is considered by the bulk of mankind to be a harmless palliative beneficial to man. In European countries this benefit is combined as food and drink in wine. The trend in wine drinking seems to indicate that this will one day be the state of affairs in Australia.

We can enjoy wine in two ways. First we can enjoy its flavour and the pleasant sensation it creates. Secondly, we can add to this an intelligent appreciation of its beauty. This is the art of the wine lover.

Wine is fundamentally a canvas on which are painted an endless variety of pictures. Wine, too, being the only beverage that blends perfectly with food, it is natural that it should become the drink over which we dwell during and after the main meal of the day.

Wine becomes the object of appreciation, just like any other work of art. Other beverages strive for consistency of flavour. Wine differs from bottle to bottle. Therefore, every glass can be discussed at length just as we might discuss a hand-carved table.

Part of the work is supplied by nature – like the wood in the chair. The artistry is contributed by the artist – the woodcarver or the winemaker.

Each wine is distinctive because of a multitude of factors: the grape variety from which it was made, the soil, the climate, the season, the maker himself, the length of time in the bottle ... Its colour will differ from dark purple to walnut brown or from the palest green to deep gold. Its bouquet will bring reminiscences of flowers and fruits, of cedar and spices. Its flavour will excite because of its depth of penetration into the palate or because of its evanescence. A district will be recognized or its affinity with the dish will be admired.

The perception of good wine from bad is not a natural gift. It is the result only of experience. But it is not the prerogative only of experts to know wine. It is the sphere of the normal educated man who prides himself on his mode of life. He has the right to nominate his favourite painter or his favourite wine because of his personal experience of paintings or wine.

Finally, it is well to remember one thing – wine is made for our enjoyment. Fundamentally, there is no other reason for its creation. A bottle of red wine with a smoking plate of roast beef and baked potatoes is one of the simple pleasures of Australian life. No knowledge of wine is required; no fear of doing the wrong thing is present; no artistic appreciation of the qualities of the wine need be noted. Eating and drinking are the most natural pleasures in the world. Drinking wine with food is simply pure enjoyment.

To come home after a hard day's work and to anticipate the evening meal is one of the rewards of the toiler. To anticipate a glass or two of wine with that meal is an added reward that only the constant wine drinker knows.

With food, wine tastes good, feels good and has a pleasant effect. There is no pleasure simpler than that.

> Alcohol unwinds us. It raises the threshold
> of sensation and makes us less sensitive to
> external stimuli, and particularly to those that
> are unpleasant. It reduces and simplifies the
> emotions. Putting a brake on all the qualities
> that enable us to get on in the world and shine
> before our fellows — for example, comba-
> tiveness, shrewdness, diligence and ambition
> — it releases the qualities that mellow us and
> make our fellows love us — amiability, gener-
> osity, toleration, humour and sympathy.
> G. K. Chesterton

1 WHAT IS WINE?

WINE is an alcoholic beverage
made by fermenting the juice of grapes.

What is the magic of alcohol? Without doubt, potable
alcohol is one of nature's greatest gifts to man.

Alcohol, taken moderately, dulls the sense of awareness
and care. It lessens the feeling of urgency of things that
have to be done, abolishes the nagging of worry, overcomes
anxiety and mental stress, relaxes our minds, makes us think
less of our problems, tends to eliminate selfconscious-
ness and shyness, thus breaking down the barriers of social
restraint and promoting conversation. It imparts a great
sense of relaxation and well-being to both mind and body.

Having consumed it, we usually feel happier and more cheerful. We are less apt to be unpleasant, nagging, ill-tempered and irritable. Consequently, it makes us more sociable people, more congenial, more pleasant companions, more tolerant husbands and wives and more understanding parents.

Unfortunately, all these benefits last only as long as the effect of the alcohol. Once it is passed we revert to our former selves. If we used alcohol to dull our sense of responsibility all day long, we should become fairly unstable citizens. If we always refused to face up to our problems we should become rather dull failures. If we were always content with our lot, we would never strive to make it better. Too much alcohol can convert the pleasant companion into the bore. All told, however, alcohol performs a useful function. It gives us a daily pause – a little freedom from the unpleasant things we have to put up with. In itself, it is not habit forming, is easy to take, operates swiftly and leaves no harmful effects.

Wine is an alcoholic beverage. It would not be interesting unless it were so. It is obvious that wine can be drunk at any time simply as such. However, the wisest drinking of wine is based around a meal. Fundamentally, it must be considered with food. Wine has always been made to go with food and the winemaker designs his wine for the meal. He makes wines which serve as an introduction to a meal (aperitives), wines that go with the meal itself (table wines) and wines that serve as a finale (dessert wines).

Wine is the fermented juice of grapes. As grapes grow almost everywhere in the temperate zone, except in the very high altitudes, it is possible to produce wine almost anywhere between the polar circle and the tropics.

But, if one with great toil and trouble attempted to make wine in Scotland or northern Canada or Norway, he would discover that the product was too low in alcohol to keep more than a few weeks. This is because there is not enough heat in the summers to give the grapes an opportunity of reaching full maturity.

Table grapes do not as a rule produce good wine. Good

table grapes are large and fleshy. Good wine grapes are small.

Soil suitable for growing the best wines is not, as a general practice, regarded as rich farming soil. Often it seems rather arid and stony. The nature of the soil has a determining influence on the character of the wine, so much so that identical grapes planted in the Hunter Valley, Rutherglen and say, the Rhône Valley of France, yield wines of widely different types.

The finest species of vines have a small yield. Hence it does not pay to grow them except in the most suitable soil.

Australian Winemaking Procedure

There are numerous varieties of grapes grown throughout Australia. About fifty varieties are used for winemaking. De Castella, who was one of the world's greatest authorities on grape varieties, discovered hundreds of varieties and sub-varieties not listed by the statisticians. However, the main types used and included under the common names by the grape growers are:

Sultana (mainly for distillation)
Muscat (Gordo Blanco)
Grenache
Doradillo
Shiraz (red) or Hermitage
Pedro Ximines
Semillon
Mataro
White Shiraz or White Hermitage
Palomino
Waltham Cross (mainly for distillation)
Rhine riesling
Frontignac
Muscat (excluding Gordo Blanco)
Madeira
Sherry (Albillo)
Tokay
Cabernet Sauvignon

When the grapes are ripe, which in Australia could be in late January or right through to May, they are hand picked. Some wineries are planning to install machine picking, but it will be some years before this is perfected.

The degree of sweetness varies with the seasons and from district to district. The grapes are checked periodically for sugar content as ripening time approaches. This content varies from as low as 9° to 12° for riesling to 16° to 18° for muscatel. The measuring instrument is a Baumé hydrometer which records the density of the juice. One degree of sugar shown on the Baumé hydrometer will produce one per cent by volume of alcohol in a fully fermented wine.

The pickers are recruited from all sources. Very often they are the members of the grape growing families, their workers and their neighbours. This small force is supplemented by casual workers from all over Australia and by office workers, factory hands and students on holiday who combine the change of atmosphere in the sunny vineyards with the chance of earning extra money.

The pickers go down the lines of the vines with scissors, clip the grape clusters and rapidly fill their buckets. These are emptied at the end of each row into horse or tractor drawn trays and finally loaded on to trucks which deliver them to the various wineries for crushing.

On arrival at the wine cellar, the grapes are weighed over a weighbridge, the varieties checked and the winery Baumé test taken. Grape growers are paid according to the variety. Rhine riesling will receive a much higher price than doradillo, for example. However, the Baumé content must be satisfactory to the winemaker before he will accept the grapes. The trucks tip their loads into hoppers and the grapes are conveyed by a moving belt to the crushing machine.

There are various types of crushers. In Australia, the most common type is the 'beater'. It consists of a large horizontal, coarsely-perforated cylinder. Inside, beaters or paddles rotate and smash up the bunches of grapes into pulp. They force the burst grape berries through the holes in the cylinder and, as the blades are set slightly off centre, the stalks, which cannot go through the holes, are forced out of one end of the crusher and carried away by another moving belt.

This is rapidly being replaced by crushers which treat the grapes much more gently. Probably the most popular is the one known as the 'roller' type. It consists of two large fluted rollers so positioned as to leave just enough room for the crushed grape to pass between. The distance between the two rollers can be adjusted depending upon the size of the bunch of grapes so that the fruit is merely given sufficient pressure to break the skin and to allow the juices to flow out without causing any bruising of the skins, stalks or seeds. This means that none of the bitter ingredients, such as oeno-tannin, are permitted to enter the 'must' apart from the natural absorption which occurs during the maceration before and during fermentation.

Attached to this type of crusher there is an attachment which consists of a rotary hub to which is fixed a series of prongs set at an angle. This is rotated through the crushed bunches and because of the eccentric movement of the prongs, the stalks are thrown out of the mass and clear of the crusher. The stalks are removed by means of a conveyor belt to be carried away and disposed of by truck.

Beneath the crusher is located a sump, usually of concrete coated with wax, into which the crushed grapes fall.

The crushed berries, which are now called 'must', comprise the juice, pulp, skins and pips.

The must is drawn through a hose by means of a 'must pump' to the fermenting vats.

If the grapes are red, the must is pumped directly into a fermenting tank.

Tremendous advances have been made in recent years in the treatment of the must at this stage. The old vats of bricks, concrete and wax are being replaced by those which are more neutral, more easily cleaned, subject to prophylactic treatment and able to exclude air. Hence winemakers, if they can afford it, are now using stainless steel or plastics of the polyester or polyvinyl group to form

the material for must sumps, fittings for hoses and fermenting tanks and for any other type of container in which
the must rests, and fittings with which it comes in contact.

If the grapes are white and the intention is to make
a dry white wine the juice is extracted from the skins and
seed. This is usually performed by means of a so-called
'air bag' press. Winemakers usually prefer to leave the skins
in contact with the juice for some hours before the grapes
are pressed in order that some of the flavour and tannin
from the skins and seeds is imparted to the juice. Where
a very fine white wine is desired the juice is passed to
a 'pre-drainer'. This is either of stainless steel or steel coated
with plastic resin and it looks like an inverted pyramid,
so that the full pressure of the crushed grapes becomes
more concentrated as the lower point of the tank is reached.
The grapes in effect therefore serve as their own press and
a most efficient extraction of juice is obtained. This juice
is then passed to the fermenter and the remaining skins
and seeds, still containing a quantity of juice are passed
through presses of some type or other and used for other
purposes such as distillation.

Fermentation
Fermentation is begun by adding what is known as a 'yeast
starter'. Yeasts belong to a broad group of vegetable growths
which do not contain chlorophyll and are, therefore,
unable to manufacture their own food. Yeasts are
simply-constructed plants, having only one cell. Each cell
consists of a transparent elastic sac enclosing a jelly-like
substance called protoplasm. When the yeast is supplied
with an abundance of nutrient material, it grows vigorously
and multiplication takes place at a rapid rate. This occurs
usually by budding or germination.

Budding consists of a bulging of part of the cell wall
and the pressing of part of the cell contents into the bulge
which is formed. This is the bud. As the bud grows the
wall between it and the mother cell constricts and finally
closes and there are two distinct cells. And so the process
keeps going as long as there is sufficient nutrient material.

During this period of multiplication chemical substances produced by the yeast and known as enzymes act on the sugar in the must and convert it into nearly equal parts of alcohol and carbon dioxide gas. This whole process is known as fermentation.

The multiplication of the yeasts and the bubbling of the newly produced carbon dioxide gas cause a disturbance in the must which is similar to boiling. Fermentation comes from the Latin word *fervere,* to boil.

Yeasts are living plants. They provide the mechanism (enzymes) to begin and operate the series of chain reactions which is fermentation. While this series may be of great interest to the chemist, it is far too complicated for the amateur wine lover to examine very closely. Fermentation is merely an operation in which the nature of sugar is changed so that other substances are formed. These substances are mainly 'ethyl' alcohol and carbon dioxide gas.

Fermentation in the form we have described can occur with any sugar, for example, cane, fruit, honey and malt sugars and, in fact, all these sugars are fermented to produce beer, fruit wines and mead. Further, the result of the fermentations can be distilled to make whisky, gin, rum, brandy and vodka.

Grapes carry yeasts on the skins of their berries. Therefore if the berry is burst open the yeasts can begin operating on the sugar and fermentation will commence. It can be seen, therefore, that the making of wine is the simplest of all alcohol-forming processes.

Pressing

As we saw above, pressing is a process whereby the juice of the grape or the newly made wine is extracted from the mass of skin and pips and residue of yeast cells. Since this mass will settle by the mere fact of its weight to the bottom of the fermentation vat after fermentation, quite an amount of wine can be pumped off or cocks can be opened in the fermenting vat to allow it to drain off freely. This first extraction of wine is known as the 'free run'. The residue of solid matter will still contain a considerable amount of wine and so it is forked on to a conveyor belt or extracted from the fermenting vat by mechanical means and taken to the press where this wine is forced out. The extract is then known as 'pressed' wine. Sometimes a pressed wine is sold as a separate product. More often, it is mixed in with the free run to give the latter more character and, if it is a red, more colour.

Ageing

When first made, most wine is harsh and yeasty to smell and taste. It must be left for a while in order to soften and to lose the yeasty character. Wine is always pleasant to drink; even when it is first made it has a great appeal to the wine lover ... But at certain stages of its life it is better than at others. There is a definite optimum period when it is at its best just as there is a period when a man is at his 'prime'.

The winemaker's task is to start the wine off well; to attend to it at its birth or fermentation and to see that everything proceeds without danger to the wine; to nurse it along in its infancy by seeing that is not attacked by harmful bacteria; and to give it every chance of maturing well and lasting a long time.

Having done this, he hands it over to a merchant who becomes the new guardian and must give it the care and protection it needs as a growing child.

Finally, it passes to its last owner who treats it with reverence and is the one who will enjoy the charms and delights that have gradually been developing.

Sections into which Wine may be Divided

There are many divisions into which we could separate wine for the purposes of discussion. Certainly, the major division as far as economists and statisticians are concerned is into 'fortified' and 'unfortified' wines.

A fortified wine is one to which alcohol has been added in its preparation as a beverage. Fortified wines in Australia are sold as sherry – sweet and dry; port; white port; frontignac; muscat and vermouth.

Unfortified wines are also known as natural wines because nothing has been added to them; and as table (or dinner) wines.

However, because wine is primarily designed by the winemaker to be drunk with a meal, we can more satisfactorily discuss wine under the headings of:

1. Wines to be drunk before a meal
2. Wines to be drunk during a meal
3. Wines to be drunk after a meal
4. Wines to be drunk at any time.

Wines to be Drunk Just Prior to a Meal

In some circles these are known as 'aperitive' or 'appetizer' wines. Aperitives are not necessarily used as an introduction to a European meal. They are usually short, sharp drinks flavoured with herbs which are used at any time of the night or day. Sometimes they have a wine base; sometimes a spirit base.

Appetizer wine is designed to prepare us physically and psychologically for a meal.

At the end of the day, it will soothe the troubled mind, settle the nerves and allow the gastric juices to flow as they should. So with mind and body relaxed we are ready to approach the coming repast with zest and eager anticipation.

In addition, appetizer wine should prepare the palate for food. It cleanses, refreshes and stimulates all nerve ends and taste buds so that our sense of taste is keener. Meanwhile, in the nether regions the gastric juices and wine are preparing the stomach for the task of digesting the food.

Wine blends perfectly with food and consequently, no disturbance in this area can be expected with a normally healthy digestive system.

Nearly any dry wine could be used as an 'appetizer' wine. The word 'dry', of course, simply means 'not sweet'. Under this division we could include dry sherry, dry vermouth, dry champagne, dry white table wine, 'aperitive' port, dry madeira, and dry red table wines.

The enthusiastic and constant wine drinker, naturally,

uses all the above-named wines for the purpose of a before dinner drink. Very few wine drinkers, however, use table wines as appetizers. In Australia the overwhelming popular vote for an appetizer wine is sherry.

Wines to be Drunk During a Meal

These will usually, but not necessarily, be unfortified wines because they are intended to be drunk in quantity and it would be impossible to have more than a small glass or two of, say, sherry with a meal.

The purpose of table wines is to provide the diner with the perfect accompaniment to his food. It is a matter of blending the flavour of the various dishes with the various wines presented. Table wines must achieve a perfect balance of flavours with the food and at the same time create in the diner a sense of relaxation and well-being.

They are called table wines because they are meant to be drunk at table and carry a multitude of designations such as riesling, chablis, claret, burgundy and sauternes.

Wines to be Drunk After a Meal

These are called dessert wines because they are intended to be drunk with or just after the dessert. Just as with an appetizer wine the intention is to stimulate the taste buds and to make us eager to partake of food, so with a dessert wine the intention is to dull the taste buds and to make us content and happy to leave the table feeling that we have had enough.

Dessert wines bear titles such as port, muscat, madeira, tokay, frontignac and marsala.

Wines to be Drunk at any Time

Strictly speaking any wine can be drunk at any time, but if we are to give these wines a particular function then we are left with other wines which perhaps could be used in a vicarious fashion to substitute for the above-mentioned wines when the occasions arose.

For example, champagne can be used equally well before, during and after a meal. Sparkling burgundy is a wine which could be substituted for a dry red wine during a meal. The Pearl wines are used by some people as a general purpose wine and some of the sweet types of wine such as Spaetlese Riesling are difficult to fit into any of the above categories. Nevertheless, each of these wines can be used for a variety of circumstances not least being the celebration of any happy event such as the birth of a child, the end of a war or the beginning of a very happy friendship. They might be used, for example, with a piece of cake or a biscuit in the mid-afternoon, or as a sort of social and continuing drink during the evening with cards, interesting conversation or any of those other pleasurable occupations engaged in by people in the evening.

And thou shalt give me health, life, long existence and a prolonged reign; endurance to my every member, sight to my eyes, pleasure to my heart daily. And thou shalt give me to eat until I am satisfied and thou shalt give me to drink until I am drunk.

Prayer of Egyptian King Rameses IV to the god Osiris

2 APERITIVE WINES

THE WORD 'aperitif' comes from the French word which simply means appetizer. It is strange that the French have over the years given a slightly different meaning to the word from the original and from what the English understand it today. They also use it to cover the snack type of food which they like to offer to guests before the entrée or soup.

Their aperitives as liquor are in some cases the very opposite to what Anglo-Saxons would regard as appetizers. For example, to a Frenchman, port is an aperitive. To an Englishman, port is only to be drunk at the end of a meal. All European nations have drinks which they call aperitives and which are not necessarily intended to be drunk before a meal, nor are they necessarily intended to stimulate the appetite ... such drinks, for example, as Dubonnet, Violet Byrrh, Amer Picon, Pernod, Saint Raphael, Ricard Pastis, Martini Elixir, Campari and the Mecsek Bitters of Hungary which are all classified as aperitives and yet more often they are drunk in the middle of the afternoon or during the long evenings of summer, while sitting at the little tables situated on the boulevards or in the piazzas or in the village square. They are more or less something to sip at while one indulges in conversation or talk of love.

Be that as it may, in English terminology an aperitive wine is still an appetizer wine and therefore it must cleanse the palate, stimulate the taste buds and start the gastric juices flowing. For this reason there must be as little sugar as possible in it because sugar coats the palate with sweetness and takes away the appetite.

There must be a certain amount of acidity because this brightens up the nerve endings and there must be a certain amount of tannin because this creates a feeling of astringency in the mouth which has a cleansing and drying effect on the palate.

Many wines could be called aperitive wines therefore because they possess all these characteristics. Perhaps the most magnificent of them is a first class brut champagne. We must remember that part of the function of the pre-prandial drink is to create a feeling of relaxation of mind and body. Any alcoholic beverage can create this condition, but not every one has the ability to prepare the palate for the meal. Dry champagne is fairly high in alcohol, is without sugar and has a most cleansing and refreshing effect on our tongue and interior surfaces of the mouth. The only difficulty is that it is always expensive.

Dry vermouth, or for that matter, any vermouth could be described as aperitive wine. Vermouth is simple to make if you know the ingredients. To make dry, or as it is sometimes called, French vermouth, you need a dry white wine in which you infuse a variety of herbs, the chief and most distinguished of which is the one known as wormwood. This herb is derived from the wormwood tree which in Germany is called 'Vermut', a most interesting bush, for from its roots, its sap and its leaves are derived the pervading, powerful and overwhelming aroma which is detected in so many alcoholic beverages. At one stage it was used for making Pernod which in those days was called *Pernod Absinthe*. In this case the flavoured element was derived from the roots of the vermut tree and Pernod Absinthe was used extensively in all countries of the world, but particularly France. However, since it tended to create addicts and its effects were most devastating on the human body, causing blindness and insanity, practically every country in the world banned its sale and that is the position today.

The extract which we call essence of wormwood, derived from the leaves of the same tree, is harmless and is used more than any other herb in the liquor industry. In addition, there are various spices and herbs derived from roots, leaves, sap of various trees and from wild flowers, blossoms, bark and so on. These include angelica, coriander, anise and peppermint.

The vermouth maker, therefore, is a specialist in his own field and he keeps close the secrets which he has had handed on to him by his family or in the confines of the laboratory of his organization. His aim is to produce a wine which is pleasant, spicy, stimulating and appetizing. The famous vermouths of the world originated in France (such as Noilly Prat) and Italy (such as Martini Rossi Vermouth).

Sweet, or as it is also called, Italian vermouth, is made from a dark wine which is either naturally or artificially sweetened. It is heavier in body than the wine used for dry vermouth. Sweet vermouth is spiced in the same way as the dry vermouth by allowing herbs and other interesting ingredients to be soaked in the wine for a period of time.

Still another variety is called Bianco. This is simply a white vermouth similar to the dry, but in this case it is sweetened.

Australia has slavishly followed the styles created by the French and the Italians, but they have done it extremely well. In my opinion the best vermouths we have are made by Wynn's under the name of Boronia, by Cinzano and by Angove's.

Still another aperitive wine is dry white wine which I shall deal with under the heading of white table wine. This has the attributes that we look for in any aperitive, but obviously a small, sharp drink with a fairly high percentage of alcohol is more useful for the purpose than anything else. What we want in an aperitive wine is simply a vehicle whereby we are transported from a state of tension, frustration and ill temper to a state of tranquillity, restfulness and bon homie and with a cleansed and zestful palate. Probably this is the reason why the English nation has adopted sherry as the aperitive par excellence and why Australia has followed England in its choice.

Dry sherry simply is an oxidized dry white wine. It is an ideal appetizer wine because a small glass contains enough alcohol to perform the psychological function of a before-dinner drink; it has a pleasant, penetrating flavour and a strong pungent bouquet; it contains elements which make it astringent, freshening up the mouth, eradicating all other flavours we might have accumulated on our jaded palate such as nicotine, petrol fumes and bad office air; and leaving us with a tongue that is cleansed and stimulated. One small glass of good sherry is not very filling, nor unduly 'heady' and, therefore, does not interfere with our intended consumption of table wines during the meal.

Types of Sherries made in Australia

The wine student will notice the frequent use of Spanish words in the nomenclature of Australian sherries. For example, there are flor, fino, amontillado, oloroso, solera or solero, jeropiga, manzanilla. Do not be deceived. These names do not necessarily mean the same as they do in Spain.

Australia has had to coin a new language for its wines and it has filched from European wine districts a great number of their terms. Very often the connexion is nebulous.

The word 'amontillado' as applied to a Spanish sherry means usually that it has been kept in wood for some years, is darker in colour than a 'fino' (the palest of Spanish sherries), and is not quite as dry as a fino. In Australia a variety of sherries appear under this name. The wine-makers of the different companies obviously have different ideas as to what colour it should be. However, they are unanimous on the point that it should be a medium dry, i.e. neither very dry nor at all sweet. In this they seem to be more uniform than the Spaniards who are as diverse in the degree of sweetness as we are in that of colour.

I have ignored, therefore, the Spanish meanings of these terms and dealt with the wines as we see them in Australia. Glossing over the great diversity of labels, I have divided sherries into the following main classes:

1. Top quality flor sherry,
2. full bodied sherry,
3. medium sherry,
4. brown sherry,
5. sweet sherry.

You will observe that we proceed from sherries that have no sweetness at all to those that are full of sugar. Some makers may have sherries which do not fit easily into the above classes but, on the whole, these are the types that are selling in quantity in Australia.

Top Quality Flor Sherry

Variously described as pale, dry, delicate, this is the highest grade sherry made in Australia. A good fino sherry is very dry; it should have plenty of flavour; it has a good, strong bouquet; it should be 'nutty', that is it should have the clean crisp flavour of nuts; it should be fairly astringent, which means it should roughen the surfaces of the tongue and back of the throat so as to cause a 'dry' feeling; it should leave a pleasant flavour on the palate after it has been sipped. In short, it should be sharp, clean, crisp and penetrating, leaving a satisfying sensation in the mouth.

All the large companies make a 'fino' sherry under the 'flor' process. I have chosen what I consider to be the best and listed them below. All told they are very similar to each other, being made of first quality material by skilled winemakers. Some are less dry than others.

Some merchants in the capital cities blend up their own 'fino' sherries from sherry material supplied by the makers listed below. These blends are usually successful and up to the standard of the ones I have listed. Although the finos are similar to one another there is just that little difference which makes one preferable to a selective drinker rather than any other.

Examples of top quality flor sherry:

Angove's	*Fino Dry*
Buring's	*Florita*
Lindeman's	*Fino Flor*
Mildara	*George & Supreme*
Orlando	*Barossa Fino*
Penfold's	*Pale Dry Fino*
Quelltaler	*Granfiesta*
Reynella	*Bone Dry & Alicante Flor*
Seabrook's	*Special Pale*
Seppelt's	*Pale Dry Solero*
Stonyfell	*Private Bin Fino, Extra Dry*
Tintara	*Flor Fino*
Wynn's	*Romalo Flor Fino*
Yalumba	*Chiquita*
Sutherland Smith	*Old Reserve*

Full Bodied Sherries

As a sherry ages in the cask it oxidizes; it acquires much of the flavour of the wood; and it undergoes quite a number of chemical changes. All of these factors result in the sherry's acquiring a much more pronounced flavour and heaviness of body. The old method of making sherry in Australia (prior to the flor method) necessitated much more ageing in wood than the flor sherries of today.

Consequently, sherries made in Australia prior to the Second World War were of the full bodied type. This style has gone out of favour.

The lists of the wine stores are not likely to show many

full bodied dry sherries. Nevertheless, there are a few available. There are a number of private binnings by the larger companies and some of the old established wine merchants in the cities have some.

They can be very interesting sherries for the person who has adopted wine as his hobby. High quality flor sherry of the 'fino' type cannot be kept long in wood because it tends to 'oxidize' and become 'bigger' and is therefore no longer true to type. The basis of all full bodied sherries today is probably fino sherry that has become too big by ageing in wood.

Some districts are such that wines produced in them tend, by their very nature, to become full bodied. Rutherglen is such a district. Hence the sherries made by Sutherland Smith, Morris, Chambers and Campbell are normally of this style although each one of these can produce excellent flor finos under modern methods. These fuller types provide excellent blending material and give character to lighter styles.

The wine lover who buys these will usually keep them in his own cask and freshen his blend from time to time with younger sherry.

Seppelt's market special bottlings of their old Rutherglen sherries and good wine merchants usually hold a few of the Rutherglen sherries from the makers I mentioned above.

Medium Sherries

These sherries appear under a multitude of names. Perhaps 'amontillado' is the most popular. A medium dry is simply a dry sherry to which a sweet fortified wine has been added. The blend is matured for some time in wood.

This is our largest selling section of sherries, perhaps because it covers the medium price range. Nevertheless, there are some extremely fine sherries to be found among them. Almost all are either made on the 'flor' system or are blended with flor sherry (and then of course, with the sweetening material).

The colour of these medium drys varies from a deep golden amber to a very pale straw.

The best examples of these medium sherries are:

Buring's	*Granada Dry*
Castle	*Spanos Amontillado*
Cohn's	*Three Palms Amontillado*
Hamilton's	*Amontillado*
Lindeman's	*Amontillado Flor*
Orlando	*Australian Medium*
Penfold's	*Mantilla Dry*
Reynella	*Del Pedro*
Seppelt's	*Dry Solero*
Stonyfell	*Pepita*
Tintara	*Amontillado*
Wynn's	*Romalo Amontillado*
Yalumba	*Four Crown*

Brown Sherries

Aged for many years in the wood, these are heavy bodied rich wines with plenty of oak character. They are all slightly sweet and all deep brown in colour. This sweetness and the brown colour undoubtedly comes from the addition of a concentrated juice from the pedro grape. This is called 'jeropigo'. Yet they are not what we would normally call 'sweet sherry'. There is a certain firmness about them, a certain 'grip' which takes them into the appetizer class in spite of their sweetness. Some of the wine merchants have blended up magnificent sherries of this style.

These sherries are much more interesting than the finos, having many more facets for the wine lover to discover. They are closely allied to the full-bodied style which I have dealt with separately.

Angoves	*Old Brown*
Buring's	*Supreme Oloroso*
Mildara	*Chestnut Teal*
Yalumba	*Autumn Brown*
McWilliam's	*Fine Old Hanwood*

Sweet Sherries

Sweet sherry in Australia is almost synonymous with other

wines called white port, muscat or madeira. There are a few made by the method of adding a sweet neutral fortified wine to a dry sherry and allowing the blend to mature in cask.

Generally, however, sweet sherry is simply a sweet fortified wine made from one or more of the following varieties of grapes: Gordo blanco, doradillo, frontignac, albillo, tokay, pedro or palomino.

The grapes named above are usually the only types used for sweet sherry although sometimes a winemaker may use some of the lesser known types of white grapes such as sultana, white shiraz, madeira and marsanne.

The use of the name 'sherry' as applied to this type of wine has been severely criticized by purists; but English is a living language and since millions of bottles of 'sweet sherry' are sold every year in Australia, we must accept the term as being incorporated in the language because of common usage. The chief objection to its being called sherry is that the wine is not made according to the sherry method.

In the making of sweet white fortified wines, the grapes are crushed and pumped to the fermenting tank. The skins are left in the vat during fermentation usually only for a short time, although this depends on the maker. Some makers prefer to extract colour and other determining characteristics from the skins by leaving them in the ferment until the end.

More commonly, the fermenting juice is run off the skins and pips early in the fermentation.

As the fermentation proceeds the sugar is rapidly transformed and the winemaker watches progress very closely by testing for sugar and alcohol content. At the stage of sweetness required he adds sufficient fortifying spirit to stop fermentation. This spirit is the distillation of suitable dry wine. Therefore, in a sweet wine, all the sugar is the natural grape sugar and of the spirit, part is produced from the fermentation of the juice and the remainder is from the distillation of other wine,

The fortified sweet wine is stored in oak casks. Small

casks give the best results and as the wine ages it becomes more mellow and the colour is inclined to darken.

As in dry sherry, sweet sherries are blended to a standard. This produces a continuity of style for a wine marketed under one particular label.

As may be expected, the various sweet white fortified wines maturing in the cellar will vary from each other because of seasonal and vineyard difference; because of the variety of grapes used and because each wine will behave differently in different oak containers. The art of the blender is to blend wines of different character to achieve the desired style and quality.

Sweet sherries, then, as dry sherries, are intended by the maker to be drunk as soon after marketing as possible. If they are kept too long in bottle they will tend to vary from standard.

A sweet wine, however, ages in bottle more graciously than a dry sherry. It will tend to soften and acquire viscosity and in general to improve. The danger is that it will probably throw a deposit. Since this is most undesirable in a glass of sweet sherry, it is not a good practice for the consumer to keep his sweet sherry for any length of time.

Sweet sherry could hardly be called an 'appetizer' wine, since it contains a great deal of sugar which is the enemy of appetite.

There is a tendency to call some sherries 'cream' sherries. These are merely a different style of sweet white fortified wine. For some peculiar reason the larger makers, like Penfold's and McWilliam's who popularized this style by advertising, have put out a wine that is very pale in colour, very strongly grape flavoured and without any woody characteristics.

I cannot see that this style can have any permanence in public favour.

The best sweet sherries are marketed under the following names:

Buring's	*Granada Sweet*
Orlando	*Special Sweet*

Castle	*Pastilla*
Penfold's	*Mantilla Sweet*
Reynella	*Hunting*
Seppelt's	*Sweet Solero*
Tintara	*Gold Label Sweet*
Wynvale	*Amber Sweet*

Objects of the Sherry Maker

The sherry maker is concerned with producing a beverage from a dry white wine which is aromatic in flavour, is fairly high in alcohol, has a typical 'sherry' flavour and bouquet and is consistent from bottle to bottle and from year to year.

He achieves this

1. by using special sherry making material,
2. by oxidation and the production of acetaldehyde,
3. by fortifying with spirit,
4. by ageing in cask,
5. by blending,
6. by asking the consumer to drink it as soon as possible after he has offered it for sale.

SHERRY MAKING MATERIAL

Sherry material is white wine in which fermentation has consumed all the sugar present in the original must and we are left with a wine which contains about 11° by volume of ethyl alcohol. The quality of the sherry will depend very much on the type of grape used. The best varieties for this purpose in Australia are pedro ximenes, palomino, semillon and doradillo.

OXIDATION

Oxidation is a chemical change involving the gain of oxygen or the loss of hydrogen. Many elements in wine are subject to oxidation e.g. tannin oxidizes and a precipitate forms and falls out of the wines; sulfurous acid oxidizes to sulphate; higher alcohols are converted to acids and acids combine with ethyl alcohol to form esters; many elements that are derived from the grapes themselves are oxidized;

the colour of the wine tends to darken and go brown because of oxidation. However, the main oxidation change is that of ethyl alcohol to acetaldehyde.

Acetaldehyde is a sweetish liquid with a strong and readily identifiable odour.

Let us return for a moment to fermentation. Fermentation is a long chain of reactions whereby grape sugar is converted to almost equal parts of ethyl alcohol and carbon dioxide gas.

During this process, acetaldehyde is produced in a reaction involving a substance called pyruvate. The last link in the chain is where acetaldehyde accepts hydrogen and produces ethyl alcohol.

In the making of sherry the process is being reversed. Ethyl alcohol is gaining oxygen and is changing to acetaldehyde. Eventually this acetaldehyde will be converted to acetic acid and acetic acid will be converted to water.

The complete evolution will take many years. In the meantime the sherry maker is concerned with the growth of acetaldehyde to give his wine the typical 'sherry' flavour. The production of acetaldehyde by oxidation of alcohol, while it is not the only reaction in the making of sherry, is a very useful measure.

The sherry maker determines from time to time by chemical means how much acetaldehyde has been built up. In a wine which contains 500 parts per million of acetaldehyde it has a pronounced odour.

FORTIFICATION

All wines, including sherry, are subject to the spoilage action of yeasts, moulds and bacteria. If ethyl alcohol at a very high strength is added to wine so that the total strength is about twenty per cent by volume of the wine, all this activity is considerably inhibited.

The alcohol so added is distilled from wine and is known as 'rectified spirit' or 'fortifying spirit'. It cannot be called brandy since it is distilled at so high a strength that all flavours which would remind us of the grape are removed.

AGEING IN CASK

Oak is the best wood in which to age wine. In small oak containers the sherry clarifies more satisfactorily and in addition acquires a slight 'woody' character. Bouquet also develops well in oaken containers. The average oak cask is rather porous. This enables air to enter through the sides of the cask and the oxygen it contains is absorbed by the sherry, thus bringing about the oxidation changes we have described above.

BLENDING TO A STANDARD

Clarets, burgundies, hocks and other table wines may differ from year to year or even from bottle to bottle. The wine lover will not complain; in fact, he will be delighted. This, he expects. But if his sherry should vary just a little from what he is used to – caveat oenologist – let the winemaker take care. Whisky, beer, gin and sherry must always taste the same.

For every label indicating a sherry made by his company the winemaker has a set standard. When the product leaves the winery he is very careful to ensure that it is consistent with what it has been from the day it was first marketed.

He keeps standard sherries always on hand and he makes these standards his target. He watches quality, colour, flavour and bouquet, tannin and acid content.

The sherry maker takes sherries of various ages and from various vats as his 'raw material'. He blends these to his standard. Since he has access to the same sherry material as he used from the beginning of a certain blend, it is not too difficult for him to arrive at his standard. His sherry materials are made from the same grapes; the same processes are employed; the same casks are used.

Particularly in the first quality range, this may result in a most complicated series of blends. He will have to use very old sherry material to give the wine character and softness; he may have to add younger material to give it life and crispness.

From this it can be seen that sherry is the most blended of all wines.

SHERRY IS MADE TO BE DRUNK
AS SOON AS IT IS MARKETED

We have seen in the brief description of winemaking and ageing given above that chemical reaction is going on continuously. This is a good thing and something for which the claret drinker is looking.

If sherry is kept in the bottle it will undergo oxidation changes. After a while it will be different from the product which left the winery. Beer is in a similar category. Old bottled beer has no merit. It tends to taste 'worn' with a slight honey flavour. The same thing happens with sherry.

Sherry, however, being heavily fortified with spirit cannot acetify or re-ferment (not for a very great number of years, at any rate). But it will deteriorate from the standard that was set by the maker if it is kept for very long.

Sherry is brought up to perfection by the maker and is meant to be drunk as soon as possible after it has been released to the market.

Very old cask-aged sherries have been developed which acquire great body and woody character. Even these have to be 'freshened up' with a little younger wine to make them drinkable. There is no point at all in keeping sherry in bottle.

Methods of Making Sherry in Australia

THE 'OXIDATION IN CASK' METHOD

Before the 'flor' process became popular in Australia all sherry was made under this method. It consists of taking a fortified dry white wine with a fortification of between nineteen and twenty per cent, drawing it off the lees or deposits which have fallen to the bottom of the vat and 'racking' into oak casks of about sixty-five gallon capacity.

These casks, called 'hogsheads', are stored in the warmest part of the winery until the wine is considered sufficiently aged. This may take anything from one to five years according to the quality of the wine and the opinion of the winemaker.

During this period the wine is taken off the precipitated lees once a year and the casks are not completely filled so that an ullage, that is, an air space between the level of the wine and the top of the cask is formed.

The result is that the wine oxidizes, builds up aldehydes and takes on some of the flavour of the wood in the cask.

The longer it is left on wood the 'bigger' or more full bodied and full flavoured it becomes.

THE 'FLOR' METHOD

'Flor' is only the Spanish word for flower and refers to the yeast film which 'flowers' on the surface of the wine during the development of the sherry.

Dry white wine destined for the flor sherry process is fermented in the normal way so that hardly any sugar remains. If the alcohol in the wine is too low, vinegar bacteria may gain the upper hand and turn the alcohol into acetic acid. Consequently, fortifying spirit is added to bring the strength to fourteen or fifteen per cent by volume of alcohol. The wines are racked (taken off the lees) after fermentation and may remain for a year or so before they are put under 'flor'.

Some winemakers place the selected material in oak casks of about sixty-five gallons capacity. Others prefer to settle it in large concrete vats lined with wax and covered with glass or wooden ceilings. As with all other winery processing it will not be long before stainless steel vats will be the only type used.

The 'flor' process is commenced by spraying the surface of the wine with a special culture. This special culture of 'flor' yeast is kept in cold storage in winemakers' laboratories or in Wine Institutes. It is very similar to the yeast which effected the original fermentation of the grape juice; but instead of operating in the depths of the liquid, it grows over the surface, appearing as a skin or film.

This film is greyish or chalky white in colour and may be somewhat rough and wrinkled. It is continuously forming.

The film yeast requires plenty of air to thrive. There must be plenty of air space, therefore, above the surface of the wine. The yeast will also consume large quantities of oxygen from the wine itself. The result is that in the depth of the wine, conditions are what the chemist calls 'anaerobic' – little oxygen is present.

This means that, although oxidation processes are going on at the surface, oxidation in the body of the new sherry is practically nil.

The characteristic of 'flor' yeast growth is the rapid production of acetaldehyde. This is so because yeast activity results in the production of aldehyde in the course of converting sugar to alcohol and because alcohol is converted back to aldehyde by oxidation.

This series of conversion and reconversion can result in the somewhat odd phenomenon of aldehyde being at a high level one day and a lower level the next, but of course the ultimate result is a fairly heavy build up of acetaldehyde. When this build up has satisfied the sherry maker and the wine has acquired the desired amount of flor character, it is further fortified with rectified spirits to bring the total content of alcohol up to eighteen or nineteen per cent.

The sherry is then transferred to oak hogsheads where it is further aged for two years or more.

This entire process results in a sherry which has a characteristic 'nutty' flavour, and none of the flat, worn or 'oxidized' flavour of a wine much exposed to air.

Thou waterest the hills from thy upper rooms
that thou mayest bring bread out of the earth
and that wine may cheer the heart of man.
Psalm ciii

3 WHITE TABLE WINES

Wines that are to be drunk with food or during a meal are called 'table wines'.

They are called 'white' or 'red' depending on the type of grape they are made from and are usually called 'dry' because they are not sweet.

Sometimes they are termed 'natural' wines. This is because they are made from the juice of grapes which has been allowed to ferment completely without addition or interference of any kind.

They are known under a variety of names – 'riesling', 'hock', 'moselle', 'chablis', 'white hermitage', 'white burgundy'. Quite often these names seem absurd when an analysis is made of their original meanings. Some of the companies seem to be completely confused. They label white wines with all sorts of odd titles which under the name of another company are quite different things.

One day something will have to be done about this naming of wines.

This present section includes wines called 'sauternes', 'graves', and 'late-picked riesling' although these are sweet and therefore barely come into the category of 'table' wines which are traditionally dry. These styles fit more easily into the section 'dessert wines' since these should be drunk after a meal.

However, I am including them here because many people drink them with meals and I wish them to be distinguished from fortified dessert wines such as 'white port' and 'muscat'.

The Making of White Table Wines

Let us return to the winery for a while and see what is the procedure in the making of these wines.

The main varieties of grapes used are 'semillon', 'clare riesling', 'Rhine riesling', 'white hermitage', 'pedro' and 'palomino'. These are well suited for making table wine. Some makers, on the other hand, are using varieties which, before table wine began to move upwards in popular demand, were used only for fortified sweet wines. These are 'gordo blanco', 'sultana', 'frontignac', 'madeira' and 'tokay'. The latter will not make *first class* table wine but, nevertheless, a good vigneron can make a fairly high average grade wine from them.

Smaller quantities of first grade wine are made from varieties known as 'pinot', 'marsanne', 'chasselas', 'traminer' and 'montils'.

The grapes, then, are fed into the crusher and after crushing and stemming are called 'must'.

Winemakers treat the must in one of three different ways, each way depending upon the equipment at their disposal and the quality of wine they wish to make.

Under the first method, the winemaker ferments the must right through to completion. The 'free run' wine is pumped off into vats and allowed to complete its slow bubbling as fermentation carries on in a much milder fashion.

The skins and pips are pressed until all the wine in them is extracted. These 'pressings' are sometimes added to the 'free run'. At other times they are kept aside for making sherry.

The vigneron who uses this method in making white table wine would be very small and would have no 'still' for distilling wine material not quite suitable for selling as wine. Nor would he be close enough to a distilling plant so that he could sell his unsuitable material.

He is concerned with fermenting every ounce of sugar that is in his grapes. Sugar is alcohol and alcohol is money. He does not wish to waste anything at all that could be fermentable.

The result will be that he will not have a wine of very high quality. The 'free run' wine will have too much colour and too much of the extracts from skins and pips. If he makes a sherry from the pressed wine it will probably be fairly coarse.

However, he can reasonably expect that there is a sale for his product at a fairly low price.

In the second method, the winemaker ferments the must for a short time on the skins. He draws off the 'free run' of fermenting juice into a separate vat and allows fermentation to proceed in this container. The remaining pips and skins are pressed and the resultant wine from them is either distilled or used as sherry-making material.

This method of fermenting on the skin for several hours results in an extraction of a considerable amount of tannin and soluble solids. The excess tannin aids in later clarification with gelatin and can be removed. This type of wine will have more colour and more character than that made from juice alone. It is likely to age more satisfactorily and to last longer than the latter wines.

In the third method the winemaker sometimes consigns the crushed grapes immediately to the press (either the hydraulic or the 'bag') * and presses all the juice out of

*See chapter on Technically Talking.

them. Usually he allows the juice to remain in contact with the skins for some hours before he puts it through the press and extracts the juice. He ferments the pure juice until completion and finally runs the newly made wine off the lees into settling tanks.

His intention is to make a wine with little colour but with great fragrance and refinement. If he is using a high quality grape he is likely to arrive at a wine that has much floweriness of bouquet and extraordinary delicacy of flavour.

Types of Australian White Table Wines

It is sufficiently accurate to divide white wines into two general styles, 'acid' and 'non-acid'. Australian winemakers endeavour to produce both these styles irrespective of the district in which the grapes are grown. They are largely successful in doing this, but naturally they have their greatest successes in making a style that suits the area.

The Swan Valley of Western Australia, for example, produces a big soft wine made into a style called by the makers 'white burgundy'. This is a most successful and beautiful wine. The sharper, firmer types made in this area are not successful.

ACID STYLE

These are variously named 'riesling', 'hock', 'moselle', or are named after the grape variety such as 'white hermitage'. The winemaker's intention is that they should be picked as early as possible in the ripening period so that there is a high percentage of acid in relation to the sugar in the must. The resultant wine will be high in acid. This gives freshness and crispness to the wine.

The wine named 'moselle' seems to have created a great deal of confusion in the minds of wine companies. One will present to the public a highly acid, metallic, firm wine distinguished from a dry 'riesling' only by the fact that it has a certain fruitiness akin to a faint sweetness. Another company will market a 'moselle' which is sugary and almost as sweet as 'sauternes'.

'Riesling' has a great diversity of interpretations. Wines

carrying the name on the label might have been made from the riesling grape. In Australia, the true riesling is called 'Rhine riesling'. 'Riesling' could also be a wine made from the 'semillon' which is a grape grown in the Hunter Valley and has for many years been called 'Hunter River' riesling. The wine could also be made from the 'Clare riesling', a grape similar to the Rhine riesling and originally found in Australia only in the Clare district of South Australia.

Finally, 'riesling' could be made from any white grape at all but is called 'riesling' because the maker thinks of this as a style of wine rather than a wine made from a certain grape.

Even here there is difficulty among makers to have them agree as to what style a 'riesling' should be. Some will make a highly tart wine entirely without sugar. Others will make a softer wine, still crisp, but with a considerable degree of sweetness.

The outstanding examples of the best acid style of wine are those made from the Rhine riesling grape picked early. They have a high acidity which makes the wine crisp and clean. There is a pleasant grape flavour about them and a certain amount of fruitiness which gives the middle palate great satisfaction.

However, this style is not at all sweet in the sense of a sugary sweetness. They are fresh fragrant wines with plenty of interest in both aroma and flavour. The 'Rhine' riesling grape makes a wine which, when young, has a scent or perfume similar to the faint smell of soap in water in which you have just washed your hands. As it grows older it loses this 'scenty' aroma and develops an odour which is clean and sharp and something like the smell of a refined kerosene sniffed at some distance.

White wines are more delicate than red, both in flavour and texture. They do not contain as much tannin nor nearly as much colouring matter as reds. Therefore, any defects will show up more obviously.

In white wines above all, then, the skill of the maker is vital. Taking these factors into consideration I nominate the following as the 'acid' style whites which are *usually* above ordinary quality.

Chateau Leonay	*Vintage Riesling & Moselle*
Chateau Tahbilk	*White Hermitage & Riesling*
Hamilton's	*Springton Riesling & Moselle*
Lindeman's	*Hunter River Rieslings & Moselles under 'Reserve Bin' label*
Mt Pleasant	*Riesling & wines from Hunter Valley under varietal names such as Montils*
Mildara	*Golden Bower Riesling*
Orlando	*Late Picking Riesling; Barossa Riesling*
Penfold's	*Dalwood Riesling. Minchinbury Rhine Riesling, Eden Valley Moselle, 'Special Bin' bottlings of Riesling & Moselle, & varietal types such as Traminer, Semillon*
Quelltaler	*Vintage Riesling*
Seaview	*Vintage Rhine Riesling & Vintage Moselle*
Seppelt's	*Arawatta Riesling & special binnings from Great Western*
Hardy's	*Old Castle Riesling & Eden Moselle*
Wynn's	*Modbury Estate Riesling & Moselle*
Yalumba	*Carte D'or Riesling*
Henschke	*Riesling & Moselle*
Tulloch's	*Pokolbin Riesling*
Drayton's	*Riesling*
Elliott's	*Riesling*
Tyrrell's	*Riesling*
Stanley	*Riesling & Moselle*
Kaiser Stuhl	*Riesling, Moselle & Semillon*

NON-ACID STYLE

These are called differently, 'chablis', 'white burgundy', 'graves', 'sauternes', or are named after the grape variety such as 'semillon'.

The maker requires that the grapes be picked later in the season so that there is a high percentage of sugar in the must and the amount of acid is proportionately less. The resultant wine will not have any 'bite' of acidity. It will tend to feel 'big' in the mouth and to be soft and round. If it is called 'graves' or 'sauternes', a high degree of grape sugar will still be present to create a sensation of sweetness.

The outstanding examples are those made from the pinot and chasselas grapes picked later in the season than the acid Rhine rieslings. Although the acid is not obtrusive, it is there in the background and the wine tastes clean and fresh. One gets a tremendous impression of softness and fullness. The grape flavour is not conspicuous; rather one gathers that it is distant and unimportant. As the wine grows older it gets fuller and develops a rich collection of flavours which is similar to a kaleidoscope in a world of taste.

The wine is not as dry as a very dry 'riesling' but there is no sensation of sweetness. Instead the palate is satisfied with a pleasant roundness which seems to fill the taste buds.

'White burgundy' and 'chablis' are interchangeable names, 'chablis' being out of fashion as a name at the present time. In the same way 'hock' and 'riesling' are interchangeable, 'hock' being out of fashion today.

'Graves' is not a popular wine because there are so many other wines which perform its function more happily. It is marketed by some makers as a semi-sweet wine with little acid.

The popular non-acid wine, apart from 'sauternes' with which I shall deal separately, is 'white burgundy'. This is extremely well made in Australia even though it is not as much in demand as 'riesling' and 'moselle'.

The maker of white burgundy or chablis is concerned with getting more flavour into his wine and probably ferments for a short period with the skins in the must. He picks his grapes later in the season rather than with his riesling-style wines so that a greater amount of sugar is present in the berry and the acid is less. Even though acid is not obvious, it is still fairly high in a young wine. This enables it to age very well. Some of the wines of this type made at Great Western both by Seppelt's and Best's have developed after five years into whites of magnificent quality.

Practically every one of the large companies has marketed a 'white burgundy' and I find it hard to think of one that is not first class. Of course, some have stood out head and shoulders above the others.

I believe that the best wines of this type come from Great Western and the Hunter Valley. 'Hunter' white wines are soft and flavourous with very great quality. As 'The Hunter' is warmer than other high quality wine districts in eastern Australia, the grapes tend to ripen more rapidly and to have less acid than in these other areas. The rieslings, therefore, are not very acidic. They are full soft wines which could very well be included in the style with which I am dealing.

North-eastern Victoria produces big soft wines of the type I am describing but to date I consider they do not have the quality which takes them into the 'above ordinary' class.

In general, Australia is more likely to produce 'soft' white wines than the crisp acid types. The summers are long and hot. Grapes always ripen and have an abundance of sugar.

I suggest that the following non-acid style whites are *usually* above ordinary quality.

Best's	*Chablis*
Chateau Leonay	*White Burgundy*
Chateau Tahbilk	*Marsanne*
Hamilton's	*White Burgundy*
Houghton's	*White Burgundy*
Lindeman's	*'Special Bottlings' of Chablis & White Burgundy*
Martin's	*'Special Bottlings' of White Burgundy*
McWilliam's	*White wines from Griffith & Hunter Valley*

Penfold's	*Dalwood Chablis & White Burgundy & 'Special Bottlings' of White Burgundy*
Seppelt's	*Rhymney Chablis & 'Special Bottlings' from Great Western of Chablis & White Burgundy*
Wynn's	*'Modbury Estate' Chablis & White Burgundy*
Hunter River	*Whites from Drayton, Elliott & Tulloch*

SAUTERNES, GRAVES AND 'LATE-PICKED' RIESLINGS
These three are related because they are white table wines which are sweet.

The German word 'spaetlese' simply means 'late-picked'. It is applied to wines made from grapes that are left on the vine long enough to dry out or 'raisin'. The sugar in the grape will develop under the influence of solar heat until it has reached maximum.

Then evaporation of moisture and dehydration will take place. Perhaps rot will set in and breach the skins. In any case we are left with a grape that is practically all sugar.

When these grapes are crushed and the yeasts are set to work alcohol is produced. There is so much sugar, however, that very soon the amount of alcohol produced is greater than the yeasts can tolerate. Hence they die. This is at an alcoholic content of about 14°Baumé.

As all the sugar has not been consumed at this stage, the resultant wine is very sweet.

In Australia, however, it is almost impossible to leave grapes on the vine until they have so 'raisined'. They have a tendency to rot or in other ways to deteriorate before they have been dehydrated. In some districts of Europe the rotting of the grape has no ill effect on the wine. In Australia it completely spoils it.

The Australian winemaker can, nevertheless, make a 'late-picked' riesling. He will instruct the growers of the grapes to leave the berries on the vines until sugar content has built up to a maximum. They will ensure, of course, that no deterioration of the grapes has set in. The winemaker will crush the grapes in the normal way and commence fermentation. As the sugar content of the must is very high he can halt fermentation while there is still a considerable amount of sugar present; but the alcoholic content will not be much less than it would be in an ordinary table wine.

There are many ways of stopping fermentation. Cooling the wine by refrigeration is one way. Allowing pressure to build up in a pressure fermenter is another. Yeast cells can be filtered out through the tight pores of filter pads or by means of a centrifuge; this stops fermentation by eliminating the mechanism of the action; or fermentation could be stopped by adding sufficient sulphur dioxide to kill the yeast. A certain amount of sulphur dioxide has to be added, in any case, to restrain the action of any stray yeast cells which might find their way into the wine which, having so much sugar still remaining, and not sufficient alcohol to inhibit yeast action, is open to such attacks.

Orlando market an excellent wine of this style, as does the Barossa Valley Co-Operative, so also does Yalumba under the label of 'Golden Ridge' riesling, and Buring's under the name of 'Chateau Leonay Late Picked Riesling'.

Nevertheless, my opinion is that this is not one of our good styles. They tend to taste a little thin and grapy, not comparing favourably with rich flavourous 'spaetlese' rieslings of Germany or the soft vinous sauternes of France. However, I must take into consideration that this type of wine is in its infancy, and that undoubtedly new methods will be found which will take us into world class.

For the same reasons our so-called 'sauternes' is a comparatively weak style of wine. Since we cannot make it inexpensively on the 'late-picking' method, we have developed a much simpler way of producing a sweet, non-fortified white.

After a dry white wine has been made in the normal way, pure concentrated grape juice is added. This grape juice is preserved by the addition of a considerable amount of sulphur dioxide and is called 'mistelle' or 'mistella'. The wine so manufactured may contain a sugar content of four per cent or more.

Another method is to add a sweet white fortified wine to a dry white wine. The alcoholic content will then be a little higher than that of an ordinary white table wine but this is desirable, in any case, for 'sauternes' as it will enable the sulphur content to be decreased.

A 'graves' is understood to be a wine that is not quite as sweet as a 'sauternes'. It is made in the same manner as sauternes.

All of the large companies and most of the small make the 'sauternes' type as this is a most popular table wine among those people who have not yet cultivated a taste for dry wines and sales are very great in this section.

A certain amount of proficiency has been acquired and I have no doubt that we shall keep on improving with new methods.

The older a sauternes is the better. Sweet wines mellow very gracefully.

Therefore a proviso of the list below is that the wines should be five years old or more. Good quality examples:

Chateau Leonay	*Vintage Sauternes*
Hamilton's	*Special Reserve Sauternes*
Lindeman's	*Special Bottlings of Porphyry*
McWilliam's	*Mt Pleasant Sauternes*
Quelltaler	*Sauternes, Graves*
Seppelt's	*Chardonnay Sauternes*
Tintara	*Golden Nectar Sauternes*
Wynn's	*Modbury Estate Sauternes*

The Present Fashion in White Wines

Are trends in fashions set by the makers or the consumers? Probably, both in the worlds of 'haute couture' and wine, the manufacturer is the prime mover.

In the matter of white wines, the producer has decided that the consumer wants wines that are young and fresh with plenty of grape aroma and grape flavour. German wine shippers have set this trend in the world and wine consumers seem to relish it.

The natural consequence of all this is that many white wines must be sold young. They are made for this purpose. A wine made from grapes vintaged in April in Australia is on the market in September and should be consumed by the following September. Thereby all the fragrance and beauty of youth is retained. Left any longer, this beauty might sag and fade away.

All the present innovations of white wine making have this early marketing as the motive . . . the cold fermentation, the pressure fermentation, the Wilmes press.

Now this, in my opinion, is a good thing. I can see no point in keeping white wines except for the occasional full-bodied white that acquires some interesting facets to its character from ageing.

The best of this young and fresh style of wine is made from Rhine riesling, semillon or pinot grapes. It is pale gold in colour, sometimes with a tinge of green. It is not altogether dry; the fruit sweetness of the grape comes through on the palate with a lightness as gratifying as a caress – different from the sickly sweetness of a sauternes.

The fruitiness of a grape is incorporated in the structure of the wine. This gives the wine a completeness and a unity which the addition of sugar cannot give.

The grapiness and fruitiness is modified and moulded into palatal shape by acid – a gentle acid that prickles the lips and tongue and sets the nerves on membranous surfaces tingling and smarting. The aroma of these lovely young wines is spicy and volatile. It seeps into the nostrils and through the soft palate filling the olfactory regions with perfume.

Will these wines last as well as those made under the older methods? The question is of not much importance if we intend to drink them young but it is of some moment if we have been left with some stocks of them. There is no doubt that almost every white wine made by modern methods and from the Rhine riesling grape grown in South Australia will age well for many years.

The Fermentation of White Wines

FERMENTING TANKS

White wines in Australia are mostly made in 'closed' vats or tanks. If they were fermented in open tanks they would lose a great deal of their bouquet and flavour.

Fermentation may begin with the skins present in an open vat but after a few hours the fermenting juice is pumped to a closed vat and fermentation completed there. It may take a week for the violent part of the operation but slight fermentation may continue for some weeks.

The small wineries ferment in oaken vats of say three hundred or five hundred gallon capacity leaving a large gap between the surface of the fermenting juice and the top bilge of the cask. The bung will be left out at the top so that the carbon dioxide gas may escape. At times the violence of fermentation will spume froth and yeast out of the bung hole in a lava-like flow over the outside staves of the cask.

Larger wineries may use wax-lined cement tanks covered with ceilings of timber or metal. These ceilings have the same effect as the closed cask of retaining a level of carbon dioxide gas over the surface of the wine and preventing the inroads of bacterial or fungoid organisms. This prevents, too, a wanton loss of fragrance and pleasant odours that are forming with the fermentation.

The best equipped wineries possess fermenters consisting either of stainless steel or of steel tanks lined with a neutral resin or wax. These steel tanks are circular and are completely enclosed on all sides and top and bottom. Adjustable valves allow the escape of carbon dioxide.

CONTROL OF FERMENTATION

One of the natural effects of fermentation is the release of energy in the form of heat. Even in cool climates, temperatures in the fermenting must can build up to ninety degrees and more. Yeasts will operate only within a certain range of temperatures. Outside this range, fermentation stops. Hence, it is very necessary to ensure that temperatures are kept down to a certain level.

In addition to the obvious need to keep the must working, there is the less apparent desirability of keeping it working, at the optimum temperature. This will be a balance between the temperature necessary to keep fermentation progressing at the fastest rate and that in which the volatile esters and flavouring elements will evaporate at the slowest rate. Obviously the lower the temperature the less fragrances and aromas will dissipate.

Wine chemists have calculated that the best results are obtained if a white wine is fermented at a temperature of fifty to sixty degrees Fahrenheit. At eighty degrees and above the bouquet and flavour is impaired.

In Australian wineries many methods are employed to cool the must from that of plunging the must with plates at the end of poles and throwing in blocks of ice to complicated refrigeration.

Some wineries cool their must by pumping it through a 'heat exchanger'. This is a metal apparatus divided into a series of compartments separated by plates. Actually there are two sets of compartments. In one set the warm must is circulating and, in the other, refrigerated brine. The coolant chills the intervening plates which then absorb the heat from the must. The fermenting must, then, is periodically pumped through the heat exchanger back to the fermenter. The disadvantage of this is that any movement of the must through hoses and pumps results in absorption of air and consequent oxidation.

Another way is to have a series of 'immersion' coils set in the fermenting vat. Refrigerated brine is pumped through these coils until the desired temperature is attained. One disadvantage of this method is that the must is cooled in the areas around the coils but not nearly so much in other sections so that an uneven fermentation results.

The most effective method is to place a hollow shell around a steel fermenter and pass a cooling material between the walls of the shell and those of the fermenter. The fermenter, in effect, becomes a refrigerator.

This method is sometimes called 'cold fermentation' although this is not a particularly accurate description since it is the jacket of the fermenter that is cold, not the fermenting must.

Constant vigilance, therefore, is required to control the level of temperature and all well run wineries keep a twenty-four hour watch, checking must temperatures and regulating the flow of refrigerated coolant.

PRESSURE TANK FERMENTATION OR CONTROLLED FERMENTATION

The German originators of this system claimed that by controlling the built up pressure of the carbon dioxide gas created during fermentation, fermentation could be controlled in such a way that the aromas, flavouring elements and other desirable constituents of bouquet could be retained in the wine.

Their theory was that pressure should be allowed to build up, be released and then built up again. This build up and release of pressure is not favoured in Australia. The Australian winemaker aims to keep pressure at about seven atmospheres.

Most Australian wineries have installed pressure fermenters. The tanks are completely enclosed metal containers with pressure dials and a valve which controls the build-up rate of pressure.

A fermentation under pressure results in a lesser growth of yeast. This gives a more efficient production of alcohol and there is, consequently, a greater yield of alcohol per gram of sugar fermented than by normal fermentation. The evaporation of alcohol also is prevented by the pressure of gas and this prevention of loss assists in a greater final alcohol concentration. Because of the inhibiting effect of pressure, pressure fermentations do not always go to completion. Therefore, there is usually a certain amount of residue sugar in these wines.

If the acid content has been high in the grapes at the time of picking this residual sugar is attractive and an addition to the appeal of the wine.

The 'late-picked' rieslings of Australia are made in this way. Pressure fermentation enables grapes fairly high in sugar content to produce a comparatively high yield of alcohol and yet retain sufficient sugar after fermentation to convey quite a sweet impression on the palate.

In spite of this, winemakers in Australia are not all convinced that this method of fermenting is of great advantage over a simple 'cold' fermentation. Basically, 'cold' fermentation performs all the functions of 'pressure' fermentation. It is not to be thought, of course, that pressure fermentation does not require temperature control. The pressure fermenter, too, is encased by a jacket and coolant flows through the hollow shell. The pressure fermenter can be used for other purposes than for making first class table wines. It is employed also for making sparkling wines as we shall see in a later chapter.

METHODS AND PROCEDURES
IN MAKING WHITE TABLE WINE

Most white winemakers today follow similar methods and procedure when they set about fermentation. The object is to keep the temperature of the grapes as low as possible from the moment the grapes are picked and to keep the juice and newly made wine at this low temperature and away from air until the final product is safely enclosed in a glass bottle.

Since the optimum amount of acid is about seven or eight grams to a litre of grape juice, the winemaker today is inclined to pick his grapes based on the acid content rather than the Baumé or sugar measurement of the juice. The longer the grapes are left on the vine after sugar has developed to about 9° Baumé, the more acid tends to be converted and to be lost in the juice. Sugar content will continue to build up as long as the grape is exposed to sunlight and warmth. However, if the winemaker should allow the acid to drop too far he will finish up with a wine that is flabby and subject to the inroads of disease, to rapid oxidation and to more rapid deterioration of the wine in other ways. Acid is the substance which holds his wine together and gives it life and interest. This is so particularly with white wines for the white wine drinker looks for a fairly high percentage of acid to make the wine more interesting, since white wines tend to lack the abundance of flavours which are found more readily in red wines.

The winemaker, if he has sufficient authority, will instruct his pickers to begin their work when the acid/sugar ratio is about 20 to 25. That is a percentage of about .7 of acid and 9° Baumé of sugar.

If it were possible the winemaker would have all his grapes picked in one day. As he cannot expect this to happen he will try to arrange that the crops in the various parts of the vineyards will be examined so that the date of the maturation of the grapes is plotted out on a chart to show the relative maturity of several different sections. For example, it might have been determined in the past that 'A' section will usually have the correct acid/sugar ratio on the 1st February, that 'B' will follow one day later and 'C', one day later than that. This is an ideal sequence, therefore, for the pickers to follow and the winemaker, if all goes well, will receive all his grapes at the correct acid/sugar ratio.

In practice he will find that this cannot be done and he is quite prepared to accept a slight decrease in acid and a slight increase in sugar during the process of picking, but it will not be so great as to interfere with his overall plan and he might finish up with an acid/sugar ratio of 25 to 30 which means that his acid has dropped perhaps to .6 per cent and his sugar has increased to 11° Baumé.

Another hazard the winemaker has to watch is the effect of heat on his newly picked grapes. Not only does heat encourage the growth of bacteria on and within his grapes, but the grape will store the heat in its pulp and skin for many hours and so when they are crushed, stored heat is released in the fermenting juice and raises the temperature of his fermentation to a far higher degree than is desirable. He can counteract this, of course, by using refrigeration but a far more effective way of overcoming the problem is to have his grapes cooled before they are crushed. Obviously there are two ways of doing this. He could have his grapes picked and delivered to his cellar before the heat of the day has become too great, or he could leave his picked grapes in a cool spot overnight so that when they are passed to his crusher in the morning they have lost their warmth.

Picking today has become far more scientific than it was even ten years ago. Far greater attention is given to picking only the best bunches and to discarding the mouldy or frost, hail or rain-spoiled bunches and the grapes are placed into containers which present a neutral surface and carry no deleterious flavours or contaminating elements such as tar, paint, ammonia, and so on, factors which were very often present in the must in earlier times.

The roller-type crusher, which consists of two adjacent fluted rollers made of rubber, between which the bunches of grapes must pass, is considered to treat the fruit gently and to extract the pulp without injuring the seeds and stalks or, for that matter, without bruising the skins. Most white winemakers then immediately transfer the pulp and skins by means of a huge pump and hose to what is known as a 'pre-drainer'. There are very many types of pre-drainers and probably the most successful is the one made by the French firm M.A.C. This is a 'V' shaped tank with hinged doors at the bottom, arranged in such a way that the whole mass can be dropped into a pit simply by opening these doors. The bottom of the tank is perforated so that the juices can drain out without any of the skins or solids.

Most of the large companies cover the whole process with a layer of inert gas such as carbon dioxide or nitrogen. This is to ensure that air comes in minimum contact with the juice and one might say that from the moment of crushing and consignment to the pre-drainer, air is completely excluded until the finished wine is bottled.

The pre-drained juice is used only for top quality white table wines. It is fermented separately in a pressure fermenter or in a refrigerated tank. The pressure fermenter is in itself temperature-controlled and is fitted with agitators which stir the fermenting wine so as to ensure that the whole body of the wine is kept at the same temperature.

Because of the lack of warmth in the fermenting must and because of the inhibiting effect of the carbon dioxide gas which is kept at a pressure of about 30 pounds per square inch above the surface of the fermentation, fermentation is very slow and it sometimes takes up to 30 days before it is completed.

In the larger wineries the newly made wine is transported through plastic tubes to a settling tank, once again being kept absolutely away from the presence of air and at a fairly low temperature. When all the lees have settled out of the wine it may be subjected to a centrifuge, which means that it is passed through an instrument which looks like a cream separator and throws out the solids in the wine to the outer limits of spinning discs and the clean and polished wine goes down the centre to be collected in a tank underneath. This process is not altogether favoured by the best winemakers since they claim that the rough handling given the wine by the centrifuge tends to damage it and in addition there is always the possibility of the wine absorbing a certain amount of air.

The wine is immediately bottled in such a way that the liquid overflows the top of the bottle and the cork which is fitted has to push the wine out of the way in order to be inserted. This makes certain that there is no gap of air between the top of the wine and the bottom of the cork.

Wine that is not intended to be such high quality is made from the juice that is left over in the skins and seeds and mass of pulp still residing in the pre-drainer. The doors are opened and they are dropped on to a continuous belt which conveys them through a 'bag' press which gently squeezes out their juice into a channel beneath the press.

Alternatively the juice-laden mass may be conveyed to a Wilmes press where a similar application of pressure is given by means of an inflated rubber bag.

In all these operations the pressure is so gentle that the skins and seeds are not bruised or broken and hence do not impart their unpleasant sap to the wine.

Grape Varieties used for White Table Wines

In the section dealing with red table wines you will see that I have dealt fairly extensively with new varieties of grapes being planted in Australia. There is an excellent book by E. W. Boehm and H. W. Tulloch published by the Department of Agriculture of South Australia in 1967 which deals with the grape varieties of South Australia. Boehm and Tulloch give the following acreages for white grape varieties:

albillo: 550 acres.

doradillo: 2,250 acres.

false pedro: 500 acres approximately. (These two writers say that the common palomino of Mildura seems to be the same variety. Presumably the grape variety known in Rutherglen as palomino would also be the same. Author's note.)

gouais: 14 acres.

muscat frontignan: 700 acres. (Boehm and Tulloch say that this is more correctly described as muscat de frontignan and shortened to frontignan. It is less correctly called frontignac. In South Australia there is a white, a red [or brown] and a black frontignan and they are often intermixed in the same planting.)

muscat gordo blanco: 6,000 acres almost. (Boehm and Tulloch note that it is South Australia's best known variety, being used for dried fruit, lexias and table raisins, for wine and for table grapes. Hence the commercial wine known as 'Lexia'. Author's note.)

ohanez, also called dira: 300 acres. (This is a white table grape only.)

palomino: 2,000 acres. (Also called paulo at Langhorne Creek.)

pedro ximines: 4,000 acres.

riesling: 1,500 acres. ('Often called Rhine riesling to distinguish it from semillon which is wrongly called Hunter River riesling in Australia.')

rosaki: 400 acres. ('Wrongly called malaga or white malaga in South Australia or Waltham cross when sold as a table grape.')

sauvignon blanc: 30 acres. (Also called white sauvignon.)

semillon: 800 acres. (It would appear that this variety is called white madeira in the Barossa Valley but, as Boehm and Tulloch remark, it cannot be separated from the true semillon on the appearance of the vine and fruit. They say that in South Australia in 1967 there were about 1,200 acres listed as semillon, but these grapes were in fact Clare riesling which has mistakenly been called semillon in the Barossa Valley and River Murray districts. Author's note.)

Clare riesling: 1,400 acres. (Boehm and Tulloch state that this variety was originally planted in the Clare district having been brought from Austria by the Jesuits about 1850. Its true identity has not been established. It was introduced from Clare to the Barossa and from there to the River Murray region but it has been mistakenly called semillon. Therefore nearly all of the 1,150 acres called riesling or semillon in South Australia as apart from Rhine riesling are actually Clare riesling. Adding to these the acres which are actually called Clare riesling, the total amounts to 1,400.)

sercial: 320 acres.

sultana: 9,300 acres.

tokay: 575 acres. (Also called white tokay.)

trebbiano: 780 acres. (Also called white hermitage.)

verdelho: 30 acres.

ugni blanc: Same as trebbiano.

In addition to the above there are also some acres of the following: *blanquette, rouschette, white grenache.*

The following new varieties are being introduced:

chardonnay (also called pinot chardonnay). This is distinguished from pinot blanc.

chasselas doro

chenin blanc

emerald riesling

flora (a Californian cross between a gewurztraminer and semillon)

folle blanche

furmint

Cabernet sauvignon grapes.
Next page: (Top) Seppeltsfield in the Barossa Valley. *(Centre)*
Well established vines showing two-wire trellising, Hanwood.
(Bottom) Fully developed vine.

gewurztraminer
marsanne
pinot blanc
sylvanertraminer (French synonym — savagnin. There is
a rose as well as a white traminer. Gewurztraminer
is probably a selection of this variety.)

In New South Wales the following white varieties are
being introduced:
chenin blanc
moscato bianco
traminer
chasselas
pinot blanc

Mr Graham Gregory of the Department of Agriculture,
New South Wales, in a talk he gave to the national conven-
tion of the Wine and Food Society of Australia in 1969
said 'the trend towards greater production of distinctive
varietal wine styles will be encouraged by the availability
of high performance clones (or strains) of the varieties
involved, the majority of which are low yielders. This was
the main reason for their lack of popularity in the past.
Clonal selection programmes which have been practised
in parts of Europe for most of this century and are now
under way in Australia, indicate that the planting of selected
vines will result in yield increases in the order of twenty
to thirty per cent over normal vine populations.'

> Before dinner he is quite dejected. But when
> he has a bottle of good wine, he begins to
> come alive, he stretches his wings, he mounts
> like an eagle.
> Boswell, on the Grand Tour

4 RED TABLE WINES

These, like white table wines, are unfortified wines but with a slightly higher alcohol strength, around about twelve or thirteen per cent by volume as compared with the ten or eleven per cent of the whites.

They are known under a variety of names in Australia – 'claret', 'burgundy', 'hermitage', 'cabernet'.

The Making of Red Table Wines
The main varieties of grapes used are 'grenache', 'shiraz', 'mataro', 'cabernet'. All of these are well suited for making red table wines although the usual practice is to mix at least two varieties together in crushing so that the deficien-

cies of one will be made up by the strength of another. Grenache, for example, is a lovely perfumed grape which is crushed together with shiraz. The combination is a happy one, both financially and taste wise, for the grenache grape is a very economic grape to produce and shiraz more often than not is better with other grapes than on its own.

The grapes are unloaded by forks or mechanical equipment and thrown into the crusher where the berries are crushed and the stalks are eliminated. The crushed berries (the must) are pumped to fermenting tanks. For red wines these are open brick pits covered with cement and lined with paraffin wax. The skins and pips of the red grapes are left in the fermenting tank for a period of time depending on the amount of pigmentation and tannin the winemaker wishes to extract from them.

Sometimes he will place paraffined boards and cross members just below the surface of the must so that the skins are forced into the fermentation instead of floating on the top and thus he will obtain a better extraction of colour.

As in a white table wine, all of the sugar in the must is fermented to alcohol. Towards the end of fermentation the wine is pumped to storage tanks or vats.

The skins and pips remaining in the fermenting tank are transferred by mechanical means to the press where the remaining wine is extracted and either pumped to the vats containing the free run or kept separately as a 'pressed' wine.

Types of Australian Red Table Wines

It would be possible to categorize Australian red wines into many different divisions. If there is anything clear about Australian wines it is that they are readily classifiable into districts. However, I wish to make a classification as simple as possible.

It is sufficiently accurate to divide red wines into two general classes – 'firm' and 'soft'. Australian winemakers endeavour to produce both these classes irrespective of the district in which the grapes are grown. On the surface they are successful in doing this but they have their greatest successes in making a style that suits the area. The Hunter Valley produces naturally soft reds which are always of a high quality. It is not able to produce firm hard wines.

Up to the present time, the Australian winemaker has had a false philosophy in making wines. Very often he has been trying to make a wine to fit a name or a style. What he should be doing, of course, is to make a wine in a natural way according to the dictates of his soil and climate and then find a name to fit the wine.

All the difficulties we have regarding Australian wine types centre around our terminology. However, I am dealing with wines as I find them in Australia and therefore shall discuss them under two headings.

'FIRM' STYLE

In some ways this is similar to what we have called in the white wines 'acid' style; but in the reds 'firmness' is more than acid. It is a combination of acid, astringency and district character.

This style is usually called by the winemaker – 'claret'. By this he intends to indicate that the wine is not noted for its heavy body because it may have quite a lightness of texture; he wishes to point out that his wine will be fairly astringent, fairly high in acid and in general give an impression of a firmness and a 'grip' on the palate and surfaces of the mouth.

If the grapes are grown in a district which naturally produces 'firm' wines they will be allowed to reach full maturity on the vine and fermented out in the normal way: Great Western, Coonawarra and Reynella reds are natural 'firm' wines.

If, on the other hand, the grapes are grown in an area where the sugar content is high at full maturity, the winemaker might see that the grapes are picked a little early so that the sugar content is less and the acid higher. In fermentation he will endeavour to extract a little more tannin so as to gain the 'firm' effect.

The best grape varieties used in this style are a mixture of the shiraz and cabernet grapes. Shiraz by itself is inclined to give too much fruitiness and too much berry flavour to the wine. Cabernet has a slight hardness and refinement about it which balances out the excessiveness of the shiraz. Even a fairly small percentage of this former grape has the desired effect. The addition of mataro to shiraz also has a desirable effect. A wine of less quality can be made from a mixture of shiraz and grenache.

You will notice that I use the word 'mixture'. By this I mean that the grapes are crushed and pumped into the same fermenting vat so that the mixture of grapes is incorporated in the wine from its birth. This gives a close knit structure which is not achieved so effectively if each grape is fermented separately and a wine made and then the different wines blended together.

In the firm type of red you will notice a very obvious presence of tannin from the very start as the wine begins to 'draw' or 'pucker up' the inner surfaces of the lips and first part of the tongue. This astringency will be felt all over the palate until the mouthful of wine has disappeared. It is a pleasant 'gripping' which should not be confused with a bitterness that is sometimes present with tannin. A sharp tingling is experienced on the tip of the tongue. This is acid. In the middle palate there is a detection of fruitiness and flavour which is satisfying and pleasing and has nothing to do with sugar content.

When young, the grape flavour, acid and tannin are a little obtrusive without being unpleasant. As the wine grows older the acid and tannin becomes less accented and a wonderful array of aromas and flavours develop. This action may continue for as much as twenty years and the quality of the wine may hold, under good keeping conditions, for another twenty.

Australia makes a wide selection of good wines of this type, their excellence depending in most cases on the skill and perfectionism of the winemaker. I have chosen what I consider to be wines which appear above ordinary in quality more often than not. Remember, however, that in odd years many other wineries can produce wines that are just as good.

Examples of 'firm' red wines which are *usually* above ordinary quality:

Chateau Leonay	*Claret*
Chateau Tahbilk	*Shiraz & Cabernet*
Hamilton's	*Springton Claret*
Lindeman's	*Special Bottlings of Claret*
McWilliam's	*Rosedale Claret*
Mildara	*Reserve Bin Claret, Cabernet Shiraz, & their Coonawarra Reds*
Orlando	*Barossa Cabernet*
Penfold's	*Special Bottlings of Claret from South Australia*
Redman	*Coonawarra Claret*
Reynella	*Vintage Claret & Cabernet*
Rouge Homme (Lindeman's Coonawarra)	*Claret & Cabernet*
Ryecroft	*Cabernet*
Seaview	*Cabernet Shiraz & Cabernet Sauvignon*
Seppelt's	*Moyston Claret & Special Bottlings of Red Wine*
Stonyfell	*Metala Claret*
Tintara	*McLaren Vale Hermitage & Cabinet Claret*
Wynn's	*Coonawarra Estate Claret & Cabernet*
Yalumba	*Galway Vintage Claret*

'SOFT' STYLE

We might have called this 'burgundy' style except for the fact that 'burgundy' is a very confusing name. To some makers it means a big heavy bodied wine, dark in colour and fruity. This is the style of wine we knew as 'burgundy' for over a hundred years. To others it is represented by a soft wine, not necessarily heavy bodied, but round and smooth without any tartness and with just a suggestion of fruitiness. This is the 'burgundy' of France.

By their very nature, the Hunter Valley, north-eastern Victoria, McLaren Vale and the Swan Valley produce 'soft' reds. However, if a maker intends to make them in, say, the Southern Vales area of South Australia he must ensure that his grapes are very ripe and that he does not extract too much tannin in his fermentation. In some years he would not be able to produce a 'soft' type. The best varieties of grapes used for this style are the shiraz or the pinot used either by themselves or as a mixture.

The bouquet is strong and honeyed rather than perfumed or spicy. When tasted there is no obvious 'gripping' on the palate but the liquid flows over the tongue with a kind of viscidity that makes it feel full in the mouth. The flavour is rich and fills all the taste buds and sends streams of aromas through the soft palate to the sensory organ of smell. Overall a sensation of great softness on the palate is experienced and at the end a slight firmness leaves it clean but with a pleasant burden of flavour.

When young the wine might not portray all these signs. But they develop very quickly. They will become softer and softer until after twelve years or so they are showing signs of being worn. They may then continue on in this stage for many years without change.

Many areas of Australia can produce this type of wine. Not all of them have been fully developed by the winemakers who do not perhaps realize fully that this style is suitable to their areas. When winemaking techniques are improved in these lesser recognized districts I have no doubt that their wines will be as good as those I am listing as being of unusually high quality.

Examples of 'soft' red wines which are *usually* above ordinary quality:

Buring's	*Leonay Vintage Burgundy*
Brown's	*Burgundy*
Lindeman's	*Special Bottlings of Hunter Valley wines & Blends of Hunter Valley and other areas*

McWilliam's	*Mt Pleasant Red Wines*
Penfold's	*Dalwood Burgundy, Hermitage & Special Bottlings of Hunter Valley Reds*
Seppelt's	*Chalambar Burgundy & Special Bottlings of Burgundy*
Stonyfell	*Private Bin Burgundy*
Tintara	*St Thomas Burgundy & Special Bottlings of Burgundy*
Wynn's	*Ovens Valley Shiraz*
Ingoldby	*Hermitage*
Osborn	*D'Arrenberg Burgundy*

'VARIETAL' RED WINES

This can scarcely be called a third division since some 'varietal' reds are 'firm' and others are 'soft'.

However, it must be included here because some winemakers have gone to the trouble to make wines out of unusual grape varieties which they think will be of special quality. In this case the winemaker has no particular style in mind but endeavours to make a wine which suits the variety and area.

Ideally, all our wines should be made this way and the concept of striving for certain styles should be abolished. Just as in architecture the formula 'form follows function' is a valuable guide, so in winemaking should we say 'districts develop distinctiveness'.

In this case, distinctiveness is not that of style but of character, and we would have just as many varieties of red wines as there are districts that grow red grapes.

Strictly speaking all wines are varietal wines since they are made from one or two or more varieties of grapes. We are using the term in Australia to denote wines made from *one* variety of grape especially one that is not commonly employed except in a blend.

These grape varieties are 'mataro', 'cabernet sauvignon', 'pinot noir', 'malbec', 'blue imperial', and several others planted in experimental patches by the large companies.

The most popular varietal wine is 'cabernet', short for 'cabernet sauvignon'.

Whether we see much 'straight' cabernet is a matter for investigation. It has such a distinctive flavour that it is detectable very readily in a blend with other varieties. It is very difficult therefore to determine by smell and taste whether a wine is a straight cabernet or not. The presence of shiraz with cabernet provides attractiveness. In France the 'merlot' is mixed in with the 'cabernet' for the same reason.

I am not giving a list of selected varietal wines firstly because there are not enough in any selected bottling to market universally and secondly because I am not sure that a wine labelled 'cabernet', for instance, is pure cabernet.

There is no law to prevent a company labelling a wine as 'cabernet' when it is a blend of 'cabernet' and 'shiraz'. However, unless the label specifically informs us that it also contains 'shiraz', it is misleading, and reprehensible.

In any case the 'cabernet shiraz' blend is considered by many as better than a straight 'cabernet'.

The wine lover who seeks out 'varietal' wines must indeed be a searcher, as the major wine companies only market them occasionally. It will be his task to keep his eyes and ears open and to ask his wine merchant to keep him informed. Let him be careful, nevertheless, that the wine company makes a specific claim on the label that the wine is made from one only variety.

Varietal wines are not necessarily first class. They are interesting.

The Grape Varieties Used

When the South Australian wineries began to expand their production in the early part of this century they realized that the demand would be largely for fortified wines like port. For this reason, red grape vines were planted in comparatively large acreages. This pattern has been followed all over Australia until recent years.

During the 1920s and 1930s very little dry table wine

of any sort at all was consumed in Australia and most of what was produced was exported to England as a cheap bulk red. There was very little encouragement therefore for the winemaker of those days to plant high quality red grape varieties. Economically he was forced into looking for grape varieties which thrived well on most soils and which produced abundantly on the vine. Those varieties which were known as 'shy' bearers went out of fashion, although a great number of cabernet vines had been planted prior to 1900.

In 1960 therefore, when the sharp upward trend in the consumption of table wines really began, the situation was that most of the red grape varieties of vines growing in all states were the prolific bearers, grenache and shiraz. There was in fact twice as much grenache produced as there was of shiraz and six times or seven times as much grenache as mataro and 800 times as much grenache as cabernet. This proved very difficult for the wine companies when they were called upon to produce wines of much higher quality in recent years. A tremendous amount of planting has gone on and I have no doubt that in the next ten years, high quality grape varieties – cabernet sauvignon, shiraz, malbec, merlot, pinot (both pinot noir and pinot meuniere) will be far more abundant than the poorer variety, grenache.

However, we must take the position as it stands and realize that most of the red wine we are drinking is either pure grenache or a blend of grenache and other varieties. Fortunately for the wine lover a great quantitiy of wine is sold by reliable companies which is either pure cabernet, pure shiraz or a mixture of the two. We might say that all Hunter Valley wines are made from high class varieties, that Tahbilk, Great Western and Coonawarra are almost entirely planted with either cabernet or shiraz. There is quite an amount of cinsaut, also called blue imperial and oeillade, in north-east Victoria, the Barossa Valley and the Adelaide and southern districts of South Australia.

In their publication, Boehm and Tulloch give the following figures for South Australia:

cabernet sauvignon: 700 acres.
carignane: 300 acres.
grenache: 10,000 acres.
malbec: 36 acres.
mataro: 3,200 acres.
oeillade: 140 acres.
shiraz: 5,600 acres.

There are also a few odd acres of *cabernet gros, dolcetto, morrastel* (this is probably described by most winegrowers as mataro since it has an identical appearance with this variety), and *port.* Take into consideration that in some areas, cabernet yields only one ton to the acre, whereas grenache will yield at least four.

Boehm and Tulloch point out that from 1894 until 1964 the entry of grape vines into South Australia was completely prohibited. A recent change in legislation now permits health-screened varieties to be introduced under Government supervision. The following is a list of the red grapes which have been introduced or may be considered for introduction in the near future:*

alicante bouchet
bastardo
emperor
barbera
gamay beaujolais
merlot
mission
mondeuse
pinot noir
ruby cabernet
rubired
touriga
zinfandel

A number of trial plantings of these new varieties has been made by all the major companies but at the date of publication of this book none of these plantings has yet been sufficiently advanced to produce crops large

*E. W. Boehm and H. W. Tulloch. *Grape Varieties of South Australia,* Department of Agriculture, S.A. 1967.

enough for any wine to be made, apart from very small sample quantities.

New South Wales has permitted a number of varieties to be planted for experimental purposes and many of the new plantings in the Hunter Valley consists of pinot noir, pinot meuniere, cabernet, merlot, and malbec. In the area once known as the Murrumbidgee Irrigation Area (M.I.A.), but now termed more euphemistically the Riverina Area, a number of these new varieties are being planted. The list of which I have set out under the chapters dealing with the vineyard areas of Australia gives a fairly accurate account of the types of grapes being planted in the various vineyards of the larger companies. It must be remembered however, that most of the grapes in Australia are grown by people who do not process the wines themselves but sell them to the wineries, and therefore the figures shown by these winemaking companies do not give a true picture of what is actually being grown in Australia.

Naturally the independent growers are being persuaded to plant more of the better class varieties and, because it must be to their financial advantage, they are not hard to persuade.

Victoria has a very large vine propagation farm at Irymple near Mildura and very many of the varieties are being nurtured here. The Rutherglen Viticultural Station is also engaged in this activity and Seppelts have begun their own nursery plantations at Ararat.

All of this indicates that in the next ten years we should be growing a much wider variety of first class grapes, both red and white, than we do today.

The wines of Champagne are far superior in richness and perfection to all other wines . . . They are pale coloured and tawny, subtle and delicate, and have a taste which is extremely agreeable to the palate . . . for these reasons they are the wines par excellence for kings, princes and great lords.

Paulmier: 'Treatise on Wines'

5 SPARKLING WINES

THE WORD 'Sparkling' is a curious though charming name used to describe wines impregnated with carbon dioxide gas in such a fashion that they will create a spectacle of bubbles cascading upwards through the wine when poured into a glass and cause a sensation of fizziness on the tongue which is rather pleasant.

More correctly and aptly perhaps, they could be called 'bubbly' wines or even, though less attractively, 'effervescent' wines.

The German 'schaum', the French 'mosseaux' and the Italian 'spumanti', all meaning the same thing – 'foaming' or 'frothy', while they may not be so pretty, are more exact. We may be tempted to call them 'aerated' or 'carbonated' wines but this would not be good English since the words are reserved for liquids which have been charged with gas, that is, those which have had the gas forced into them, as opposed to wines in which the gas has been created by fermentation.

In Australia, we know sparkling wines under the titles of 'champagne', 'sparkling burgundy', 'sparkling moselle', 'sparkling hock' and 'pearl' wine.

We can quite conveniently divide sparkling wines into three classes according to the methods by which they are made. They are made by

1. Bottle fermentation
2. Tank fermentation, or
3. Carbonation.

Bottle Fermentation Method

The most precise description is 'the slow fermentation in bottle with long ageing on yeast' method.

First of all a base wine is clarified and filtered. For champagne, a dry white wine without much flavour is the best. Winemakers consider the 'pinot blanc' the most desirable grape for this purpose. 'Sparkling moselle' and 'sparkling hock' may have more definite grape flavour. 'Sparkling burgundy' is best made from a neutral dry red wine.

A fermentable material is prepared by mixing cane sugar with wine and this solution is poured into the base wine. At the same time yeast is added. Immediately the wine is filled into very strong champagne bottles and secondary fermentation begins. Usually these bottles are made so as to take the 'crown' seal which is completely air tight and can be removed with the minimum of trouble.

All the bottles are stacked on their sides in a suitable cellar and, as fermentation proceeds and carbon dioxide is produced, a considerable pressure is created inside each bottle. Sometimes the weaker bottles will burst.

On the completion of fermentation, the bottles are all individually shaken, re-stacked and stored for some months so that the wine can mature on the lees.

Each container now holds a considerable quantity of dead yeast cells and other solids produced by fermentation. Hence after this first ageing period, they must be removed. There are two ways of doing this.

The first is known as *Disgorging*.

DISGORGING

In this method the bottles are placed upside down in special racks. Every day for several weeks an operator shakes each bottle and gradually works the deposits down the neck of the bottle until all the sediment rests on the cork.

Usually, after this, the bottles are placed neck downwards into a freezing agent and a small amount of wine containing the sediment is frozen.

At this stage there is a pressure of about one hundred pounds per square inch in the bottle. The operator will hold it at a forty-five degree from vertical angle into a timber receptacle and remove the crown seal. The plug of frozen sediment is forced out by the pressure of gas.

The bottle is quickly returned to a vertical position and any yeast adhering to the neck is removed by the wine flowing out from the top of the bottle.

The wine has been exhausted of all sugar by fermentation and is, therefore, at this stage, completely dry. A predetermined amount of sugar syrup to sweeten the wine according to the demands of the existing market is added to each bottle which is then topped up from another bottle, corked and the cork is wired down.

After this, the syrup is shaken through the wine and the bottles again placed in stacks to allow the wine to mature for some time longer.

The second way of removing sediment is known as the *Transfer System*.

TRANSFER SYSTEM

The system of disgorging is a time consuming, difficult and expensive way of cleaning a bottle of its deposit. Moreover, it is very hard to obtain suitable operatives.

The transfer system has been designed to retain the traditional method of making champagne while introducing more efficient and less expensive ways of finishing the process.

Under this mode of operation, fermentation takes place in the bottles as described above. The bottles are not placed in racks but are emptied by inserting a tube into the neck of the bottle and siphoning out the contents.

These contents are pumped into a settling tank under pressure. Obviously, unless means are taken to prevent it, the pressure in the bottles will be greater by far than the pressure in the receiving tank and much gas would be lost.

Therefore, there must be a counter pressure in the receiving tank. This is obtained by means of a complicated arrangement of valves which permits carbon dioxide from artificial sources to provide counter pressure without being, in any way, absorbed into the wine.

The wine, now transferred, has all sediment filtered out and is bottled bright and clear after the 'liqueur d'expedition' (as the sweetening syrup is called) has been added. Bottling is done under pressure and the wine now finishes with a pressure of seventy-five to ninety pounds per square inch.

COMPANIES EMPLOYING TRADITIONAL
BOTTLE FERMENTATION METHODS
Seppelt's have their champagne making plant at Great Western, western Victoria. They market their champagne as

> Great Western 'Extra Dry'
> Great Western 'Brut' (Vintage)
> Great Western 'Imperial Brut'

The term 'brut' on a champagne label means that the wine is 'natural' or rather that it has had no 'liqueur d'expedition' added to it. Therefore one would expect it to be completely dry. In practice the so-called 'brut' champagnes are not as dry as this but have just the slightest trace of sugar in them to make them palatable.

The words 'extra dry' indicate that the champagne is much less dry than 'brut'.

Harvesting grapes at Penfold's, Nuriootpa *(left)*, and Wynn's Modbury Estate *(right)*.

The fermenting must.

Crushing grapes.

Seppelt's make the base wine for the champagne largely from the 'Irvine's white' grape which they grow at Great Western. The result is a sparkling wine of great quality and with a remarkable cleanness on the palate. Seppelt's use the transfer system for all champagne except the 'vintage brut'.

'Great Western' Sparkling Burgundy is made from a variety of red grapes including the 'pinot meuniere'.

Penfold's have one champagne making plant at Auldana near Adelaide and another at Minchinbury near Sydney.
The sparkling wines are labelled
    Minchinbury Private Cuvee Champagne
    Minchinbury Sparkling Burgundy
    Minchinbury Sparkling Moselle
Penfold's use the 'transfer' system for clarifying the wine after secondary fermentation.

Hardy's make their sparkling wines in their Mile End cellars in Adelaide from a base wine made from riesling and semillon grapes.
The sparkling wines are labelled
    Tintara Champagne
    Tintara Sparkling Moselle
    Tintara Sparkling Burgundy
    Tintara Sparkling Hock
Hardy's use the traditional disgorgement method.

Wynn's make their sparkling wines at Magill calling them
    Romalo Brut Champagne
    Romalo Cuvee Reserve Champagne
    Romalo Sparkling Burgundy
It is common practice for some of the larger companies and wine merchants to ask Wynn's to make champagne and other sparkling wines for them and to label it with their own label. In some cases the company or merchant provides the base wine so as to give the finished product a closer relationship to the label. Wynn's (Romalo) use only the 'disgorgement' method.

McWilliams make their sparkling wines at Yenda Cellars in the Riverina and label them as
>Imperial Reserve Champagne
>Imperial Reserve Pink Champagne
>Imperial Reserve Burgundy
>Imperial Reserve Moselle

McWilliams's use the traditional 'disgorgement' method.

Barossa Valley Co-operative make their sparkling wines at Nuriootpa in the Barossa Valley and market them as
>Kaiser Stuhl Champagne
>Kaiser Stuhl Sparkling Burgundy
>Kaiser Stuhl Sparkling Moselle

They use the transfer method.

Lindeman's make their sparkling wines in Sydney as
>Private Cuvee Champagne
>Sparkling Burgundy
>Sparkling Hock
>Sparkling Moselle

Gramps make an excellent wine by the transfer method which they call Orlando Champagne.

Tank Fermentation
As with bottle fermentation, a base wine is clarified and filtered. Fermentable material or yeast food is added in the form of a mixture of sugar and wine. Starter yeast is added and the wine is pumped into the fermenting tank where fermentation begins.

Normally, all the gases produced by fermentation are permitted to escape into the atmosphere. The 'pressure' tank introduced a new method of making sparkling wines. As the tank is completely sealed, the gases are retained in the tank and hence in the wine.

The pressure tank, as used in Australian wineries to make sparkling wines, is also used to produce the so-called 'pressure fermented' white table wines. It is equipped with valves, gauges and a temperature control system.

The 'secondary' fermentation in the tank is completed in about two weeks. The wine is chilled and transferred by pumping from the lees of yeast and other sediment into another container where it is cooled further to about 25°F so as to cause precipitation of tartrates.

After this, sugar is added if necessary to bring the wine to the desired degree of sweetness and it is filtered and bottled.

If the sparkling wine manufacturer wishes to make a champagne type beverage, he bottles at a pressure of about ninety pounds per square inch.

If he wishes to make a 'pearl' wine he bottles at a pressure of about twenty pounds per square inch.

'Pearl' is rather an odd title to give a wine; it comes directly from the German 'perlwein', the Germans being the people who developed this method. The little bubble created when the pressure is released after the seal is taken off the bottle is apparently likened to a bead.

With the greater pressures employed in the champagne type wines, a very strong bottle has to be used and cork has to be wired to the bottle in the same way as bottle fermented champagne.

With 'pearl' type wines ordinary table wine bottles can be used and a plastic seal is employed which is held in position with a screw cap or metal foil.

TANK FERMENTED wines are made by
Cinzano under the name of 'Santa Vittoria' Champagne.

Gramp's (Orlando) under the name of 'Barossa Pearl' and 'Blue Ribbon Barossa'. They also make a champagne-type wine in tanks which they call 'Sparkling Carte Blanche'.

McWilliam's under the name of 'Chateau Gay'.

Penfold's under the name of 'Mardi Gras' and 'Tiffany'.

Barossa Valley Co-operative under the name of 'Kaiser Pearl'. This firm makes for a number of other firms who market the wines under their own labels.

Thumm, who markets under the name of 'Yaldara' calls some of his wines 'Sekt' which is another German name for champagne. He also makes for other firms who use their own labels.

Buring's under the name of 'Sparkling Rinegolde' and 'Sparkling Liebfraumilch'.

Carbonated Wines

Carbonated wines are sparkling wines atrificially charged with carbon dioxide gas instead of by fermentation.

The quality of carbonated wines can be quite high especially if the base wine is made from the same grape varieties as are used for champagne.

A skilful winemaker can produce a carbonated wine that is almost identical with a sparkling wine made by bottle fermentation. However, there is an almost infallible method of detecting it from the real thing. The carbon dioxide produced by fermentation is more closely knit with the wine than that injected from outside. Therefore a carbonated wine loses its bubbles much more quickly than a sparkling wine made by fermentation.

The following are CARBONATED WINES of high quality:
Best's   Golden Vintage
           Sparkling Burgundy
           Pink Cham
           Golden, Pink or Crimson Bubbly
           Baby Bubblie

These are made at Great Western in Victoria by the Thomson family. The base wine is placed in a stainless steel tank, sweetening material is added and gas is induced into the wine from steel cylinders as the wine is bottled.

The Legal Definition of Champagne

Naturally a legal definition by a State authority does not

necessarily create a case for the authenticity of any article. Even if champagne were defined by an Australian Act of Parliament the definition may not be accepted by the majority of wine drinkers.

There are innumerable Australian sparkling wines on the market made by various companies by different methods and from different material.

The question, therefore, is twofold: can any Australian wines be called champagne? If so, which ones?

Let us first look at the law. Legal descriptions of wine are found in the Health Acts. These are not uniform in all States although the wine industry hopes to reach uniformity before long. The South Australian Act demands that any wine labelled as champagne must be made by the 'bottle-fermentation' method. In Victoria this is not necessary and so any wine could be called champagne as long as it is not carbonated.

A French wine made by the 'methode close cuve', that is by tank fermentation without any bottle fermentation, could be legally labelled champagne in Victoria but, it could not be so labelled in South Australia and some of the other States. Any wine made by the 'champenoise' method, that is by bottle fermentation, even though made in France in an area outside the delimited (see p.86) area, legally could be called champagne.

The incongruous situation exists, therefore, that French sparkling wine which cannot be called champagne in France can be described and labelled as champagne in Australia.

In practice, Australian wine merchants eschew the temptation. It does point up, however, the inconclusiveness of our definitions of champagne.

If we are not going to abide by *French* legislation on champagne then we must be fairly accurate in our own description of the wine.

We find 'champagne' a very useful word for a certain type of wine. The fact is that we do make a wine which is very similar to that made by the French and which they call champagne. Take any one of our first class champagnes and mask it. Put it against one of the best of the French. It is very difficult to say which is which. Quality considerations aside, we have learned the secret of how to capture that faint but easily recognized flavour which is peculiar to genuine champagne.

If we are to be precise in our definition, therefore, we should have to use a description which went something like this: *champagne is a white sparkling wine made by secondary fermentation in the bottle with long ageing on lees and which has the typical flavour of sparkling wine made in the Rheims-Epernay region of France.*

This typical flavour, incidentally, is not the flavour imparted to the wine by grape variety or district. It is the peculiar 'freshly made bread' or 'leaf vegetable' aroma and taste which is created in the wine by the long ageing on lees.

We may not like this taste but if we want to call our wine champagne it must taste like champagne and so must have this peculiar flavour.

Technically, the French get the flavour and quality of their champagne by centuries old techniques which are now prescribed by French law for French champagne makers and are supervised by the Comité Interprofessional du Vin de Champagne. These laws fix the boundaries within which champagne grapes may be grown; impose obligations that the wine shall be composed only of the grape juices from the vine plants mentioned above; fix the types of wine plants which may be grown, the maximum yield of the harvest and prescribe the methods of making. All vineyards within the defined boundaries are declared to be within the 'delimited' area.

In France the wine is often left in contact with the yeast which created the second fermentation for at least a year. This ensures that the fermentation will be complete, allows the yeast cells to die and permits development of the 'champagne' bouquet and taste. These are created mainly from the autolysis or disintegration of the yeast cells.

Indubitably many of our Australian sparkling wines are made in the same manner as and taste similar to French champagne. I include Great Western, Minchinbury, Tintara, McWilliam's and Romalo.

Some of our 'champagnes' are, just as indubitably, made from grape varieties which are far too obtrusive to make champagne. Others have not had sufficient time on the lees to acquire the champagne flavour.

As for sparkling wines made by the tank method or any other method which is not by bottle fermentation, they do not even slightly resemble champagne. They may be attractive in their own way and have appeal for a great number of people but they certainly do not possess the typical champagne flavour.

If we are to call a wine 'champagne' because it looks like genuine French champagne, smells like genuine French champagne and tastes like genuine French champagne then we must have a code of labelling which provides for these primary requisites. Let us call wines which do not taste like champagne, 'bubbly' or 'mousseux' or anything you like but please let us not call them 'champagne'.

Few things surpass old wine;
    and they may preach
Who please, the more they
    preach in vain, –
Let us have wine and women,
    mirth and laughter,
Sermons and soda-water
    the day after.
Lord Byron: 'Don Juan'

6 DESSERT WINES

THE WORD 'dessert' comes from
the French 'desservir' meaning 'to clear the table'. Hence
it is a peculiarly apt word to use for wines to be drunk
after a meal.

These 'dessert' wines are fortified wines like sherry, that
is they have had 'fortifying' spirit added to them in order
to preserve them.

In Australia we include under the name of 'dessert' wines
the following:

Port, White Port, Frontignac, Muscat (or Muscatel),
Madeira, Tokay. All of these wines basically are made
the same way.

The grapes are picked at a maximum degree of sweetness, crushed and pumped to the fermenting tank. Fermentation is initiated and as it proceeds the sugar is transformed. At the stage of sweetness required, the winemaker adds sufficient 'fortifying' spirit to stop the fermentation. This spirit is distilled from suitable dry wine and has an inhibiting effect on the action of yeasts when added to bring the strength of the fermenting wine up to about sixteen per cent by volume. In practice, fortified wine is about twenty per cent by volume of pure spirit (or alcohol).

Therefore, in a sweet wine or dessert wine such as we are discussing, all the sugar present is natural grape sugar, and all the alcohol is derived from the fermented grape.

Port

Basically in Australia there are two types of Port, 'Tawny' and 'Vintage'.

A *tawny* port is simply one aged in oaken casks. It may be a blend of several years.

A *vintage* port is one of special quality, all the wine of one year, bottled early in its life and aged in bottle.

TAWNY PORT

Tawny port is usually made out of a red grape like shiraz but extremely beautiful wines called 'port' have been made from white grapes like tokay.

This makes the definition of Australian Tawny Port extremely hazardous.

As a fortified wine made from *red* grapes grows older, it becomes lighter in hue and develops a light brown colour.

As a fortified wine made from *white* grapes grows older, it becomes darker in hue and also develops a light brown colour.

It is impossible, therefore, after a certain age, to tell by colour alone whether a fortified wine is made from white or red grapes. This comes about even earlier if the wine has been aged in oaken casks as opposed to ageing in bottles. In spite of this, *most* Australian ports are made from red grapes – shiraz, grenache and mataro.

The best 'tawny' ports on the market, whether they be made from red or white grapes, are listed below. It must be realized, however, that Australia has been producing fairly good wines of this type for over a century and therefore nearly every winemaker can produce from old stocks a tawny port which may not be very much different from those I have selected.

Red grapes give a greater extraction of tannin. This gives the port a firmer 'grip' on the palate and helps the wine to longer life.

In early life, therefore, port is usually purplish in colour. Later it becomes dark red and loses its violet overtones. At this stage it begins to appear on the market under such names as 'Invalid', 'Royal Reserve', or 'Gold Label' Port.

As it grows older and the red pigmentation oxidizes to dark brown it might be called 'Tawny' or 'Liqueur' Port. The final stage is light brown and then it might be called 'Very Old Tawny' or 'Vintage Tawny'. This latter name is very misleading as it can confuse the consumer into thinking it is a 'Vintage' Port which is a very different thing.

A tawny port is aged in cask until the day when the winemaker decides he is going to sell it. During this process of ageing he is periodically pumping the wine off the 'lees', that is he is transferring it from one cask to another in order to separate it from the solids that have deposited at the bottom of the 'ageing' cask. This precipitate is simply a natural process of ageing and consists of tartaric acid, precipitated pigmentation and other deposits created by oxidation.

Precipitation can continue in the bottle, of course, and for this reason, the winemaker desires that a tawny port should be sold and consumed as soon as possible after bottling. There is no point in keeping a tawny port in bottle. Its life has been planned as a life in cask and it will not gain anything from bottle ageing.

Good examples of Tawny Ports are:

Bleasdale	Pioneer
Lindeman's	Macquarie, El Rey
McWilliams	Fine Old Hanwood
Mildara	Reserve Bin
Morris	Special Old Tawny
Orlando	Vintage Tawny
Penfold's	Club
Reynella	Port Royal
Seppelt's	Para Liqueur, Mt Rufus
Stonyfell	Old Lodge
Tintara	Coronet
Yalumba	Galway Pipe, Directors Special
All Saints	Tawny

VINTAGE PORT

Vintage port is always made from red grapes. There are very few Portuguese variety grapes about but sometimes a few of these are crushed with shiraz to make vintage port. Cabernet is occasionally used in small quantities together with shiraz.

After about eighteen months the wine is bottled, corked with a long 'straight' cork similar to that used in red table wine bottles and the bottles are stored away on their sides.

Because the wine is intended to last a long time it is usually of better quality than that used for tawny ports. Not every year is a good year for vintage port. The vintage port maker must wait for a vintage when everything is 'just right'.

The wine must be of a very deep colour – dark crimson with possibly a lot of purple. It must have a high sugar content, very high tannin content and high acidity. In spite of its sugar, the tannin will make it appear not so sweet. It will be very rich and flavourous but will seem to be rough and astringent. This is necessary if it is successfully to negotiate its long journey in bottle. After many years it will be soft and velvety and a very much better article than a tawny port of similar age.

Because ageing in bottle is much slower than that in cask the dark red colour remains for many years so that the average consumer might think that it never changes. It will seem to be lighter in body than the tawnies which acquire a 'liqueur' character as they grow older; the finish will always appear to be firmer and much of the grape flavour will be retained for a long time.

Eventually however, a vintage port will change to a brownish colour and be indistinguishable in appearance from a 'tawny'. This may be when it is twenty years old.

At this time it will have reached maturity and its flavour and bouquet will be enriched with a myriad of aromas and a bountiful supply of taste variants which a tawny port can never have.

The best vintage ports I have known were made by
Reynella
Hardy's (Tintara)
Seppelt's
Martin's (Stonyfell)
Sutherland Smith's

A vintage port must be labelled 'vintage port' and the date of the vintage must appear. Sometimes you will see ports without the date. They are not vintage ports. Sometimes a vintage year will appear on the label of a wine that is obviously a tawny, that is, it has been aged in cask. This is not a *vintage* port.

A vintage port cannot be unsealed once it has been 'put down' until the day it is ready for consumption. Therefore, since it must throw a deposit as it ages, it will leave a layer of sediment along the lower side of the bottle as it lies in the bin. This sediment is easily disturbed and when the bottle is raised to an upright position will probably fall through the wine and create a cloudy appearance. The port, therefore, must not be poured until this cloudiness has precipated again to the bottom of the bottle.

Other Dessert Wines

Undoubtedly to the great irritation of English purists, the word 'port' in Australian wine language, simply means a reddish coloured, sweet, fortified wine.

Other dessert wines derive their names mainly from the grape from which they are made. For example there is *muscat*.

MUSCAT

Also known as 'muscatel' or 'muscadel' it is a sweet fortified wine made from one of the branches of the muscat grape family. There are quite a number of branches and not all of them are classified. The two main divisions are the white muscat which in Australia is known as the 'gordo blanco' or the muscat of Alexandria and the 'brown muscat' or 'frontignan'. All these wines have one thing in common. It is the characteristic and unmistakable flavour of the muscat grape.

Muscat is made very well in Australia. The rich soil of the Murray and Murrumbidgee Valleys; the hot summer sunshine, and a plentiful supply of water from irrigation seems to be the ideal combination for making this type of wine.

The overladen burden of the fruit, the heaviness of the bouquet and the syrupy sugar contained in the wine make it a great favourite with those who like sweet wines.

As a muscat grows older in cask, its texture thickens and it acquires a viscosity which is akin to the honey-like flow of a liqueur. Hence it is that it is given the name of 'liqueur' muscat.

All Australian muscats are good. Many sweet wine drinkers consider that Rutherglen muscats and frontignans are the best. Certainly this type of wine from that area has a strong, perfumed and distinctive flavour. Nevertheless, the more subdued tone of South Australian muscats appeal more to those who like a glass of muscat after dinner as a change from port.

It is hard to select any maker as outstanding since every company has a superb example, but to take a few of the very best I would name:

| Morris | *Liqueur Muscat* |
| Lindeman's | *Raisin Liqueur Muscat* |

| Seppelt's | *Special Bottlings of Old Muscats* |
| All Saints | *Liqueur Muscat* |

FRONTIGNAN

As I have explained, this wine is a member of the muscat family. Even this branch of the family has several sub-divisions. The name is not popular on company labels because people are hesitant on how to pronounce it. Good frontignans are sold under the name of

Seppelt's	*Frontignac*
Lindeman's	*Frontignac*
Hardy's	*Frontignac*

As explained previously, frontignac should more correctly be called frontignan, the abbreviation of muscat de frontignan.

TOKAY

Tokay, of course, is made in Hungary. A long way back in our history some Australian winemaker produced a wine which he considered similar to the Hungarian product. As is usually the case with our Australian winemakers, it was not long before others copied him and Australian 'Tokay' became an accepted wine.

What is strange about this development is that a certain grape grown in Australia became known as 'tokay'. Nothing much is known about it though it may be the Hungarian Harslevelu. Today only wine made from this grape is called 'tokay'.

There is little justification for the name because, although the wine is somewhat the same colour as the European article and it is sweet, the similarity stops there. Hungarian Tokay is made like a German Spaetlese Riesling or a French Sauternes. Hence it is not fortified. Australian tokay is fortified to about twenty per cent by volume of alcohol.

It is however an excellent product and a useful change from port or muscat as a dessert wine since it does not have quite the definition of port nor the overpowering flavour of a muscat. Good examples are:

| Morris | *Tokay* |
| Orlando | *Gold Medal Tokay* |

WHITE PORT, MADEIRA

These are now almost obsolete names in the industry. In between the two World Wars, port, white port, and madeira formed the bulk of sales. Today wine sold as 'sweet sherry' has almost eliminated wines under the name of white port and madeira. They are simply sweet white fortified wines made from any white grape – the most popular being gordo blanco, sultana, muscat de frontignan and tokay.

I do not intend to give any example of these wines on the principle that what nobody misses is well forgotten.

MARSALA

The popular marsala made in Australia is the type known as 'Marsala All' Uovo' 'egg Marsala'. This is a thick, heavy and syrupy wine made by adding to a sweet base wine concentrated grape juice, herbs and other flavouring elements such as egg. If we did not have an Italian community, it is doubtful whether this wine would be popular. It contains a high percentage of sugar and is so strongly flavoured that a little is usually enough. The best and original example is

| Wynvale | *Boronia Marsala All' Uovo* |

OTHER PRODUCTS

The remaining types are the proprietary lines of the various companies. They differ from other sweet white fortified wines only because they are made from different grape varieties. Examples are:

Hardy's	*Tintara Sauvignon Blanc*
Leonay	*Maywine*
Houghton's	*Liqueur Hermitage*

No nation is drunken where wine is cheap:
and none sober where the dearness of wine
substitutes ardent spirits as the common
beverage. It is, in truth, the only antidote to
the bane of whisky.
Thomas Jefferson. 1818

7 THE WINE SCENE IN AUSTRALIA

THE AUSTRALIAN winemaker is
usually a company. Some of the wine companies possess
as many as seventeen or eighteen wineries in different areas
all over Australia. Very few of them are specialists in the
sense that they make only one wine in one area, a practice
observed in Europe.

On the whole, the Australian winemaker is concerned
with making a large variety of wines. Even the smallest
will produce red and white table wines, red and white
fortified sweet wines, dry sherry and vermouth and, in very
many cases, champagne. This great variety may be produced
in one winery from grapes grown in the district, or it may

be the result of blending the grapes of several districts.

Let us not be critical of this. This is Australia, not Europe. We can do these things because of a most equable climate; because our vineyard areas are very few; and because public demand is for this great variety.

Australian Winemaking Background

The great Australian wine companies are very strong financially, even by European standards. That is, they possess, quite often, very large acreages of valuable land. They are all equipped with the most expensive winemaking plant; and all hold enormous stocks of maturing wine.

These companies do not really need vast areas of vineyards held in their own name.

The whole industry relies on the small independent grower, who does not make wine himself at all, but sells his grapes to the large companies or co-operatives. In the non-irrigated areas, such as Barossa Valley, this independent grower, in addition to grapes, may grow vegetables or crops of wheat or oats; or he may run sheep or cattle. He is in fact a small 'mixed' farmer.

In the irrigated areas of the Rivers Murray and Murrumbidgee, the 'block-holder' usually has only a very small holding which produces, nevertheless, a prolific crop of grapes. It might also produce oranges and grapefruit. This small land owner has the opportunity of selling his grapes as fresh fruit to the large cities; as dried fruit – he dries it himself – mostly for export; or to the wineries to be made into wine or distilled into brandy.

Most of the wine sold in Australia is retailed under the name of these companies. Their large advertising campaigns and their highly efficient selling and merchandising organizations see to this. The wine need not be made from their own grapes; it might not even be the wine they have made themselves. Many of the larger firms purchase their wine from the co-operatives or from other private companies because they have not made enough to satisfy the demand for the product under their own name. Wine in Australia is made by one of the following three groups:

The Large Private or Public Company. This includes Pen-
fold's. Seppelt's, McWilliam's, Lindeman's, Hardy's,
Gramp's, Wynn's, Mildara, Smith's (Yalumba), Reynell's,
Hamilton's, Martin's, Angove's, Leo Buring's.

As I have said, these companies need not necessarily
grow their own grapes. In fact, several of the companies
named above have very small holdings of vineyards indeed.
They all have
1. extremely efficient wineries,
2. very capable technical staff.
These two factors enable them to produce the great
varieties of wines and give them the ability to 'blend'
skilfully. Hence, even though a company may be lacking
a certain wine for which it has a demand, it can buy in
wines from wineries all over Australia and blend these
up to its own requirements.

Some of the companies I have listed under the 'large
private or public companies' do not in any way compare
in financial size with, say, Penfold's or Seppelt's. I have
included them here because they have products that are
marketed nationally.

Again, one or two of these companies own large tracts
of vineyard area near Adelaide. This land is gradually
becoming surrounded by residential areas as the city
expands. They are finding that they are worth hundreds
of thousands of dollars more as potential land developers
than as winemakers.

Certainly, the vineyards in these areas will be swallowed
up and it is more than likely that the winemaking practices
of the companies will be given up.

However, the development of new areas is an unending
process and the loss of old areas will be more than taken
up by the planting of the new.

The Co-operative Winery. These are at Waikerie, Berri,
Loxton, Renmark, Nuriootpa, Clare, and McLaren Vale
– all in South Australia.

They were formed to take the produce of the local growers
– to make it into wine or brandy. Even though a grower

owns shares in a co-operative he need not necessarily sell his grapes to it; nor is the co-operative bound
to buy his grapes. Nevertheless, the scheme operates to
buffer the producer against the hardship which could be
endured because of lack of demand in a period of over
supply and gives him a certain control, although very
remote, over the price of his grapes.

The co-operatives produce enormous quantities of wine.
However, since they do not have effective merchandising
or selling sections, most of what they produce has to be
sold to the private companies to be marketed under company labels.

Technically, the co-operatives do not have to bow to
the private companies. Their laboratories and winemakers
are just as efficient; their wines just as well made. The
co-operatives have often received government guaranteed
loans in order to buy the latest equipment and to establish
their wineries as the most modern in Australia. In some
cases the co-operative can obtain quality grapes from the
grower who is a shareholder at times when the private
company cannot.

The great difference between the two is that the co-
operative is not interested in making wine except from
the produce of its members; nor is it interested in buying,
from other areas, wine for blending; whereas the 'company'
winemaker is primarily interested in marketing a standard
product under its own label and where the wine comes
from is a secondary matter.

The wine of the co-operative, therefore, is the wine of
the area.

The Small Family Concern. Australia began her winemaking history with the small family concern. Some of
the families grew to become the big companies of today.

The tendency was until recently for the small family
winemaker to disappear. This was largely because he found
it too difficult to compete with the highly advertised products of the large companies.

With the rapidly rising interest in table wines in recent

years the tide has changed. The small maker who has some skill in making table wines has found that there is a renewed demand for his product. High quality table wines do not necessarily need advertising. They are sought out.

The firms, then, who have remained and look like remaining, as small family concerns are those who are making a high quality table wine and who have enkindled in oncoming family members a strong interest. These families can see in winemaking a profitable independent business.

The following are examples of this type:
1. Hunter Valley Area: Families of Elliott, Drayton, Tyrrell, Lake.
2. North-Eastern Victoria: Families of Sutherland Smith, Chambers, Buller, Brown, Bailey, Booth, Campbell.
3. Great Western, Victoria: Thomson.
4. Barossa Valley (South Australia): Thumm, Basedow, Henschke, Hoffman, Falkenberg.
5. Southern Vales Area (South Australia): Ingoldby, Chaffey, Kay, Osborn, Potts, Johnston.
6. Clare (South Australia): Birks, Knappstein.
7. Mount Lofty Ranges (South Australia): Tolley, Hodges.
8. Goulburn Valley: Purbrick, and groups of families of Italian descent.
9. A group of families in the Swan Valley of Western Australia.
10. Groups of families in the Murrumbidgee irrigation area.

The Winemaking Areas
It can be seen from the foregoing that in the investigation of winemaking areas it is not the existence of the wineries or winemakers that matter so much as the existence of the vineyards. Grapes can be processed anywhere; or a winery set up in a few months. It takes three or four years to get a vineyard into production.

Many of the grape growing areas in the irrigation districts of the Murrumbidgee and Murray were, undoubtedly, set up more with the dried fruit market in view than winemaking or distilling. As wine drinking became more popular in

Australia and dried fruit marketing more hazardous, accent on winemaking became very much stronger.

The maps I have included showing the wine areas of Australia are based on where the grapes are growing, not on the existence of wineries.

It is probable that many a small maker will commence business in these areas in future years.

The Wholesale Wine Merchants

The capital cities of Adelaide, Melbourne and Sydney are the wine cities of Australia. Here you will find, as in many other fiscal matters, the financial strength of the wine industry. Every one of the large winemaking companies has its economic roots deep in one of these cities.

However, in addition to the winemaking companies there are quite a number of firms in Adelaide, Melbourne or Sydney who do not actually make wine but have a large sale for products under their label. They are, in effect, wine blenders and wine bottlers. In some cases the blending is very skilful and the blender has in fact added something of his own skill to the winemaker's product. Usually these wholesale wine firms have one product which stands out and for which it has a large sale. Sometimes the mere power of advertising and merchandising has effected a big demand for their products.

Many of these wine merchants have a larger output than some of the small wine companies. Almost universally they are national advertisers and market their products in every State.

In Adelaide there is Woodley Wines, recently taken over by the chain store operator, Crooks National Holdings Limited. This company markets such well known products as 'Three Roses' Sherry and 'Est'.

In Melbourne, Nathan and Wyeth have a large sale for 'Castle Vintage' wines; Max Cohn and Company for 'Three Palms' Amontillado Sherry; and W. J. Seabrook and Son for their 'Pale Dry' Sherry.

In Sydney, Rhinecastle Wines market a large number of table wines under their label.

The large winemaking company in many instances acts merely as a wholesale wine merchant. It buys large quantities of other winemakers' products, blends them and sells them under its own label.

This is a process of development. A progressive wine firm will find that there is a greater demand for its products than its own winery can supply. Rather than under supply this demand it will endeavour to blend wines up to the standard which it has been maintaining. This does no harm to anybody except in the circumstances where a firm tries to convey the impression that a wine comes from a certain area when in fact it is a blend from several areas.

The next logical development is for the company to purchase new vineyards and construct new wineries. This has happened in the history of nearly every large company.

The Wynvale organization is a remarkable example of development along these lines. Once Wynn's had no vineyards or wineries. They were merely wine merchandisers. Today they have two vineyards in South Australia and large wineries at Magill, Modbury, Coonawarra and Yenda (Griffith), besides their large blending cellars in Melbourne.

Even Nathan and Wyeth who are typical wine and spirit merchants in Melbourne have deemed it wise to plant their own vineyards at Avoca in Victoria, and to take over Buring and Sobels of South Australia.

The question is sometimes asked, 'Why do the large co-operatives not market their produce under their own label?'

The answer is that they do. Every co-operative has its own labels and endeavours to sell as much wine under these labels as it can. The great difficulty is that they have no selling organizations. The large private companies have devoted many years to selling wine as well as to making it. They have concentrated on getting their names known to the public; they have devoted a large segment of their profits to national advertising. This policy has paid off. Today they can afford to spend literally hundreds of thousands of dollars on advertising annually; whereas the co-operatives find it difficult to allocate even a small amount for this purpose.

During this period of intensive selling, the production side was not neglected. My point is that no company can market wine under its own label unless it has an effective selling organization. This is far more important in wine marketing than the excellence of its products.

If with water you fill up your glasses,
You'll never write anything wise;
For wine is the horse of Parnassus,
Which hurries a bard to the skies.
Sir Thomas Moore

8 THE VINEYARD SOILS OF AUSTRALIA

In the previous pages I have listed wines which I considered to be of unusually high quality. Do not take these names as always representing the best wines or think that there may not be others just as good. Hundreds of Australian wines which I have not listed are made similar to those mentioned. Each particular district has its own characteristics. For all styles of wine made, some districts will have years when they cannot produce top quality wines. To search out the best wine of its style, knowledge of the best years of any area is desirable. A good wine merchant should be able to help you here.

On the other hand, very many districts produce wines

that are similar to those of other districts. All of New South Wales, north-eastern Victoria and Western Australia tend to produce big, soft white wines with not too much acid but full of flavour and perhaps not altogether dry. The fact that a certain acidity is found in them at times is due, no doubt, to the careful attention given to picking the grapes a little early so that the ratio of acid to sugar is higher than it would be in a normally ripe grape.

South Australia and southern Victoria can make wines that are naturally acid and firm. This is probably because of the higher latitude of Great Western in Victoria and the higher altitudes of those parts of South Australia where the grapes used for making acid-style wines are grown. Both these factors make for lower ranges of temperature which in turn creates conditions where grapes are produced with a higher percentage of acid to sugar at ripening time. Nevertheless soil and other climatic conditions have something to do with it. Both these areas can produce high acid white wines of great quality. Firm Rhine rieslings and semillons are natural to the districts.

There is a great similarity among all South Australian wines made in the hills we know as the Mount Lofty Ranges, ranging from the Clare district about eighty miles north of Adelaide to McLaren Vale about thirty miles south. The French would call this similarity of flavour 'gout de terroir' – the tang of the soil. Even though the best tasters can pick a Keyneton red wine from a McLaren Vale, the similarity is too close always to be sure. It is quite often a knowledge of the individual winemaker's idiosyncrasies that enables the expert taster to establish the wine's identity.

No list of first class wines can ever be complete. Every year another maker provides us with a wine which is better than he ever made before. Some of the wines on such a list will not always be outstanding. Finally, every year new areas are coming into production and old areas which formerly did not make high grade wines suddenly have begun to make them. For example, the Griffith district in New South Wales, once considered to be a producer of only mediocre wines, has proved to be capable of making very high class whites from Rhine riesling, pinot and semillon grapes.

The conclusion we must draw is that we must not be too rigid about defining areas of quality. In the forties and fifties we were very apt to despise wines made in the irrigation areas. It is no longer considered a correct premise to argue that irrigated vines cannot produce good table wines or that because water is applied artificially to soil that, therefore, the grape is inferior. It is soil, climate and the maker that really matter. It is up to the viticulturalist and the winemaker to work in co-operation to bring out the best in the grape.

The Vineyard Soils

Soils in general are created by the breaking up of rocks which make up the earth's surface into smaller and smaller fragments. Rocks were originally what is called 'igneous', that is they have bubbled up in molten form from deep down in the earth's surface. Igneous rocks are either basalt or granite, and are known as 'primary' rocks.

Gradually, these primary rocks are broken up by such things as frost, rain, wind, flowing water and the actions of carbon dioxide and oxygen. The resultant particles are scattered over the surface of the earth by wind and streams. Some of them settle on the beds of seas or lakes. Pressure of water forms them into 'secondary' rocks such as lime-stone, sandstone and slate.

Sometimes a sea or lake bed is forced upwards by movements of the earth's surface and the process of wearing down and breaking up begins again.

Soils consist of these broken down particles. They fall into two easily distinguishable types. Extremely fine particles form into a stiff tenacious material called 'clay'. Coarser particles form 'sand'.

Sand and clay mixed together are called 'loam', although this name is usually applied to soil in which there is 'humus' content, that is, decayed vegetable or 'organic' matter.

The proportion of sand to loam will determine the soil's physical properties or its texture, which, in turn, determines the ease with which a soil can be worked and with which water penetrates it.

The classic wines of the world do not seem to require much soil. The beautiful white wines of Germany are grown on the slate slopes of the Rhine Valley. The refined red wines of Bordeaux are grown on heavy gravel. The slopes of the famous Cote d' Or of Burgundy are almost completely lacking soil. The roots of the vines used for making the outstanding Portuguese ports penetrate into almost pure slate and granite.

Soil, or lack of it, is an important factor in determining what is a quality vineyard. It is difficult to know what it is in soil that gives a wine refinement. In the Murray Valley near Renmark the soil is pure sand. Watered by irrigation the vines produce prolifically. The grapes are big and plentiful and the sugar content is high.

At Great Western in Victoria, the soil is granite gravel completely lacking in humus. The grapes are small and the yield of the vines is meagre. The sugar content is low.

Wines made in the first district are of good colour and have a fruity bouquet and flavour; but the taste is of poor quality and the wine is lacking life. On the other hand, wines made in the second district are light in colour and body. The nose is fragrant and the taste is full of flavour with interesting facets. In short, they are quality wines.

This pattern of quality is typical of Australian wines. Rich soils, sandy soils produce mediocre wine. Rocky soils, volcanic soils, slate, laterite and limestone produce high quality wines.

If the grapes are big and full of sugar they do not produce quality wines. Of course, it is not only a matter of soil. Heat and water, together with a soil suitable for fruit growing can produce this result in the grape.

If the grapes ripen completely without being too rich in sugar and still contain a high degree of acid there is a good chance that they will make first class wine.

In many parts of Australia, soils are found rich in iron-stone either as a capping or in the form of gravel. This 'laterite' is usually a remnant from a geographically ancient formation which once constituted the whole area.

Very often outcrops of granite or basalt will occur in areas which otherwise consist of loamy soil. These also are resistant residue from older formations.

Ancient structures and laterite cannot be classified together with other soils of the locality. Vineyards closely adjacent to each other in Australia are, therefore, likely to produce completely different wines. A vineyard on the hill with scarcely any topsoil and with the roots of the vine delving down into pure rock (skeletal soil) will produce a non-comparative wine to the vineyard on the plain below with plenty of rich topsoil and with the roots supplied with abundant nourishment. Even different sections of the same vineyard will, perhaps, produce dissimilar wines.

The feature of many Australian vineyard soils is their calcareous (lime carrying) nature. Again and again, you will come across the parent limestone rock. It is common in the Mount Lofty Ranges.

The presence of laterite is a distinctive feature very often found in vineyard soils. This red friable material is characterized by the presence of particles both large and small of ironstone in layers beneath the surface. Beneath laterite, usually the presence of white or nearly white clay is detected. In addition, there sometimes occur intermittent layers of siliceous material such as quartz. These clay and siliceous layers are termed 'companion' materials.

In other places disintegrated laterite with some soil material and organic matter will be found together with traces of the original surface. This original surface will have been badly leached and will consist principally of light coloured and coarse textured material with which some organic matter will be associated. This structure is called 'lateritic podzolic soil'.

In addition to the above, the following vineyard soils are found:

BROWN FOREST SOILS

These, naturally, are brown in colour and are of medium to fine texture. Usually, they are not very deep and free lime occurs in the lower sections. They are found in the more humid part of the Mount Lofty Ranges near Adelaide.

TERRA ROSSA SOILS

They are reddish brown to red in colour, are generally shallow in depth and occur exclusively on limestone as parent material. The soil is developed in humid to sub-humid conditions on the residue left after the solution and leaching away of the parent limestone. Many of the vines at Coonawarra are grown on this soil.

RENDZINAS

These are black to very dark grey, shallow in depth and resting on limestone. Generally, they are of medium to fine texture. Like terra rossa, they are developed on the residue of parent limestone. They sometimes occur simultaneously with terra rossa. Evidence indicates that terra rossa soils are confined to harder limestone and rendzinas to the soft. The remaining vines at Coonawarra are grown on rendzinas.

RED BROWN EARTHS

At the surface these are brown to red brown in colour. At a slightly lower depth they are brighter and redder and vary from red brown to dark red. Textures vary from sand to clay loam becoming pure clay at a greater depth. They occur on a wide variety of parent materials such as igneous and sedimentary rocks, alluvium and colluvium. A good example of red brown earths is the Barossa Valley.

GREY CALCAREOUS SOILS

These are shallow soils of grey to grey brown colour being medium textured of weakly developed structure. They are inclined to powder when dry. The soil is produced by the weathering of the parent lime bearing material after the lime has largely been removed by leaching. The grey appearance and powdery nature are due to the low accumulation of organic matter, this being prevented by the high temperatures in the districts where the soils are found. They occur in South Australia on lime bearing materials in districts largely occupied by the red brown earths; for example, in the 'Southern Vales' area, south of Adelaide.

ALLUVIAL SOILS

These are not only associated with rivers and creeks but for our purposes we are not concerned with other forms. Along streams alluvial soils normally occur on the levee banks and the first terraces. Along the Murray River there are very many different types of sand. According to G.W. Leeper in *Introduction to Soil Science,* 'In the irrigation districts ... ease of drainage is the most important feature for distinguishing types. This may be seen in a given table which compares four types from an irrigated area of country typical of the Victorian Mallee where sand ridges alternate with flats. The first type, Murray sand, is found in the highest level of the ridge. The other three types commonly occur in succession in passing down the ridge towards the flat. Barmera sand and Barmera sandy loam being found on the upper slopes and Coomealla sandy loam below them, with still other types on the flat itself.'

Sandy soils found alongside creeks are not usually very deep. Very quickly the roots of the vine find their way down to the subsoil as at the Concongella ·Creek at Great Western where there is a clay; or ironstone soil as in the Hunter Valley creeks. Deeper alluvial soils are found alongside the Goulburn and Ovens Rivers in north-eastern Victoria.

> It is an established fact that wine and, above
> all, great wine is partly a matter of good luck.
> Luigi Veronelli, 'The Wines of Italy'

9 THE VINEYARD AREAS OF AUSTRALIA

**A Discussion of
Quality Vineyards** ALL WINES produced in Australia
are of a comparatively high standard; comparatively, that
is, with high volume producing countries like France and
Italy where there is a demand for cheap inferior wine as
well as for high class wine. In Australia, the poor beverage
wine seen in wine drinking countries would not have a
market. The winemaker, therefore, must produce good wine
simply to remain in business. Areas that have been proved
to be unproductive of good wine have been given up and
more profitable pursuits such as general farming and grazing have been substituted.

Australian wines, therefore, are soundly made, with good

flavour, good colour and lasting qualities. However, only a very few reach such a high standard that we could confidently show them against the best wines of other countries.

Although Australia is such a large country, the soil and climate of areas very many miles apart can be similar and the wines that are produced in these areas are very much alike. Yet, on the other hand, wines made within a small area can differ vastly in quality. Quality depends mainly on climate. Grow the same variety of grape in different soil and a different climate and you will get an entirely different wine. For example, shiraz grapes grown at Tahbilk in Victoria ripen to a Baumé (measure of sugar content) of 11°. At Rutherglen only about a hundred miles away, they ripen to 16 or more degrees. The difference in the wines produced is remarkable. Tahbilk makes a light, firm claret. Rutherglen makes a heavy, soft, sugary style of dry red.

If we took the prize lists of the wine shows over a period of years we should soon find out what vineyards were regarded by the judges as the best. Here and there we find an anomaly, but on the whole we would see that the judges were fairly consistent in giving prizes to wines from the same vineyards. From these prize lists we should be able to discover the vineyard districts which produce the best of Australia's wines.

Another way of deciding on quality vineyards is to look at wines after they have been in bottle many years. If they have lived a long time and retained their charm it is because they are basically well made classic wines.

This criterion does not mean that a wine of twenty years or more is necessarily better than one of only five years. Whether or not one likes old wines, provided they are sound, is a matter of choice. We can exclude some vineyards about which we are in doubt as to whether they are classic or not by looking at some of their wines that have been in bottle for twenty years or more.

Just as Australian classic wines are all very similar and taste very much the same after many years of ageing.

so do old first quality wines of any country grow more like one another. It is more difficult to separate an old Hunter River from an old French Burgundy or an old Bordeaux than it is to separate the five year old counterparts of these wines. After a great deal of sniffing and sipping, a good wine taster can, eventually, delineate the fine differences of flavour; but it is much easier for him to pick up a young wine and declare it to be a Bordeaux from its bouquet.

Australian wines from average quality vineyards do not grow old gracefully. If they are overloaded with sugar in the first place, this sugar becomes more apparent with age and the wines, if they are dry table wines, become intolerably and nauseatingly sweet. If they are lacking in acid, they become oxidized and undrinkable.

Quality Australian wines, on the other hand, show their class by retaining all their beauty and adding to it the refinement of maturity.

Below are listed the wine growing areas as though they were thickly populated areas like the wine districts of France or Italy. This is done only to give an idea of locality. The districts in most cases are so small that it would be more realistic to show a list of wineries. However, the aim is to show areas where wines are grown exhibiting a similarity of character.

It would probably be misleading merely to list wineries. The use of the word 'winery' as opposed to 'vineyard' is desirable. For the purpose of categorizing districts, the place where the grape was grown is the important thing. In most instances, the vine grower is a distinct identity from the wine maker. Australian practice generally is to buy grapes from a man who has no interest in them once they go to the winery. The exception is the high quality vineyard and winery where it is essential to operate growing and making as one unified whole. Even this winery will supplement its supplies by purchasing grapes from one or two smaller growers who are independent of the winery.

Australia has the soil and climate for producing top quality wines. It has the economic resources, trained manpower, techniques and, above all, the willingness to succeed. Several areas are capable of and do occasionally produce table wines of top world quality.

The Vineyard Areas
The vineyard districts may be conveniently divided as follows:

SOUTH AUSTRALIA
1. Clare-Watervale
2. Adelaide Environs
3. Barossa Valley
4. Springton-Eden Valley
5. Southern Vales
6. South-East South Australia
7. Murray Valley

VICTORIA
1. South-West Victoria
2. Goulburn Valley
3. North-East Victoria
4. Murray Valley

NEW SOUTH WALES
1. Hunter Valley
2. Riverina

WESTERN AUSTRALIA
1. Swan Valley

To understand why the vineyards of Australia are where they are it is necessary to know the history of the development of the wine industry in Australia. In the last century and in the period between the two World Wars many vineyard areas had been developed and many had been discarded.

The new settlers in the colony often chose wine as a primary product most likely to produce income. As time went by many realized that it produced much less than wheat or sheep or dairying or other forms of agriculture or horticulture. Only those districts in which viticulture proved economically preferable to other forms of land utilization have survived as vineyard areas. The basic reason why vineyards continued in existence was that they paid better than farming.

Since the end of the war, the large wine companies have begun replanting and extending old areas and opening up new. Today, the finance, the keenness and the techniques are here, but there is still not sufficient demand for our product either here or overseas.

The large wine firms possess the most modern equipment and their men are well trained. Their winemakers are highly qualified, highly intelligent and very experienced. Their executives are shrewd men of sound judgement. Overseas developments are watched very carefully and improvements incorporated in Australian methods. There is a constant exchange of information, of details about improved techniques and new equipment.

These companies investigate, subject to experiment and test in every way potential areas for the growing of grapes. If initial tests prove satisfactory the land is purchased and different varieties of grapes are planted to discover which is most suitable in the particular type of soil and climate. Finally, the whole vineyard is planted with these selected varieties.

There is a certain fallacy which circulates among Australian amateur wine circles, irritating to knowledgeable wine men. It is to the effect that we do not make the great wines we used to make years ago, more specifically, that, since the death of Maurice O'Shea, no great winemaker exists in Australia; that with the going out of the districts of Lilydale and Whittlesea, Victoria does not produce wines of anywhere near the same quality.

This theory is unadulterated sentimental nonsense. Never before in the history of Australia have we developed better districts for wine growing; never before have we had better winemakers; never before have we had better wines.

I have not the slightest doubt that sometime during the next century Australian wines will be recognized as being among the best in the world, ranking equally with the best French and German wines.

Blended Wines

Indubitably, our best wines come from one area (provided it is a first class area) and are the wines of one year.

At the same time many of our first class wines are blends of wines from different areas. We saw in the discussion on sherries that the large companies believe in 'blending to a standard'. Although this practice applies primarily to fortified wines it has been applied very successfully to table wines like riesling and claret.

Men who have had years of experience in the Australian wine trade have found that there is one striking difference between European and Australian wines. It is that Australian wines are remarkably even from year to year. This factor applies with little difference to every area on the continent of Australia. There may be variations in acidity, sugar and colour but one vintage will not have a remarkable superiority over another. No difference in vintage compares with the big annual differences experienced in Europe. There is rarely any question, therefore, of winemakers in Australia blending the poor vintage of one year with the good vintage of another year. Coonawarra and areas of the same or higher latitudes may be an exception to this rule. Australia is such a huge country, with so large a variety of soils and so many contrasting climates, that it is only to be expected that it should produce wines exhibiting tremendous difference in type, flavour and character.

Wines from north-eastern Victoria, for example, are very strongly flavoured and yet are remarkably soft. Wines from areas near Adelaide are sometimes mild in flavour but are consistently firm in body.

Experience has shown that the good qualities of one district combine effectively with those of another. Blending of different districts, therefore, has been employed to a great extent and with very great success. The 1942 'Hock' of Thomas Hardy & Sons, for instance, was a blend of Hunter Valley and South Australian riesling. It won prize after prize in the three capital cities in which it was exhibited.

It may be that in the future, certain of our wines will become renowned, not for the fact that they come from a certain area but for the fact that they are a blend of two areas that complement each other. In this we shall differ considerably from other countries. Just as France ultimately discovered that her best wines came from individual vineyards in the Bordeaux and Burgundy districts, so we may finally discover that our best wines are blends of wines from selected vineyards in different areas.

This blending of districts naturally presents considerable difficulties to those who would like to name all our wines after the grape variety and locality. To be utterly faithful to this method with a blended wine would mean an intolerable and cumbersome jumble of words on the label.

Quite obviously, a few of our large firms are endeavouring to create impressions that some of their wines come from certain prestige districts when in fact they are either blends of that area with wines from other areas or are blends but do not contain any of the wine of the prestige area at all.

This chicanery is only to be condemned. It eventually tears down the prestige of the high quality areas.

Every wine drinker has high praise for a successful blend of, say, Angaston and Coonawarra wines when this blend is clearly stated on the label. There is great dismay at the thought that a poor Coonawarra blend should be sold as a 'straight' Coonawarra. Once it comes in for criticism because of its inferior quality from people who know, the reputation of the district suffers.

Apart from the outright faking that goes on where blends and other non-district wines are represented as the wines of the district, there is the quasi deception that takes the form of naming a wine after an extinct vineyard or point of interest associated with the district. Even an existing vineyard might be named without claiming that the wine comes from the district. Consumers will, perhaps quite unjustifiably, assume that the wine comes from the high quality district.

Actually, all this misrepresentation is entirely unnecessary. The average table wine drinker does not care very much whether his wine is blended or not. On the contrary, he is more likely to expect his claret always to be the same high quality if it is.

Successful blends have been those of Colin Preece of Seppelt's with his magnificent reds in the forties and fifties where he put north-eastern Victorian wines with Great Western; there were the outstanding wines of Roger Warren of Hardy's who blended Hunter Valley with McLaren Vale; there is the series of beautiful reds of Mildara using Hunter Valley and Coonawarra which we saw in the fifties; Maurice O'Shea blended Junee and Goulburn Valley with Hunter Valley; Yalumba blended, very successfully, Angaston with Coonawarra. John Davoren of Penfold's successfully blends today various districts of South Australia. Lindeman's have a wonderful range of blended wines with an outstanding example using Hunter Valley and Clare.

All these blends are and have been openly explained to the consumer and have been marketed successfully.

Not every blend is great or even good. Some commercial wines that have been marketed as blends have been complete failures. The rewards go to the skilful cellarman in blending just as they go to the clever winemaker in winemaking.

We look timidly forward,
With a spark of hope to where
the new lands, already weary of producing
gold, begin to green with vineyards.
Robert Louis Stevenson

10 THE VINEYARDS OF SOUTH AUSTRALIA

Clare - Watervale   EARLY settlers apparently considered the Mount Lofty Ranges ideally suited to the cultivation of the vine. When we look at this area, and also at the country near Clare, we are not surprised that at least the German migrants thought so, because some of the hills are so steep that it would be extremely difficult to cultivate them for any other purpose. It would remind the German settlers that part of the Rhine Valley was useless for anything else but vines. However, there are many flat fields where you can see the farmers ploughing on the more rounded contours of the range.

Clare is on the great northern road that eventually finishes up in Darwin. About seventy miles from Adelaide, the gently undulating countryside deepens its character and becomes hilly. The road sinks between green fields which unexpectedly become textured with the geometrical criss-crossing of vines. This is the introduction to the pretty little town of Watervale. Tall pines outline the path to Quelltaler winery. Here, poplars, Australian gum trees, mown paddocks of hay and white ridges of limestone give a peaceful atmosphere.

Quelltaler is built over artesian water and all water used for winery operations is supplied from bores. The limestone soil, the hilly contours and the climate produce grapes eminently suited for dry wines. For the whites, semillon, pedro and Rhine riesling are used; for the reds, shiraz and grenache. This is the home of the famed 'Granfiesta' sherry which was the first 'flor' sherry of any consequence to sell generally on the Australian market. H. Buring and Sobels owned Quelltaler but it has been taken over and is now wholly owned by Vignerons Distillers and Vintners Limited, a holding company for several liquor companies. Nathan and Wyeth Pty Ltd, of Melbourne and Remy Martin of France are the two major shareholders. The total acreage is 480 of which 60 are non bearing, but planting is proceeding at the rate of 20-30 acres per year. Soils are red brown loam over soft limestone, shale and deeper still, clay. Rainfall is twenty-five inches. One-third of the grapes are purchased from local growers. Quelltaler still have about 200 acres available for future plantings.

Another ten miles along the road brings us to the township of Clare. Clare wines are very distinctive. Each winery buys its grapes from the growers in the district but a good wine taster can detect the differences in style between the three makers.

Birk's of the 'Wendouree' vineyard make a dry red from shiraz and mataro which is full, rich and flavourous with a very dry finish. They have seventy-one acres under production. Grape varieties grown are grenache, shiraz, doradillo, pedro, mataro, Rhine riesling, Clare riesling, albillo, tokay, cabernet sauvignon and malbec. Birk's purchase fifty-three per cent of the grapes processed. They are planting at the rate of two acres per year.

The Stanley Wine Company makes similar reds of outstanding quality with perhaps a little more fruit in the middle palate. From Rhine riesling, Clare riesling and semillon, they make highly acid whites, which are fresh and attractive and among the best in Australia. This company is owned by the Knappstein family. In the Leasingham/Watervale area they have 537 acres; at Clare itself they have 100 acres and at East Clare they have 46 acres. The grape varieties grown are cabernet sauvignon, grenache, mataro, shiraz, Rhine riesling, Clare riesling, tokay, white sauvignon, pedro and malbec. The soils at Leasingham are red clay over limestone; at Clare acid-type sandy loam and at East Clare, clay over limestone. Irrigation is not used. Sixty per cent of the grapes processed are purchased. For future development, 150 acres have been set aside at East Clare and planting is being carried out at the rate of fifty acres per year.

The Clarevale Co-operative situated right in the centre of Clare has a large market for a lower priced, but high quality beverage made from shiraz, mataro and grenache grapes. All these grapes are purchased from the Co-operative's grower/shareholders.

At Watervale, the height is 1,200 feet above sea level. The rainfall is twenty-six inches per annum.

At Clare, the height is 1,310 feet. In addition to the ever present limestone, there is a considerable amount of sand-stone.

In the centre of a cluster of little hills, between Watervale and Clare, there is a tiny hamlet. This is 'Seven Hills'. A rough side track takes you up to an ancient stone church. It was built over a hundred years ago by Jesuit priests and brothers who laboured with their bare hands to cut the stone and erect the church and the neighbouring monastery and winery which are fashioned in the same way. A great variety of grapes are grown in the little vineyard but they are not catalogued. Most go into making altar wine for sacramental purposes. A Jesuit lay brother is winemaker. He makes a passable dry red out of the red varieties and a dry white out of a patch of straight Clare riesling. This grape bears no relationship to the Rhine riesling and it produces a flat, fruity type of wine, soft and flavourous but without great quality.

Adelaide Environs

As you drive out from the city of Adelaide, you sometimes pass directly from city to vines, just as you might in Melbourne walk from a street of suburban houses into a market garden.

This rather startling transition from residences to vines is no better exemplified than at Magill. This is a pretty little suburb nestling at the foot of the ranges. You can catch a tram here and almost immediately walk through large gates strikingly marked in yellow and black with 'Penfold's Wines'. Immediately you are among the vines. Across the road from which you enter is the old cottage built by Dr Rawson Penfold in 1844. It is still in good order and today is maintained as a kind of Penfold museum.

At Penfold's at Magill, which is the South Australian headquarters of the organization, the aspect that impresses most is the storage capacity. As you wander from building to building you are confronted again and again with huge redwood storage tanks, concrete vats and oaken casks. Money has not been spared in installing the latest in machinery, equipment and scientific apparatus. This winery is situated on the 'Grange' Hermitage.

Extensive mechanical conveyors carry in the grapes to the fermenting vats as they come in from the surrounding vineyards a few miles to the north-east. Yet the vineyards around here in the immediate vicinity are very few. Magill is a kind of blending centre for Penfold's. With so many vineyards, wineries and cellars in South Australia there must be some place where all the different wines are blended so that there is a uniformity of product.

Close to Grange, is the Penfold's 'Auldana' vineyard and winery where Minchinbury Champagne and Sparkling Burgundy are made. Like all Penfold's wineries, this is a picture of efficiency and modern equipment. First class wines made here and at other wineries are blended and aged in the cool cellars dug into the hillside.

Auldana makes a little wine, including St Henri Claret, from the vineyards on the adjacent hills. Land is too valuable for the cultivation of vine and it will not be long before all these vineyards in the city environs are gone – Penfold's at Magill, Hamilton's at Glenelg, Martin's at Burnside, although the wineries will remain.

Penfold Wines were established by Dr Rawson Penfold in 1844. Today they are a public company which owns many wineries in Australia and many thousands of acres of vines. The wineries are at Kalimna, Nuriootpa, Magill, Auldana, McLaren Vale, Griffith, Rooty Hill, Branxton, Penfold Vale and Wybong Park. They are vineyard proprietors in the Barossa Valley, Adelaide environs, McLaren Vale, Coonawarra, Griffith, Rooty Hill and Hunter Valley areas. They have offices and distributing centres in every State in Australia and in New Zealand and agents in very many countries of the world. Their main bottling and distribution centre is at Tempe near Sydney, which is a giant complex of cellars and bottling equipment, probably the largest and most spectacular in Australia. The company shifted its main operations from Adelaide which had been its headquarters for well over one hundred years to Sydney in 1968.

Hamilton's were established in 1837 by Richard Hamilton at Glenelg a few miles out of Adelaide. The vineyard was called 'Ewell' after his former home in Surrey. Today the vineyards are entirely surrounded by suburban houses and only 45 acres of vineyards remain out of what once was 156 acres. However, the company has purchased 110 acres at Springton in the Barossa Ranges. Probably the most famous of Hamilton's products is their Extra Fine Moselle which is made from the pedro and verdelho varieties of grapes grown only at the Ewell vineyards.

Hamilton's also are the owners of 55 acres of grenache and pedro ximenes at Happy Valley (near Reynella) and about 54 acres of pedro, palomino, gordo blanco, grenache, cabernet sauvignon, malbec and shiraz at Nildottie in the Murray Valley. This, of course, is irrigated. They have set aside another 150 acres at Swan Hill in Victoria and 400 acres at Nildottie for future development. They are partners with The Adelaide Steamship Company in a large new project in the Hunter Valley.

If you look across to the ranges from the centre of Adelaide, you can see a quarry that has been blasted into a corner of the lovely hills. If you direct your path towards this quarry, your road takes you through the beautiful suburb of Burnside. Suddenly, right at the base of the mountain, with the quarry stretching up sheer before you, you realize that you are at a winery too. This is 'Stonyfell', the stony mountain.

The Martins (proprietors of Stonyfell) bring in many of their grapes from a vineyard near Langhorne Creek close to Lake Alexandrina. They call the excellent claret made from these 'Metala'. Some of the wines are made from grapes grown at Burnside but the winery is also a blending station for wines brought in from Martin's winery at Angaston. In 1902 Henry M. Martin and his son Ronald H. Martin took over the winery established by a certain Henry Septimus Clark in 1858. In 1926 a limited liability company was formed as H. M. Martin and Son Ltd. The company owns 95 acres of vines at Langhorne Creek comprising shiraz, cabernet and paulo (palomino). It also owns 36 acres of tokay, sweetwater, pedro and grenache at Stonyfell (Burnside). The soil here is a deep red loam over limestone and slate schist. Like most other successful companies in the business of making wines, H. M. Martin and Son plan to buy further properties for future expansion. They are proprietors of W. Salter & Son at Angaston.

Wynn's, too, have a winery at Magill. They bring in their grapes from Modbury. Between the Wynvale and Penfold wineries at Magill, is the Romalo Wine Company where, stacked high around the thick concrete walls are over half a million bottles of ageing champagne. S. Wynn and Co. Pty Ltd, have their headquarters in Melbourne and have vineyards at Modbury and Coonawarra in South

Australia and at Yenda in New South Wales. They have wineries at Magill, Coonawarra and Yenda. At Modbury they have 447 acres bearing the following varieties: grenache, pedro, semillon, Rhine riesling, palomino, doradillo, cinsaut (also called 'ouillade' or 'blue imperial'), shiraz, white hermitage and mataro. The soil at Modbury is mostly Bay of Biscay red clay on limestone sub-soil. Other sections consist of gravelly loam and sandy loam. Modbury is not irrigated. Wynn's became a public company and obtained listing on Australian Stock Exchanges in 1970.

On the main north-eastern road a few miles out of Adelaide there are three or four vineyards on the lower slopes of the Mount Lofty Ranges. Among these are C. J. Hodges and Douglas A. Tolley at Hope Valley and Angove's at Tea Tree Gully. The soil here is a heavy loam and the rainfall is between twenty and twenty-five inches. Angove's have 240 acres comprising pedro ximenes, Rhine riesling, shiraz, cabernet and grenache. These vineyards are not irrigated.

In previous years the main interest was in producing fortified wines but with the upsurge in the demand for table wines about ten years ago, production has been switched to red and white table wines of medium quality.

Barossa Valley

The first Surveyor-General of South Australia was Colonel Light. He had fought against Napoleon in the Peninsular War and considered that an area north of Lyndoch about thirty-five miles from Adelaide was similar in appearance to the Barrosa Valley which he had seen in Spain at the time of the war. Both the town which he named after his old commander, Lynedoch, and the valley, which he named after Lynedoch's victory of Barrosa, are now misspelt.

The Barossa Valley was formed by the North Para River which has its source in the ranges just north of Nuriootpa and follows a south-west course approximately through the towns of Nuriootpa, Tanunda and Lyndoch and joins the Gawler River at the town of Gawler.

Wine men often refer to the Barossa Valley as though

the term covered not only the district of the North Para Valley but the regions in the so-called 'Barossa Ranges' where grapes are grown. This would include Keyneton, Springton and Eden Valley.

This may be convenient as a term to cover a group or society of agricultural people doing the same thing. It cannot suffice for a description of two areas different in so many respects. As we shall see, the soil, the climate and the altitude of the North Para Valley is quite different from those of the areas in the ranges.

Therefore, for the sake of homogeneity, we shall treat the Eden Valley-Springton regions as being a different district to the Barossa Valley. We shall do this, fully conscious of the fact that wine men include them in the title of 'The Barossa' because they are grape growing areas closely related to the valley. Very often the grapes are gathered in these higher vineyards and taken to the valley wineries for processing. However, if we are to give a description of the character of districts we must confine ourselves to where the grapes were grown, not to where they were made into wine.

The soil in the Valley consists of red brown earths, disintegrated sedimentary rocks such as limestone, sandstone and ironstone, and alluvial sands along the sides of streams. Throughout, various secondary rocks are found beneath the surface. At Angaston limestone in the form of marble can be seen besides layers of quartz.

The rainfall is about twenty inches. Tanunda, in the centre of the valley is 864 feet above sea level.

With the several varieties of soil, there is naturally a variety in the quality of wine made. The Barossa was and to a certain extent still is an area for the production of fortified wines such as port, sweet and dry sherry, tokay and frontignac. Of their style all of these are excellent. Seppelt's, Penfold's and Gramp's are the giants of the Valley, making millions of gallons of wine a year.

The latter day habit of drinking table wines has compelled the Barossa Valley firms to convert their plants to the making of a fairly high percentage of dry wines.

On the whole the quality of dry reds and whites made from grapes grown in the Valley is only average. The really high quality table wines are made from grapes grown in the hilly areas. Many of the Valley wineries are proprietors of vineyards in these hilly areas or have firm arrangements with growers on these localities to supply them with grapes.

On the other hand, there are undoubtedly some outstanding wines made from some grapes actually grown in the Valley. There are obviously patches of soil with elements of quality that other areas do not have even in the immediate surrounds. Gramp's, for example, make a lovely dry red which they call 'Barossa Cabernet'. It is made from cabernet sauvignon and shiraz grapes grown in the Valley.

No doubt the fact that many of the red varieties of grapes were planted to make port wine in economical quantities has a tendency to level out the quality of the reds. These grapes, mainly grenache and mataro, are now used largely for making claret. Very often shiraz is mixed in with them at crushing and tones up the quality, but, other factors aside, it is necessary to have quality grapes like shiraz and cabernet to make quality reds.

Penfold's have an immense winery at Nuriootpa where they make excellent flor sherries, ports and sweet wines. Throughout the Valley and surrounding areas, Penfold's have smaller wineries and stores and vineyard plots all contributing to the output at Nuriootpa. Better quality grapes for making table wines are treated at Penfold's high quality centre at Auldana near Adelaide. They are now a public company still controlled by the Penfold-Hyland family who have the largest block of shares. The policy of the company is not to divulge acreages, but nevertheless it is well known that they have at least 1,000 acres under vines in the Barossa Valley, 700 acres being in the northern section of the Valley at a vineyard they call 'Kalimna' which is claimed at present to be the largest single vineyard in Australia. This claim will be over-ridden by the still larger vineyards being planted by Penfold's at Wybong Park in the Hunter Valley. All told, Penfold's have eighteen vineyards and wineries in Australia.

Next to Penfold's huge establishment at Nuriootpa is the Barossa Valley Co-Operative Winery. Naturally, a smaller concern than the 'giants', it has nevertheless achieved remarkable success in its history since its establishment in the middle thirties. Today its net assets amount to $5 million. The specialty of the company is sparkling wine. Much of the 'pearl' wine seen under various labels is made by the Barossa Co-Operative. Its own label is 'Kaiser Stuhl' named after a peak in the ranges overlooking the Valley.

Seppelt's who have various wineries throughout Australia, have their headquarters and main operations centre at Seppeltsfield near Greenoch in the Valley. The thousands of acres of land owned by Seppelt's surround the winery and are beautifully maintained. The winery and store rooms are built from bluestone. The fermenting vats are set into the side of a hill so that all settling operations may take place by gravity. Naturally, many thousands of tourists visit Seppeltsfield every year and I doubt if any winery in Australia is more worth a visit. It is beautifully run and the whole complex is a most picturesque sight. Seppelt's make only fortified wines here: at Tanunda they distil a well known product – Chateau Tanunda Brandy, and at Great Western in Victoria they make their champagne. Seppelt's is a family concern and was established by Mr Joseph Ernst Seppelt at Seppeltsfield in 1851. They have 500 acres of vines at Seppeltsfield, the soil type being red/brown earth. Grape varieties grown are grenache, mataro and palomino. Seppelt's consider that the economics in the marginal areas in the Barossa Valley are not attractive and consequently have reduced acreage here considerably. This is because many of their holdings were fragmented and mostly on poor soils or in marginal rainfall areas. They have reduced their interest to the immediate areas around the Seppeltsfield, Dorrien and Chateau Tanunda wineries. It is not their intention to expand operations in the Barossa Valley at the moment other than to maintain their gardens in good condition by a thirty year rotation programme. The Barossa Valley wineries of Seppelt's process the grapes grown by this company in the Waikerie area. As we shall see in our descriptions of the other areas, Seppelt's have large areas of vines and many wineries in the various States of Australia. Twenty per cent of the grapes processed are purchased. Nevertheless, in the next few years the present tonnage will nearly double due to the new gardens coming into bearing. The average planting for the last ten years has been in excess of 100 acres per annum and will continue at that rate indefinitely. They still have about 1,000 acres of first class land which can be developed. Seppelt's are continually evaluating areas for vineyard development. They have at least five possible spots located in South Australia for further investigation should they wish to progress further. Most of these are now in natural rainfall areas where at least twenty-five inches per annum can be expected and all with some possibilities of supplementary watering. Seppelt's floated as a public company this year (1970) and expect to seek stock exchange listing late in 1973.

Gramp's (Orlando) are the proprietors of a winery, tremendous in size, at Rowland Flat. They have won fame with their 'Barossa Pearl' but deserve high praise for their wonderful white table wines such as 'Barossa Riesling' made from the Rhine riesling grape grown in the ranges and for their most successful 'Late picked' Riesling. This is slightly sweet in the German 'spaetlese' style. Once again it is a family concern established by Johann Gramp in 1847 at Jacob's Creek, a mile north-east of the present winery. The company has over one thousand acres of vineyards in full bearing both in the Barossa Valley and near Ramco on the River Murray. The highest vineyard is known as the 'Steingarten', which is more or less an experimental vineyard of Rhine riesling grown by Gramp's at about sixteen hundred feet on top of the mountain immediately behind Rowland Flat. Steingarten has an area of six acres. The vines are pruned on the basket system and the soil is schist rock. This is new soil of decomposing soft rock, a shale type which splits fairly easily. At Rowland Flat the soil is a gravelly sandy loam overlaying both red and yellow clays; Bay of Biscay loam in patches;

white podzolic soils overlaying a yellow clay (these are not particularly fertile); heavy alluvial soils alongside the Para Creek near Lyndoch (these are heavy, black soils not particularly suited to quality grapes). Gramp's grow grapes also at the top end of the Valley which are on red/brown earths with lime structures underneath.

In 1953 Orlando (Gramp's) revolutionized table wine production in Australia by adopting the cold and pressure-controlled fermentation that was being practised by both West German and Austrian wineries. Since that date extensive buildings and installations of the latest and best procurable winemaking techniques and equipment have been introduced and today the storage capacity of Orlando cellars exceeds four million gallons. In 1956 Orlando made further history when it introduced the first naturally sweetened effervescent wine in Australia, the world-wide registered Barossa Pearl. Except for a little irrigating, the Barossa Valley vineyards depend on the natural rainfall together with intense cultivation. By far the greatest tonnages of grapes processed are purchased from outside growers. Grapes grown by Orlando include Rhine riesling, cabernet sauvignon, shiraz and trebbiano. In 1969 a new vineyard property of 253 acres was acquired at Eden Valley. 180 acres of this is suitable for growing vines. The soil here is of the skeletal group with several outcrops of siliceous rock, average rainfall is twenty-six inches. Rhine riesling, gewurztraminer and frontignan are being planted.

Smith's (Yalumba) are in the hills just out of Angaston. They make fine white wines under the name of 'Carte d'Or' Riesling. Flor Sherry is an outstanding product of theirs under the name of 'Chiquita'. Yalumba make a group of excellent light tawny ports from grape varieties such as shiraz (red), dolcetto (red) and tokay (white). 'Galway Pipe' and 'Directors Special' are two. Yalumba is a family company owned by the Smith family. Mr Wyndham Hill Smith is managing director and Mark Hill Smith, his nephew, is manager. The company was established by Mr Samuel Smith at Angaston in 1849. They are the proprietors of 401 acres of vineyards in the Barossa Valley area and 372 acres at Qualco (Oxford Landing) in the Murray Valley. In the Barossa Valley they grow the following grape varieties: madeira (it is difficult to know what is meant by this grape variety – according to Boehm and Tulloch, it cannot be distinguished from the 'true' semillon), mataro, tokay, white sauvignon, shiraz, white hermitage, pinot, pedro, sweetwater (it is difficult to find out what exactly this grape is), sherry (this is probably the albillo), temperano (more exactly temprano – probably the panse precose), Rhine riesling, cabernet sauvignon, semillon, grenache and dolcetto. The soil varieties are mostly sand or sandy loam over clay.

At one of the peaks of the Barossa Ranges, Yalumba has gone into partnership with the proprietor of a property called 'Pewsey Vale', a Mr Geoffrey Angus Parsons. Yalumba are responsible for the planting and care of the grapes and for the making of the wine. The soil here is a gravelly, sandy loam with some very dark loam in patches. The sub-soil is very pebbly and consists of decomposed stone, basalt boulders and limestone structures. Pewsey Vale is largely planted out with Rhine riesling and cabernet sauvignon, with some semillon. It is considered by Yalumba that this area will produce the best white wines they make. The height above sea level is 1,600 feet and the rainfall is twenty-five inches.

The company have set aside 200 acres at their River Murray vineyard and 1,700 acres at Pewsey Vale for future development and they plan to plant these acreages at the rate of 100 acres per annum. All grapes are processed at the winery at Yalumba including those grown at Qualco and seventy-five per cent of all grapes processed are purchased from outside growers.

Chateau Leonay, owned by Leo Buring Pty Ltd, is a winery on the outskirts of Tanunda. This company has had remarkable success with their Rhine riesling white wine which has won several gold medals in the agricultural shows. The grapes for these come from the ranges north of the valley. Much success, too, has been gained with the dry reds made at this winery. Rinegolde, still and sparkling, is made here. It is a sweet wine which comes under the category of sauternes. Leo Buring Pty Ltd, formerly a public company was taken over by Lindeman's and is now a wholly-owned subsidiary of the latter. Leo Buring's was founded by the man of that name, a cousin of the Burings of Buring and Sobels. He established Chateau Leonay near Dorrien just after the Second World War. The company owns sixty-five acres of vines at Watervale and fifty-four acres in the Barossa Valley. The grapes grown include grenache, shiraz, pedro, palomino, Rhine riesling, Clare riesling, and white hermitage. It is planting another six acres of vines and has the purchase of other properties for expansion under consideration. Ninety per cent of all grapes processed are purchased.

In the Valley, also are to be found Tolley, Scott and Tolley who make a first class brandy: They were formed in 1858 with the object of purchasing grapes from the growers of the surrounding district for the manufacture of brandy and fortifying spirit. At that time the name of the company was the East Torrens Wine Making and Distillation Co. Ltd. In 1888 it came under the control of Thomas Scott and Ernest and Douglas Tolley. In 1904 the present distillery at Nuriootpa was built and today all the brandy and spirits is made here. The company is now owned by the Distillers Co. Ltd, of Britain. It has 800 acres of vineyards at Waikerie on the Murray River comprising grenache, doradillo, cabernet sauvignon and a few odd varieties. Here the soil is sandy loam and limestone marl and it is spray irrigated. The company has set aside another 200 acres for further planting.

Salter's which is a division of the firm of H. M. Martin and Son, of Adelaide are also in the Valley. Salter's market their product under the name of 'Saltram'. There is a very attractive red under this label made from shiraz grapes grown on the limestone and quartz near Angaston. W. Salter and Son Ltd, was founded in 1859 by William Salter and his son Edward. In 1941 H. M. Martin and Son Pty Ltd, purchased a controlling number of shares in the company.

They own 105 acres of vineland near Angaston. Grape varieties grown are semillon, grenache, pedro, shiraz, palomino, cabernet sauvignon, Clare riesling, dolcetto, Rhine riesling and tokay. Most of the areas get supplementary watering from Saltram's own bore – in winter by spraying and in summer by flooding. Although H.M. Martin and Sons do not own property under their own name in the Barossa Valley, most of the wine sold under their name is made by Saltram's under the general supervision of the H. M. Martin directors. Up to ninety per cent of the entire production of both Saltram's and Martin's is from grapes grown on properties other than their own.

In addition there are several other small makers whose labels are not known nationally. It may seem unjust to pick out one or two special wines from each maker's range and to give prominence to only these. Every company wishes to be known not only by one product which happens to be more than usually excellent but by all their products which they will quite justifiably claim are just as excellent. However, we are dealing with districts rather than makers. Our aim is to seek out the outstanding wines of these districts but not to give a list of all the wines that are made there.

Every year at the beginning of the vintage, a Vintage Festival is held in the Barossa Valley. This is a revival of similar festivities indulged in by the ancestors of the present Valley people most of whom are of German descent. It consists of marching bands, beautiful and elaborate floats festooned with grapes and grape leaves and pretty girls in gaily coloured traditional costumes. The carnival is celebrated with dancing in the streets and parks and, of course, with gusty drinking of the Valley's beverage.

Thomas Hardy and Sons are the proprietors of a vineyard at Dorrien which they call 'Siegersdorf', which was the old name for Dorrien. They obtain the grapes for their winery in the Eden Valley/Springton area. They make a most magnificent white wine which is named after the vineyard as 'Siegersdorf Riesling'. For details of their operations in the Southern Vales area see pages 137-8.

Another grower in the Barossa Valley is P. T. Falkenberg, who has 112 acres of the following varieties: muscatel, grenache, pedro, mataro, semillon, madeira, frontignac, white hermitage, sercial and carignane. Seventy per cent of his production is from purchased grapes and he has set aside sixty acres for future plantings.

Other smaller firms in the Barossa Valley are Basedow Wines Ltd, Chateau Yaldara Pty Ltd, St Hallet, R.H. Binder, Chateau Rosevale, North Para Vineyards (E.& L. Hoffman), B. Leibich and Sons, Paradale Wines and Wilsford Wines.

Springton-Eden Valley

This district runs along the watershed of the Barossa Ranges, as the Mount Lofty ranges are called in these parts. Some of the peaks in the locality are over 2,000 feet above sea level. Eden Valley and Springton are 1,400 feet. Rainfall is about thirty inches per annum. We can include in this district because of similarity of soil, rainfall and altitude, the valleys and hills along the north-eastern road as it swings in an arc from Springton to Keyneton. Pewsey Vale is an old area now being revived.

Pewsey Vale Vineyard is at a point about 1,600 feet in the ranges overlooking the Barossa Valley. The land is owned by a man called Geoffrey Angus Parsons. The venture is a partnership between him and Yalumba Wines, the property being planted out, cultivated and managed by Yalumba. (See section on S. Smith and Sons, Barossa Valley.) There are 106 acres of Rhine riesling, 5 acres of cabernet and 17 acres of semillon.

The soil is podsol, a sandy loam sometimes on limestone, sometimes on ironstone, quartz and clay which, as we have seen under 'Vineyard Soils', is known as 'lateritic podzolic soil'.

There are quite a number of independent growers in this district, all of whom grow high quality grapes such as Rhine riesling, and all of whom are intensely proud of their grapes. Usually, the cultivation of vines is only part of their activities as in addition, they engage in pastoral or agricultural pursuits. From their grapes are made some of our best quality white wines. Shiraz is also grown and new areas are constantly being planted with these two high quality varieties.

Hamilton's have a winery in Springton from whence comes their 'Springton' Riesling, Graves and Claret, all beautiful wines. Hamilton's Ewell Vineyards Pty Ltd, are dealt with more fully under the Adelaide environs area. They were established in 1837. Hamilton's have forty acres of Rhine riesling, shiraz, white frontignac, grenache and cabernet sauvignon at Springton where they had taken over an old winery in 1965.

The other winery in the hills, at Keyneton, is the property of C. A. Henschke. He built up an enviable reputation with his steely, highly acid rieslings which he makes 'from grapes grown in the ranges. These whites are characteristic in style, appealing to those palates which find acid a pleasant accompaniment to the highly refined flavour of the Rhine riesling. Henschke makes, in addition, white wines from other grape varieties and a very distinguished red from shiraz grapes. The firm C. A. Henschke and Co., was established by his great-grandfather in 1868.

Many of the famous makers, such as Penfold's, Hardy's and Yalumba purchase grapes from this region, preferring to process them in their own wineries in other areas. Orlando purchased 253 acres here in 1969

Southern Vales
REYNELLA – MCLAREN VALE

The Mount Lofty Ranges continue their rolling path parallel to the gulf as you go to the coast along the road that travels from Adelaide to Victor Harbour. Between the ranges and the sea there is a low level undulating stretch of country where vines are spread out like patchwork against the green cloth of orchards and cereal crops. Here are Reynella, Glenloth, Benjamin Chaffey, Tintara, Johnston, Ingoldby, Horndale and a few smaller wineries. Probably the better definition of this area is 'Reynella-McLaren Vale'. It is more descriptive than the old-fashioned term 'SouthernVales'. The two vales concerned are Morphett

Vale and McLaren Vale but the district of Reynella, as distinct from the wine firm known under the same name, embraces most of the vineyards in the Morphett Vale area and the term 'Southern Vales' has become unpopular with wine men as the term for an area because it can become confused with the winery which is called Southern Vales Co-operative. Langhorne Creek is usually included in the area called Southern Vales.

In the Reynella area the most important vineyard, of course, is that of W. Reynell and Sons Ltd, which was established by John Reynell in 1838. (Walter, incidentally, was the son of John and much of the success of the firm is attributed to him, although undoubtedly there would have been no firm of this name if it had not been for the pioneering efforts of his father.) In April 1970 W. Reynell & Sons sold their assets excepting the vineyards at Reynella to Hungerford Hill Ltd.

The sub-soil at Reynella is basically limestone, either pure limestone, marl or chalk. At Reynella itself the company (W. Reynell & Sons) has 430 acres under vine and at McLaren Flat (Wylpena) it has 61 acres of vineyards. The grape varieties grown include 72 acres of cabernet sauvignon, which acreage is being increased annually. The rest comprises shiraz, mataro, grenache, Clare riesling, gouais, white hermitage, pedro, palomino and doradillo. The doradillo and white hermitage are slowly being replaced with better varieties. Reynells have set aside 60 acres at Reynella and 20 acres at McLaren Flat for future development. Irrigation is not used. Sixty per cent of all grapes processed are purchased.

Glenloth is a company which has now been purchased by Seager Evans and Co. of London. At the present time it comprises simply a winery and distillery and much of the wine made is exported to England in bulk. Therefore, all of the grapes processed are purchased from outside growers. However, the company has purchased 400 acres in the Keppoch area of south-eastern South Australia and they will be planting there at the rate of 100 acres a year.

Edwards and Chaffey Pty Ltd, is a company wholly owned

by Benjamin Chaffey who is a grandson of one of the two brothers who established the irrigation project at Mildura in the 1880s. He is a member of the Board of Directors of Mildara Wines Pty Ltd. The name of the vineyard is 'Seaview' and it was established in 1850 by English settlers. There are 180 acres under vines comprising cabernet sauvignon (50 acres), Rhine riesling, sauvignon blanc, palomino, pedro ximenes, albillo, shiraz, mataro and grenache. The vineyards are five miles inland from St Vincent Gulf and 550 feet above sea level. The proximity of the sea is said to have an ameliorating effect on the climate. Spring frosts are seldom experienced and the summers are fairly mild. The resulting long, cool ripening period, therefore, has an influence on the quality of the grape harvested. The land is undulating and of a gravelly nature. Ironstone impregnated gravel predominates in the topsoil, which is shallow. The sub-soil is chalk-impregnated soft marl. Chaffey's property is on the hills which form the southern part of the valley of the Onkaparinga River which divides Morphett Vale from McLaren Vale.

Right next door to Chaffey is the Amery Vineyard owned by Kay Brothers Pty Ltd, of which Cuthbert Kay is the principal. This company has 130 acres of vines and plan to plant another 100 acres. They grow 17 acres of cabernet sauvignon as well as grenache, shiraz, mataro, Rhine riesling, pedro ximenes, sauvignon blanc and frontignan. The soil is mostly sandy loam with some ironstone boulders and a clay sub-soil. There are some patches of Bay of Biscay loam. Neither of the above two vineyards are irrigated.

The largest company in the area is that of Thomas Hardy and Sons Pty Ltd. This company has its headquarters in the city of Adelaide. It has branches in every State of Australia and agencies in various countries overseas. It is also planting vineyards at Keppoch in south-east South Australia and has 106 acres at Waikerie in the Murray Valley. Hardy's are perhaps more noted for their blending ability than for their straight wines, although they are making a reputation for themselves these days with their unblended McLaren Vale wines. At McLaren Vale there is a very large winery called 'Tintara' and it was this name that for very many years was the title under which Hardy's wines were sold. More recently the company has realized the value of the name Hardy and slowly the name Tintara is being taken off the labels. The Tintara winery is a very large one and handles grapes grown in the McLaren Vale area by a great number of growers who do not have their own plants. Hardy's themselves are the proprietors of 319 acres in this region of cabernet sauvignon, doradillo, grenache, malbec, palomino, pedro, Rhine riesling, semillon, shiraz and sauvignon blanc. The soil is largely sand or light loam over limestone and there are quite large sections where clay is the sub-soil. Some areas have an ironstone content. Most of the area is not irrigated but the poorer varieties such as doradillo and palomino are given supplementary spray irrigation. The high quality vines receive none. McLaren Vale is noted for its dry reds more than any other type of wine and Hardy's use their Dorrien vineyard in the Barossa Valley for making their high quality whites. Probably the most famous of Hardy's reds are the wines they have put out as cabernet sauvignon with a special code number. At one stage the central figure of this number denoted the year in which the wine was made but readers would be well advised to ignore the significance of the number system as the code is not based on vintage years. The code number is merely an arbitrary one to distinguish the bottling among its fellows. The cabernet sauvignon wine is usually a blend of wines from various areas and it must be admitted that Hardy's have achieved great success in blending softer and fuller areas with those that produce hard and firm wines. The Hardy's straight 'McLaren Vale Hermitage' is made only from shiraz grown in the area and is an extremely good example of an unblended wine of great quality and ageing potential. Most of the blending of Hardy's high quality sherries is done at the Mile End cellars in Adelaide. Hardy's were established in 1853 by Thomas Hardy of Devon, England, at a place called Bankside on the bank of the River Torrens three or four miles west of Adelaide.

Ryecroft Vineyards Ltd is owned by the Ingoldby family and James Ingoldby Jnr is the managing director. The company owns 277 acres of shiraz, cabernet, grenache and pedro at McLaren Flat, the soil of which is mainly red clay and some of which is fairly sandy. Irrigation is not employed. Of the grapes processed by the company, fifty per cent are purchased from outside sources. Jim Ingoldby, in conjunction with Egerton Dennis, a local vineyard proprietor, formed McLaren Vale Wine Pty Ltd. This company purchases wines from other wineries in the McLaren Vale area and bottles them at the winery of Ryecroft. They then sell the wine under the label of McLaren Vale Wine Pty Ltd and on the label they give details of the person who grew the grapes, the winery which made the wine, the grape varieties which made up the wine, the vintage year of making and any other interesting details. The object of the exercise is to bring attention to the fine wines made in this area by placing accent on the name McLaren Vale. It was felt by the directors of the company that too much wine was removed from the area in bulk and sold under the name of other companies located in areas very far removed from McLaren Vale. The Ryecroft vineyard was established by Frederick Wilkinson in 1884 and was sold to James Ingoldby Snr in 1919.

F. E. Osborn and Sons Pty Ltd, is headed by d'Arenberg Osborn, who is the son of the original founder. The company owns 130 acres under vines which are shiraz, grenache, mataro, doradillo, palomino, albillo and cabernet sauvignon The vineyard is known as 'd'Arenberg Vineyard' and is situated in the hills overlooking McLaren Flat. The soil is largely ironstone over a clay sub-soil. Supplementary spray irrigation is used if necessary on most of the vineyard.

A. C. Johnston Ltd own a vineyard called 'Pirramimma'. It was established in 1892 by Mr A. C. Johnston who was the father of Alex and Digby the present proprietors. There are 150 acres under vine including shiraz, grenache, pedro, palomino and three acres of cabernet sauvignon. Situated at McLaren Flat, the soil varies from sand on the high rise to Biscay loam in the hollows, with a red clay sub-soil over limestone marl. The whole area is referred to as Willunga Plains. The rains come from the ranges and looking across to the latter one can see why, because the Willunga Escarpment rises suddenly out of the ground as though it has been thrust sharply upward by some earth movement millions of years ago.

Horndale is simply a winery and distillery which processes grapes purchased from the local growers. It is a subsidiary of Gilbey's.

In the same area is J. C. Sparrow and Co. and a winery called Valle d'Oro.

In the township of McLaren Vale there is the fairly large winery known as Southern Vales Co-operative which was formed for the purpose of taking the grapes from the local growers who had no winery of their own.

Obviously, with the growing popularity of wine, grape growers who at one time gave their produce to wineries outside their properties to process will set up their own plants and make wine themselves.

For example, there is the firm of G. A. Pattritti at Dover Gardens. This firm was founded by the father of the present proprietors in 1926. It processes several hundred tons of grapes of which approximately one-third is supplied from their own vineyards. It is planting another 25 acres of shiraz.

LANGHORNE CREEK
Strictly speaking this does not come into the Southern Vales area but as it is set among the hills and vales south of Adelaide, geographically speaking, at least, it fits the description of a Southern Vales vineyard. Wine men usually refer to the area as 'Langhorne's Creek' and even in the township today there are signs which still have this spelling. Apparently at some stage in South Australian history one of the state authorities decreed that the apostrophe 's' should be eliminated from all place names and hence Langhorne's became Langhorne and we had the nonpossessive Rowland Flat and O'Halloran Hill.

There are quite a number of vineyards in this area which

sell their grapes to the local winery known as Bleasdale or to wineries outside the area such as Martin's at Burnside. The main varieties grown are shiraz, palomino (this is known locally as paulo and it is more than likely that it differs considerably from the palomino grown in other parts of South Australia because of the tendency for grape vines to develop their own strains according to area), muscat, grenache, doradillo, verdelho, cabernet sauvignon, and frontignac. The soil is a deep rich alluvial silt caused by the continual flooding of the Bremer Creek alongside which the vineyards are planted. The rainfall of this area is only 13.5 inches and therefore irrigation is absolutely necessary. The Bremer Creek, which has its source in the ranges around Mount Torrens, flows strongly during most winters. The Potts family, very many years ago, hit upon the idea of creating a weir. This is a very simple affair consisting mainly of a large steel plate which can be raised or lowered when required. It blocks off the creek which then floods over its banks and the floodwaters spread themselves over the surrounding vineyards. The depth of water can be as much as three or four feet and as flooding continues for some weeks, the ground receives sufficient moisture to last the whole year.

Just as in other areas, many vineyards in the Southern Vales area have disappeared. For economic reasons Emu and Stephen Smith and Co. gave up their holdings. Others, like Hamilton's found that they were in the path of the expanding city of Adelaide.

This is a quality area. The reds develop great colour, are astringent and rich, sometimes a little too rich. In particularly good patches such as at Reynella, the reds have a clear cut refinement with good middle flavour and a firm finish. Shiraz and cabernet grapes combine together very effectively in this district. First quality whites have been made by Benjamin Chaffey, Amery Winery and by d'Arenberg Osborn.

South-East South Australia
In our discussion on soils we saw that the underlying rock

of all this area was limestone and that it was not very far below the surface. Technically speaking, the area is podzolic soil associated with old sand dunes and sand sheets. There are occurrences of small to large swamps and at Coonawarra small areas of terra rossa and rendzina soils.

Generally, because of the higher southern latitude and the proximity of the ocean from which cold winds blow, the area is not one where the summers are very hot. The altitude is not even 200 feet above sea level. We can conveniently divide the region into two sections – Coonawarra and Keppoch Valley.

COONAWARRA

Prior to Wynn's purchase in 1950, the winery now used for making Coonawarra Estate red wines was engaged in producing wine from the local grapes mainly to be distilled into brandy. A little wine was sold in bulk for blending and an Adelaide company bottled some of it straight and it was marketed under the name of this company as Woodley Claret.

Mr Sam Wynn had a number of bottles of wine originally made by Redman's in 1932 and was impressed by their remarkable quality even after eighteen years' ageing. He attributed the success of the wine to the fact that it was given five years' ageing in wood.

Convinced that Coonawarra was a quality area, he purchased the winery and several acres of vines in 1950 for his company, S. Wynn and Co. Pty Ltd. The company marketed the red wine under a striking new label as 'Coonawarra Estate Claret'. The first Coonawarra Estate Claret was the 1950. It was not made by Wynn's as they did not purchase the vineyards until after the vintage. Coonawarra reds have done very well in wine shows over the years.

As a newly made wine, a Coonawarra is deep purple or heliotrope in colour. This changes in a couple of years, usually to dark red. As a rule the young wine has a spicy aroma, the body is light but the flavour is strong and rich. The tannin grip is satisfying. The wine ages well. However, there are several undesirable features about them which deserve attention.

The first is that they require several years ageing in wood. Their acid content is high. They suffer from the malo-lactic fermentation which, if it occurs in bottle, creates an unpleasant turbidity and carbon dioxide gas which gives a disturbing fizziness to the wine. The pre-Wynn Coonawarras suffered from this defect mainly because of too early bottling. The suggestion that they spend up to three years in wood is a good one. The malo-lactic fermentation is now induced artificially immediately after the yeast fermentation so that there is no chance of its occurring in the bottle.

The second feature is that a cold summer will produce a very poor Coonawarra red. Wynn's did not bottle some years at all because of their thinness and lack of quality. In a cold year the grapes do not ripen sufficiently to produce sufficient body in the wine. Even when the year is not too cold, the wine can turn out thin and acid.

The third feature is that the hardness and acidity of Coonawarra reds do not appeal to all wine drinkers. Women, as a rule, do not like them.

Summing up on all this, we find that Coonawarra produces red wines which are certainly in the top bracket of Australian clarets. In a good year, with correct treatment, with sufficient ageing in wood and with sufficient bottle ageing after that, they can compare favourably with the best reds in the world.

The blending of Coonawarras has been engaged in most successfully. The high acid, voluminous flavour and spiciness of the area combines well with reds from other areas that are well made, full, rich and soft but perhaps lacking in interesting flavour or acidity. Many companies have used Coonawarra reds in their blends in order to make their own wines more interesting. The fact, of course, does not appear on the label. The most successful blend is Hunter Valley-Coonawarra, but blends of Coonawarra with north-eastern Victorian reds and Barossa Valley reds are pleasant.

The original winemaker in the area was William Redman

who made wine for the first developer at Coonawarra, John Riddell. Eventually Redmans set up their own winery which they called 'Rouge Homme' and this was eventually purchased by Lindeman's in 1965. Owen Redman then set up another winery which he operates under the name of O. & L. Redman, a partnership of himself and his wife.

Wynn's now have 345 acres under vine at Coonawarra, of which 121 are planted with cabernet sauvignon, 122 with shiraz and 46 with Rhine riesling. They also have various plots of pedro, palomino, doradillo and Clare riesling. Great importance is attached to the difference of the two soils, the red terra rossa and the black rendzina. Wynn's cabernet, incidentally, is all grown on the red loam. For some reason or other grapes grown on the red soil develop more quickly than those grown on the black. Perhaps it is something to do with the refraction of sunlight. The result is that in a cloudy and cool year good wine may be made from grapes grown on the red soil but the grapes grown on the black soil never completely ripen and hence the resultant wines made from them are full of malic acid and they are too light and thin.

The area has many summers when the skies are cloudy and rain falls. Hence the grape grower becomes quite anxious about the sugar content in his grapes. He knows that time is running out and once the temperature drops to 50°, as it will in late April and May, any further accumulation of sugar will not occur.

The virtue of this region is partly attributable to the fact that it is a place of slow ripening and hence there is a very satisfactory balance of acid and sugar in the ripened grape. In addition, the fact that the grapes are mature and hence are harvested in May, and sometimes even in June, means that the weather at fermentation time is cool and a cool fermentation is natural. This of itself must result in a more perfect wine. I feel that the hazards of growing grapes on the black soil are well balanced by the rewards that are obtained in the many good years seen in the area.

Wynn's have a total area of 1,059 acres of vineyard land and are planning to develop a further 714 acres.

30° South

LAKE
FROME

LAKE
TORRENS

RANGES

LAKE
GAIRDNER

32°

FLINDERS

PORT
AUGUSTA

SOUTH AUSTRALIA | N.S.W.

Clare —
Watervale

Murray
Valley

34°

CLARE

MURRAY RIVER

RENMARK

WAIKERIE

BERRI

PORT
LINCOLN

Barossa
Valley

EDEN VALLEY

GAWLER

SPRINGTON

LOXTON

ADELAIDE

Springton —
Eden Valley

Adelaide Environs

Reynella

McLaren Vale

Langhorne Creek

SOUTH AUSTRALIA | VICTORIA

KANGAROO
ISLAND

MT. LOFTY RANGES

Southern
Vales

36°

THE VINEYARD AREAS OF
SOUTH AUSTRALIA

Keppoch
Valley

NARACOORTE

South East

Coonawarra

Major Districts

Minor Wine Growing Districts

CITIES AND TOWNS

South Australia

MT. GAMBIER

MOUNTAIN
RANGES

VINEYARD
AREAS

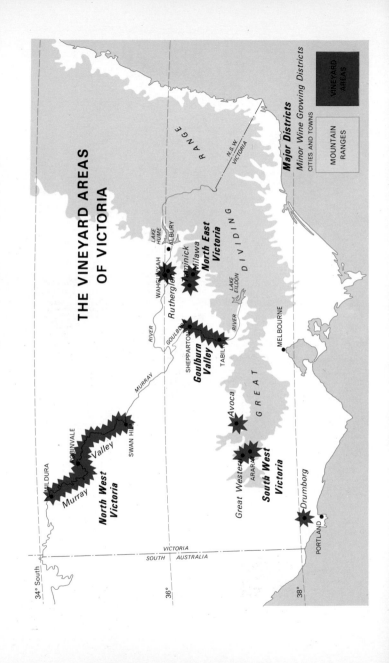

THE VINEYARD AREAS
OF VICTORIA

North East Victoria

WAHGUNYAH

Rutherglen

Corinick

Milawa

Goulburn Valley

SHEPPARTON

TABILK

North West Victoria

MILDURA

ROBINVALE

Murray

Valley

SWAN HILL

Avoca

Great Western

ARARAT

South West Victoria

Drumborg

PORTLAND

MELBOURNE

GREAT

DIVIDING

RANGE

LAKE
HUME

ALBURY

LAKE
EILDON

RIVER

GOULBURN

RIVER

MURRAY

RIVER

N.S.W.

VICTORIA

VICTORIA

SOUTH   AUSTRALIA

34° South

36°

38°

Major Districts

Minor Wine Growing Districts

CITIES AND TOWNS

MOUNTAIN
RANGES

VINEYARD
AREAS

Lindeman's purchased some acres of vines with the 'Rouge Homme' property but in addition have acquired a large property at Keppoch Valley near Naracoorte and are beginning the planting of this property immediately.

Mildara Wines Ltd purchased vineyards at Coonawarra in 1954 and since then have proceeded with a planned programme of vineyard development. They now have over 300 acres planted, the majority of which are red grapes about evenly divided between cabernet sauvignon and shiraz. They have planted test areas of malbec, Rhine riesling, Clare riesling, sauvignon blanc, semillon and palomino. They plan to plant a further 200 acres in the next two years and wish to continue to extend their plantings until their total holding of over 700 acres is in production. All Mildara land is on the 'red bank'. Like most of the wine growers in the area they use supplementary watering during the first two years from planting to assist in the establishment of the vines. This water is pumped up from the underlying reserves which are fairly close to the surface. Irrigation, however, is not practised otherwise in the area as all the winemakers believe that it deteriorates quality.

In addition to the superb dry reds, the Coonawarra area is now producing some of the best rieslings we make in Australia. Both Wynn's and Mildara have marketed Rhine rieslings in recent years from Coonawarra which compare favourably with the Rhine rieslings made in the Eden Valley-Springton area.

Other winemakers at Coonawarra are Penfold's, who at this stage have no winery, but quite a large vineyard. The grapes are harvested and sent by road transport to Magill.

Eric Brand has a very small vineyard of several acres and an equally small winery. Brand, incidentally, is the son-in-law of William Redman. His red wines are up to the best standard of wines from the area and he has won several awards at the shows for them.

A private company headed by Peter Yunghanns, Melbourne restaurateur, has purchased about 500 acres situated between Lindeman's and 'Rouge Homme' for the purpose of planting vines.

KEPPOCH VALLEY

This area has become the centre of attraction for a number of companies who have bought large tracts of land. The land skirting the area is not attractive country to look at, being considered in past years as almost desert with sparse vegetation and very often showing no signs of growth whatsoever. The region was rehabilitated after the Second World War mostly by the Australian Mutual Provident Society and with a great deal of success. Trace elements were introduced to the soil which enabled trefoil to be planted which in turn produced the nitrogen which was so lacking up to this stage. Sheep grazing, therefore, is the industry of the area. The winemaker, however, became interested in the Keppoch Valley not because of the soil reclamation which had been practised but because of the sub-soil of limestone and the fairly high water table. In addition, it had been proved at Coonawarra that extremely high quality table wines could be produced. It is hoped by the companies who are developing the area that with Coonawarra, it could become the premier quality district of Australia.

Seppelt's have purchased 500 acres of land at Keppoch which is about thirty-five miles north of Naracoorte. Although the whole of this area possesses similar characteristics of climate and sub-soil to Coonawarra it is wise to regard the Coonawarra section as quite separate from the Keppoch Valley region because of the great differences in the surface soil. There may also be other differences such as that created by wind patterns and frost which make Coonawarra what it is, and which may possibly make Keppoch Valley wines quite different. Incidentally, the name *Keppoch Valley* is more correct than the term *Padthaway* which is the proprietary name of the family which owned the land which the wine companies are now developing and who still own the original homestead.

The present intention of Seppelt's is to transport grapes from Keppoch to their winery at Great Western. The grape varieties planted are cabernet sauvignon, shiraz, malbec and Rhine riesling. Seppelt's intend to plant tokay and the new varieties which have recently been brought into Australia such as pinot noir, gamay Beaujolais, silvaner, and gewurztraminer once they have been evaluated in the area. The soil type of the Seppelt property is red brown earth over clay and limestone. This surface soil, therefore, is different from the red soil of Coonawarra which is terra rossa.

Thomas Hardy and Sons have purchased 300 acres and Glenloth Wines 400 acres in this area. Hardy's have 80 acres of shiraz and 20 of cabernet sauvignon.

Murray Valley

Undoubtedly, the characteristics of every area along the Murray Valley are different because the soils are different and there are slight climatic differences.

However, the general conditions of growth are the same. The soil is alluvial sand, the temperature in summer is in the high nineties, the vines are 'flood' or spray irrigated and the same varieties of grapes are grown.

At Renmark, Berri, Loxton and Waikerie, there are huge co-operative wineries and distilleries. Although these co-operatives market wines under their own labels, the market for these name brands is particularly small and the product is sold in bulk to nationally advertised companies.

A very large private company, Angove's Ltd, with a winery at Renmark, markets wine and brandy under its own label with considerable success. It has a substantial export market for its product in bulk in England. The company has 60 acres of cabernet, shiraz and Rhine riesling at Renmark and 2,000 acres at Murtho of various varieties. In spite of this huge area, ninety per cent of the production at Angove's is obtained from grapes purchased from properties not their own.

There are one or two smaller wineries owned by private individuals at Moorook and Berri. Many of the grapes grown in the Murray Valley are trucked to the wineries in the Barossa Valley and further south for processing.

Although table wines had not been well received as quality wines until recently, experiments have been successful and now we are seeing something of more than ordinary quality from this area. Sweet fortified wines are well made and one or two muscats are of superb quality.

Enormous quantities of brandy are distilled and have a good market throughout Australia under various labels which do not give any indication as to where they were made. They have a lightness and cleanness of flavour which is highly suitable to the Australian palate, quite different from Australian brandy made from material grown in other areas and, of course, tremendously different in flavour from French brandy.

Many of the famous makers, such as Penfold's, Hardy's, and Yalumba purchase grapes from this region, preferring to process them in their own wineries in other places, although Hardy's have their own winery at Waikerie.

Seppelt's have purchased 1,100 acres in the Qualco (Waikerie) area and have planted 500 acres of palomino, white hermitage, shiraz, doradillo, malbec, cabernet sauvignon and tokay, and intend to plant albillo, Rhine riesling and one or two of the recently imported varieties. Their property has a soil type of coarse red river sandy loam over limestone and marl with fossil shells. Irrigation is by means of permanent and portable overhead sprinklers. Seppelt's remark that as the vines mature in these Murray Valley areas they have seen the quality rise in table wines and with improved equipment in the wineries they expect to see some premium wines coming from the district. All the grapes grown by Seppelt's or purchased by them in this area are transported to their Seppeltsfield winery in the Barossa Valley for processing.

Hardy's have 106 acres at Waikerie consisting of shiraz, pedro, doradillo, palomino, Rhine riesling, grenache, sultana and gordo.

Yalumba have 372 acres at Qualco of doradillo, gordo, palomino, pedro, riesling, semillon, white sauvignon, sultana, cabernet gros, cabernet sauvignon, grenache, malbec, shiraz and dolcetto.

> Look not thou upon the wine when it is red,
> when it giveth his colour in the cup; ... at
> the last it biteth like a serpent, and stingeth
> like an adder.
> Proverbs xxiii. 31

11 THE VINEYARDS OF VICTORIA

South-West Victoria AT THE present time, the most important grape growing area in south-west Victoria is at Great Western, a little township on the Western Highway mid-way between Ararat and Stawell; but there are several new areas which are attracting a great deal of attention.

DRUMBORG

Seppelt's have planted vines recently at Drumborg near Heywood. This is just outside the town of Portland, almost a degree further south than Great Western or Coonawarra and a little further south than Melbourne. Remembering that Lilydale once produced magnificent wines in almost the same latitude and that Coonawarra wines have difficulty with frost and cool summers, this should be a very interesting area when developed. The soil is different from all these other districts being of volcanic residue over leached clay, with some underlying granite in places on the hills and good red clay on the flats.

Seppelt's have the same plans as they have for Keppoch Valley. In other words their intention is primarily to produce grapes here of high quality most suitable for making their Great Western Champagne. Probably, as time goes on, they will make wines which can be sold as dry table wines such as Rhine riesling and pinot. The main grape they grow at Drumborg for champagne was formerly thought to be the pinot blanc of France, sometimes called chardonnay. Eventually it was found that the grape was not this variety and it acquired the new name of Irvine's white, a tribute to the man who obviously planted the grape at Great Western and from whom Seppelt's purchased the vineyard in 1918, Hans Irvine. The property consists of 450 acres, 200 of which are planted with Irvine's white, Rhine riesling, tokay, miller burgundy, chasselas, sylvaner, gewurztraminer and pinot chardonnay.

AVOCA

Another new, or rather revived, area is at Avoca which is, like Great Western, in the range of hills which form the Great Dividing Range, the height being 790 feet above sea level. It is about forty miles north-east from Great Western. Here you have a joint venture between Remy Martin of Cognac, France, and Nathan and Wyeth of Melbourne in planting a vineyard of about 200 acres. They have planted 150 acres of white hermitage and 50 of doradillo, these being considered the most suitable for making high quality brandy.

Perhaps it is pertinent to note that white hermitage is also called trebbiano which is the grape grown in the Cognac area of France where it is called St Emilion. Nathan and Wyeth plan also to plant 40 acres of vines annually.

Wal Henning, by profession a teacher, by business an

earth-moving contractor, and by choice, a vigneron has purchased 400 acres of arable land which he is planting out with white hermitage, doradillo, Rhine riesling, malbec, pinot, shiraz and cabernet. His land has a subsoil of quartz and limestone.

GREAT WESTERN

Great Western is set in hilly country with the ranges of the Grampians in the background. The height above sea level is 900 feet. The soil is comparatively infertile but sheep grazing is apparently a paying industry in the district and the great wheat fields of the Wimmera are not far away. The rainfall is about twenty-two inches.

The soil, generally, is gravel and sand formed by the erosion and disintegration of the original granite rock and red brown volcanic ash over clay and granite soils.

Best's vineyard flanks the Concongella Creek. The soil just here is a clay loam and a yellow clay subsoil. Best's have fifty acres of vines consisting of shiraz, malbec, pinot meuniere, esparte, chasselas and Rhine riesling.

Seppelt's winery and main vineyards are on a hilly slope just above the township but Seppelt's have vineyards also which stretch southward at different points along the road that leads to Moyston. Their other vineyards border the Western Highway near the township and run along the banks of the Concongella Creek. They have 1,500 acres of which 500 are under vines which are Irvine's white, shiraz, cabernet sauvignon, pinot blanc, semillon, malbec, miller's burgundy, pinot noir, cinsault, Clare riesling, Rhine riesling, esparte, tokay and white hermitage. With only a few minor variations they are using only Irvine's white for the champagne and shiraz for the reds.

The combination of soil and climate produces wines that are highly acid, light bodied, astringent and firm. Although the flavour is quite different, Great Western red wines are similar in many ways to Coonawarra wines. Not every year is a good year. Some years are definitely thin, acid and unremarkable. In other years frost will destroy the buds and there will be no vintage. A good year will result in beautiful reds and whites which will last for many years.

Like Coonawarra reds, Great Western clarets are inclined to give an impression of lightness of character and usually the colour is light without any purple at all. A three year old Great Western usually has the colour of pigeon's blood – pure red without any trace of blue or yellow. In a good year it can be classic in character with a deep crimson colour, a good flavourous centre palate, a good balance of acid and a fine astringency.

To be any good at all the reds need at least three years in wood before bottling. To bottle any earlier means a hard acid wine.

Great Western wines, therefore, like Coonawarra wines, are useful for blending. If a maker cannot wait the time to age them correctly he blends in heavier, fruitier and less acid material. Great Western reds, because of their delicacy and great refinement, contribute tremendously to a blend.

In a good year, the whites are full of flavour, crisp and strikingly clean to the palate.

Both reds and whites of Great Western need many years in bottle before they show their full perfection and then they develop tremendous perfume and flavour.

The Thomson family, who are the proprietors of Best's, bottle a little of their dry reds and whites to sell under their own label, but dispose of the bulk to merchants. Best's also make at Great Western their popular carbonated Sparkling Hock, Burgundy and 'Cham', and the 'Baby Bubblie' in the small bottles.

Here Seppelt's make their world renowned 'Great Western' Champagne and Sparkling Burgundy. Their vineyard and winery are called 'Great Western', a name they took over from Hans Irvine when they purchased the property in 1918. Best's call their wines 'Great Western' because of the overriding right of the wines of the district to be sold under the name of the district.

Seppelt's use the winery at Great Western as a centre for their 'prestige' table wines in the same way as Penfold's use their Auldana Winery. Wines receiving cellar treatment and bottled here are: Chalambar Burgundy, Moyston Arawatta Hock, Rhymney Chablis, Chardonnay Sauternes and Melita Moselle. Seppelt's make no claim whatsoever on the labels as to where the wines come from. The labels themselves are simple, intelligently set out and attractive in appearance and carry the vintage year of the wine. As there is a general consistency in their character and their overall excellence does not vary from year to year, it is more than probable that the wines of the district are blended with wines of other districts to balance the lack of body and excessive acid which characterizes Great Western wines of a poor year.

It is not to be thought that Great Western wines always need blending. In most years they can stand up in their own right.

North-East Victoria

RUTHERGLEN

Rutherglen is at the northern point of this district. The most southern points are Taminick, about ten miles west of Glenrowan and Milawa, ten miles east of Wangaratta.

Like so many other Australian soils, the soil in the district is based on primary volcanic rocks both basalt and granite, with a scattered mixture of secondary rocks like sandstone and limestone. Most of the vineyards are grouped around three rivers, the Murray, the King and the Ovens. Consequently, many of the vines grow on the sandy loam flats of these water courses.

Most of the country is flat and only a few hundred feet above sea level. A low range of hills (the Warby Range) is seen near Glenrowan, while at Milawa the foothills of the Australian Alps are not far away.

Agriculturally, the area is rich. Grazing is the main industry. 'All Saints' at Wahgunyah use spray irrigation with water pumped from the Murray on the sandy section of their vineyard next to the river. All the other vineyards depend on rainfall which is about twenty-five inches a year.

Seppelt's is the only large company in the area. They make the heavy, fortified wines so useful for blending and a beautiful full-bodied sherry which is aged in oaken casks of Spanish origin. The other wineries are controlled by families who usually have other interests besides the making of wine. The winemakers at Rutherglen are largely mixed farmers. Booths and Bailey are pastoralists. On the other hand, Sutherland Smiths', Morris' and Brown's have large properties and are dedicated winemakers with no other interests.

The winemaker in the north-east is, like his counterpart in the Hunter Valley, also the grower of the grapes. A few tons are brought into the area from the irrigation districts but do not go to make up the 'prestige' wines. He does not like his product to be thought of in the same terms as 'irrigation' wines.

The grapes are mainly shiraz and grenache with a little of cabernet, blue imperial, alicante bouchet and durif for the reds and Rutherglen pedro (different from pedro ximenes), Rutherglen muscat and white hermitage for the whites. In recent years Rhinè riesling has been planted.

Before the great upsurge in the demand for table wines, heavily fortified wines like port and muscat and full bodied sherry were the chief wines. A very heavy and fruity red table wine made from shiraz was the distinctive wine of the district. These wines still represent a large proportion of the production. However, competition from the more cheaply produced irrigation wines resulted in a decline in the demand for fortified wines and the north-east has swung across to producing table wines sometimes very different from the heavy reds of former years.

Rutherglen and Milawa sherries tend by their very nature to be 'bigger' than South Australian. Yet, in their own style, they are first class. The ports and muscats of the north-east are magnificent. They are weighty and full of colour, rich in sugar and flavour. The dry reds have a tendency to go the same way. Those made by Chambers and Campbell are like non sweet ports. The reds of the north-east are readily identifiable. The berry flavour is most pronounced, similar in its strongest examples to blackberry jam. The body is big and soft and there is just a suggestion of sweetness.

The winemakers of late, particularly the Sutherland Smiths and John Brown, have been endeavouring to eliminate this 'bigness' from their reds. To a certain extent they have succeeded but the berry flavour remains. The shiraz grape has been tempered by these two makers at times by the addition of cabernet and mondeuse. The effect is good, but a straight north-eastern shiraz has an appeal that will never be equalled. Its distinctiveness is an asset.

The dry whites of the area are generally too 'big' and have too much flavour. Skilled winemakers have endeavoured to overcome this tendency. Morris is making crisp light wines from the white hermitage. Brown is very successful with his Rhine riesling and has made very interesting whites from combinations of various sorts including the white frontignan, white hermitage and white grenache grapes. Sutherland Smiths are making superb rieslings with somewhat more of a fruity flavour than other districts.

Seppelt's have 500 acres at Rutherglen of which 250 are planted with brown muscat, grand noir, grenache, pinot noir, shiraz, tokay and port varieties. Their soil is of the red brown earth type on most vineyards and river sandy loam on flats. They employ irrigation on the river flats but there is only natural rainfall on the high ground.

The Rutherglen area has presented practically every problem known to viticulture in Australia and for this reason Seppelt's were inclined to proceed slowly with the area over the last decade but because they feel that it can produce unsurpassable sweet wines, sherries and some types of table wines they have revived interest of late. Most of their vineyards are being reconstituted with virus-free stocks and selected clones. A clone, incidentally, is a strain of any particular variety of grape which has shown particular characteristics such as immunity from most diseases or the ability to produce fruit more abundantly than its brothers and sisters in the same family.

G. Sutherland Smith and Sons who are the proprietors of 'All Saints' vineyard at Wahgunyah have 350 acres of vines including shiraz (130 acres), cabernet sauvignon (20 acres), pinot, Rhine riesling, semillon, marsanne, chasselas, white hermitage, white grenache, palomino, doradillo and tokay. Most of these vines are grown on alluvial soil with the balance on sandy or clay loam. They use supplementary irrigation, that is they add eight to ten inches by spray in summer to the natural rainfall of twenty-two inches. Sutherland Smiths have set aside 750 acres for future development but not all of it is suitable for grape growing.

'All Saints' was established in 1864 by George Sutherland Smith who is the great-grandfather of the present generation who run the vineyard, namely George Jnr, Ian and Peter. Traditionally the Sutherland Smiths have been the leaders in the area for over a century with their great castle-like structure which is their winery. Although they are not the ones to boast, their production of wine is both great and of high quality. The label perhaps is not as well known as those of the giant companies but as the years pass it is becoming more and more popular.

C. H. Morris and Sons Pty Ltd, have 110 acres at Rutherglen consisting of blue imperial, shiraz, cabernet sauvignon, durif, alicante bouchet, brown muscat, tokay Rutherglen pedro, white hermitage, pinot blanc (this appears to be a different variety from the chardonnay) and palomino. All these are grown on a red clay loam. Across the river in New South Wales Morris' have 120 acres at Balldale comprising grenache, Rhine riesling and Rutherglen pedro. These are grown on sandy soil. There is no irrigation used at all by Morris'. The Morris family process quite a considerable quantity of grapes they purchase from the irrigation areas of the Murray.

W. H. Chambers and Sons have 70 acres at Rutherglen of various varieties including Rutherglen pedro, Rhine riesling, gouais, brown muscat, tokay, shiraz, mondeuse, grenache, alvarelho, touriga, blue imperial, alicante bouchet, doradillo, palomino and cabernet sauvignon.

Stanton and Killeen have 30 acres at Rutherglen of

muscat and shiraz grown on sandy loam, some of which is flood irrigated.

Campbell's who own the 'Bobbie Burns' winery have 110 acres at Rutherglen of shiraz, brown muscat, white hermitage, malbec, blue imperial, Rutherglen pedro and cabernet sauvignon. These are grown on red clay loam, 40 acres of which is flood irrigated. Campbell's have 600 acres of land available for further development.

Just near Rutherglen there is a little township known as Barnawartha. There is a property here of 36 acres owned by the Gehrig brothers growing shiraz, white hermitage, palomino, Rutherglen pedro, cabernet, Rutherglen pinot and Rhine riesling. These are irrigated from the Murray River. The soil is of a clay loam nature.

Other vineyards in the area are R. S. Buller and Son, L. Jones (Rutherglen); C. Conte, V. Curcio, G. and V. Scrimizzi (Ardmona) and R. N. and K. B. Gayfer (Chiltern).

MILAWA

Brown Brothers have a property at Milawa which is about ten miles to the east of Wangaratta. The main plantings are shiraz (43 acres), Rhine riesling (23 acres), cabernet sauvignon (10 acres), and there are similar plantings of mondeuse, grenache (red and white), white hermitage, tokay, brown muscat, chasselas and graciano. The soil here consists of clay loam over river gravel. There is limited irrigation from underground sources. At Everton which is situated on the foothills of the mountains making up the Australian Alps, Brown's have a small area of shiraz, cabernet, Rhine riesling, palomino and white hermitage. Here the soil is sandy shale with a loam mixture. Brown's also process a certain number of grapes which they buy in from irrigated areas only for the purpose of making sherry. On the whole the wines made at Milawa by Brown's are lighter in character than those made at Wahgunyah and Rutherglen. They have such a distinctive style that the area really could be considered as separate and on its own. Brown's have established several acres and a small winery at Beverford near Swan Hill in the north-west.

TAMINICK

Bailey Brothers (Bundarra Vineyards) have 230 acres of vines most of which are at Bundarra which is four miles due west of Glenrowan but they have in addition 140 acres of shiraz at Huceynia which is nine miles west of Glenrowan. Irrigation is not used and the soil is a deep red gravelly loam. Booth's also have a winery and some vines here. Allan Watson, restaurateur, has 8 acres of vines near Bailey's.

Goulburn Valley

Tahbilk Pty Ltd, is situated in the Goulburn Valley near the township of Tabilk. This again is close to the town of Nagambie. The vineyard is approximately thirteen miles from Seymour and therefore quite a distance from the other vineyards of the north-east. One could not describe the wines of Tahbilk as typically north-eastern and once again we must say that the area should be described as one which is quite separate from any other. It is only north-eastern Victorian because geographically that is where it is situated. Chateau Tahbilk has a 2,800 acre property but only 100 acres are under vines. These are Rhine riesling, white hermitage, shiraz, cabernet sauvignon and marsanne. The soil is partly sandy loam and partly clay loam. The area is irrigated. The wines could be described as high quality.

Mr Ross Shelmerdine is developing 500 acres of vineyards very close to Chateau Tahbilk under the direct supervision of Mr Colin Preece who was formerly Seppelt's manager and winemaker at Great Western.

Also within this area are the vineyards of Gravina and those of Darveniza. The Darveniza brothers have a vineyard near the township of Mooroopna a few miles from Shepparton. They have about 40 acres of vines, most of which are shiraz but they make sweet fortified wines from grapes they bring in from the Murray Irrigation Area.

Gravina's have 15 acres of grenache and shiraz on a loam soil which is flood irrigated from the nearby Goulburn River. They also process large quantities of grapes brought in from the Murray Valley irrigation areas.

North-West Victoria

Although the districts covered by the townships of Rutherglen and Corowa are in the Murray Valley, they are not usually included in the division known as 'Murray Valley'. The reason for the distinction is 'irrigation'. Most Murray Valley vineyards are on the sandy loam flats of the river and are irrigated by flooding with water pumped up from the stream. The vineyards of the north-east of Victoria and Corowa (in N.S.W.) are grown on the heavier soil away from the river and are not irrigated. The exception is that of All Saints at Wahgunyah.

Grapes are grown along the Valley in settlements. Hence there is a collection of grape growers at Lake Boga, Swan Hill and Robinvale, as well as at the very large irrigation area covered by Mildura, Merbein and Red Cliffs.

The grape grower here, as along the Murray in South Australia, is not necessarily growing grapes for winemaking. On his block of land he might be cultivating citrus trees such as oranges and grapefruit or even vegetable crops such as peas. Certain grapes cannot be used for anything else but winemaking. Take shiraz and semillon, for instance, which are grown extensively in the irrigation areas. Other varieties, such as sultana, waltham cross and gordo blanco, can be used both as table grapes and for winemaking. Others, again, such as currant, can be used only for dried fruits. The grape grower, therefore, is an independent horticulturalist who sells his product on the best market. There are wineries at Lake Boga (Thomson's), Beverford (Buller) and Robinvale (McWilliam's). They use the locally grown grapes both for making wine and for the distillation of brandy and fortifying spirit. Wine made from shiraz and semillon in these areas is usually of good average quality. They give promise of greater things, and under certain conditions it is possible that high quality wines might be made from time to time.

Winemakers from other areas, such as Griffith and, to a much smaller extent, Rutherglen, move into this area at harvest time and purchase vast quantities of grapes for their own wineries.

At Mildura, or rather, at Merbein which is more like an outlying suburb of Mildura, there is a large winery owned by the public company of Mildara Wines Ltd. This company buys its grapes from the local growers. Because of the very real dependence of the growers on the company, the latter can exert quite a control over them as to what type of grape they should grow and how they should cultivate it.

Average red and white table wines are made in this district and a flor sherry of outstanding quality is made from the local grapes. Mildara Wines, in addition, blend and bottle red and white table wines from other areas which they sell under the label of Mildara. The company owns a vineyard and winery at Coonawarra and has blended Coonawarra Claret very successfully with Hunter Valley reds and reds from other areas. These blended clarets are sold under the Mildara 'prestige' label with the vintage year and bin number appended. The Mildara 'straight' Coonawarra clarets are marketed under their own label. 'Golden Bower' Riesling is a beautiful wine, usually a Hunter Valley, given expert selection and cellar treatment and of extremely high quality. The company makes a beautiful 'brown' sherry, slightly sweet, under the name of 'Chestnut Teal'. For the rest, like almost all Murray Valley wineries, the product is sweet fortified wines and an average quality sherry. The company is a large distiller of grape material and has several excellent brandies marketed under its label, the best of which is an outstanding spirit known as 'Mildara Pot Still Brandy'.

At Irymple the company has storage cellars and vineyards. There are 140 acres of listan (or palomino) and Clare riesling, varieties introduced by the company; cabernet sauvignon, malbec, and Rhine riesling.

A new company, Hungerford Hill Pty Ltd, was formed in 1969 to develop vineyards in the Hunter Valley region of New South Wales. They have also established a winery at Buronga which is in New South Wales quite close to Mildura. Hungerford Hill have a fifteen year contract with local growers under which these growers have agreed to

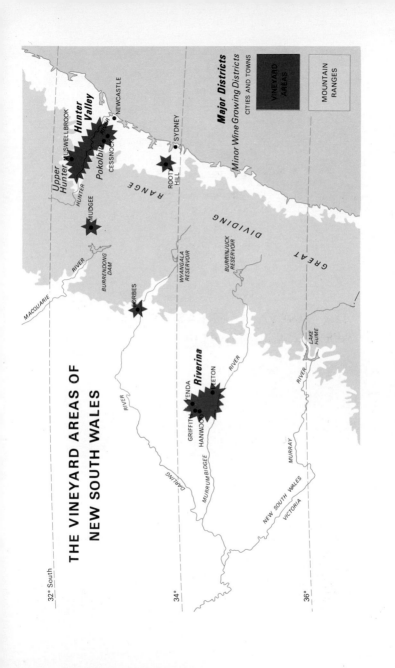

THE VINEYARD AREAS OF NEW SOUTH WALES

Major Districts

CITIES AND TOWNS

Minor Wine Growing Districts

VINEYARD AREAS

MOUNTAIN RANGES

Hunter Valley

Upper Hunter

Pokolbin

Riverina

SCONE

MUSWELLBROOK

MUDGEE

CESSNOCK

NEWCASTLE

SYDNEY

ROOTY HILL

FORBES

GRIFFITH

YENDA

HANWOOD

LEETON

GREAT DIVIDING RANGE

MACQUARIE RIVER

BURRENDONG DAM

WYANGALA RESERVOIR

BURRINJUCK RESERVOIR

LACHLAN RIVER

MURRUMBIDGEE RIVER

DARLING RIVER

MURRAY RIVER

LAKE HUME

HUNTER RIVER

NEW SOUTH WALES

VICTORIA

32° South

34°

36°

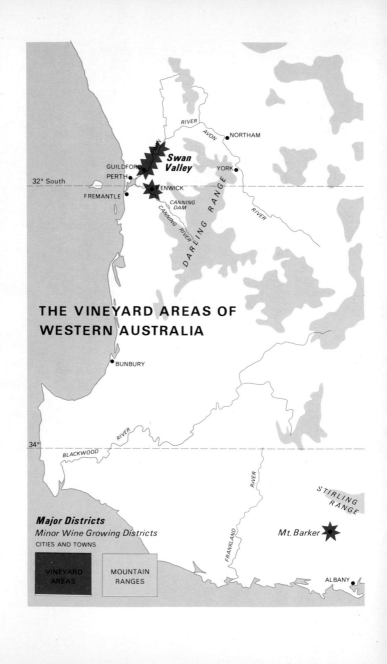

THE VINEYARD AREAS OF
WESTERN AUSTRALIA

RIVER
AVON
NORTHAM
GUILDFORD
PERTH
32° South
FREMANTLE
Swan Valley
YORK
FENWICK
CANNING
DAM
CANNING RIVER
DARLING RANGE
RIVER

BUNBURY

34°
BLACKWOOD
RIVER

FRANKLAND RIVER
STIRLING RANGE
Mt. Barker
ALBANY

Major Districts
Minor Wine Growing Districts
CITIES AND TOWNS

VINEYARD
AREAS

MOUNTAIN
RANGES

plant and cultivate 230 acres of cabernet sauvignon, 220 acres of shiraz, 25 acres of Rhine riesling and 50 acres of semillon and to plant further acreages as required. The winery at Buronga is an open air affair with Whitehill roller crushers and fermenting tanks of the 'controlled fermentation' type sitting out in the open. It will be capable of handling 2½ million gallons of wine. Although the company has some control over the methods of cultivation of the growers, they have not at this stage any clear idea of what is required. All they are looking for is that the company's standards of colour and acid and sugar content in the grapes should be adhered to.

Other Areas in Victoria

The Yarra Valley which won for itself a reputation of producing some of the greatest white wines made in Australia naturally attracts a lot of attention from amateur winemakers who envisage building up similar vineyards for the future. To date, not one of the traditional and established winemaking companies or families have endeavoured to enter this area but there are a great number of small properties which have been planted with vines of the winemaking type.

At Vermont, Lilydale and Yarra Glen there are sporadic outbursts of planting. I feel that these are more in the nature of horticultural gardens and are not really serious attempts at establishing vineyards. The area obviously suffers from the defect of being too cold in the summer months for the grapes to ripen every year and traditional winemakers consequently are very cautious.

At Bendigo a similar situation exists. Amateur grape growers have planted out several acres of vines and courageous as these attempts are I feel they are largely based on a nostalgic desire to re-create vineyards which existed last century. We could not in all fairness list them as serious attempts at viticulture, at least not until far more money is made available to develop them. Similar ventures have been started at Waurn Ponds near Geelong, at Keilor and at Kyneton.

I believe that wine is to those senses (of taste and smell) what music is to hearing and painting to seeing, and, just as a catchy tune or pleasing picture may have its passing appeal, it is only those works of art (or those wines) behind which an intense effort and singleness of purpose is sensed, that can ever achieve greatness.

David Wynn, 1956

12 THE VINEYARDS OF NEW SOUTH WALES

Riverina THE WORD 'Riverina' as applied to the wine growing district is of comparatively recent usage. Formerly this region was called the M.I.A., that is the Murrumbidgee Irrigation Area. Winemakers in this part dislike the term because it lays too much stress on irrigation and the general name of the area, Riverina, was applied specifically to the wine growing district even though of itself it covers a very much larger stretch of country, including the district around Deniliquin. Thus, if Deniliquin begins a vineyard area it would have to be included under the general description of Riverina.

The Burrinjuck Reservoir which has a capacity of 772,000

acre feet was completed in 1913. It catches the water from the Snowy River Mountains, or part of it, as some of the water is deflected to the Murray. Water released from this storage is first used for the generation of electric power. After this it flows down the Murrumbidgee for 240 miles to a movable weir near Narrandera. Here some of the river is diverted into an artificial river which is called the Murrumbidgee Main Canal. This conveys it to the irrigation areas which are situated around the towns of Narrandera, Leeton and Griffith.

In 1967, 42,000 tons of grapes were supplied from the vines in this area to the wineries. The New South Wales Conservation and Irrigation Commission will permit any one person to hold either 300 acres of irrigable grazing land or 75 acres of land irrigable as a fruit block, the fruits being citrus, apples, pears, apricots, peaches or grapes. Irrigable land can be held only by persons, not by incorporated companies.

After the First World War the New South Wales Government developed the M.I.A. as a soldier settlement area. As the time went by immigrants, particularly those from Italy, settled here and there was a general flow to the district of people from surrounding non-irrigated areas.

The plain of the M.I.A. was built up over the ages by the gradual breaking down of the comparatively close Kosciusko Range. Soils tend to vary considerably. They range from a heavy clay loam difficult to work and drain, to a light sandy loam very friable and easily drained. Occasionally there are stretches of sandy soils built up by windblown sands in hollows and small vales. Mostly the sub-soil is clay which helps with drainage and holds the irrigation water.

In 1910 the Murrumbidgee Irrigation Act was passed by the New South Wales Government. In 1912 McWilliam's established a winery at Hanwood and in 1913 Penfold's began one at Griffith. A C.S.I.R.O. laboratory was established in the area in 1926. McWilliam's today have another winery at Yenda and still another at Beelbangera. Wynn's have one at Yenda.

Among the smaller makers are the Italian group. They are Rossetto's, De Bortoli, Calabria and De Angeli, Miranda's and Franco's. Then there are Charlie Morris from Rutherglen and Dorowen Wines.

By and large it is a McWilliam's area. When he was still only a lad Jack McWilliam was sent by his father to begin the winery at Hanwood. It still stands, basically the same as when he constructed it, a huge wandering building with steel reinforcing projecting out of every concrete wall where Jack had left room for expansion or continuation of the wall. There are four brothers, the sons of the original owner, all of the same character, dedicated to their business and incredibly hardworking. They tilled the soil, planted the vines, picked the grapes, crushed them and made wine.

McWilliam's today is among the four largest wine companies in Australia. It is still a family concern and there are many McWilliams in the business. The four brothers have sons who are in the various wineries helping their fathers and uncles. The company has a huge centre at Pyrmont in Sydney and many acres in the Hunter Valley. At Griffith, Stewart, the son of Jack, is the vineyard manager. As the company is not permitted to own irrigable land there are five blocks of vines, each of 50 acres, each owned by a McWilliam but all running as one vineyard.

The entire M.I.A. is occupied by small landowners who are absolute masters in their own affairs. They are able to grow what types of grapes they choose, they pick them when they choose, they can sell them where they please. This situation could inevitably create difficulties for wine makers in the area. Fortunately there is a tremendous amount of co-operation between growers, winemakers, the Department of Agriculture, the Water Conservation and Irrigation Commission and the C.S.I.R.O. A committee comprising all these interests meets once a month to sort out any problems and to decide appropriate remedial measures. It is called The Irrigation Research and Extension Committee (I.R.E.C.) and is under the chairmanship of a grower. The grape growers of the M.I.A. have always grown grapes suitable for making high quality wines. This contrasts with the situation in the Murray irrigation areas where there are enormous plantings of gordo blanco, sultana and doradillo. In the M.I.A., on the other hand, there is no gordo blanco or any of the types of grapes used for processing into dried fruit but there are many acres of shiraz and semillon and every year there is an increase in the number of acres of cabernet sauvignon, Rhine riesling and some of the more recent additions to Australian viticulture such as pinot noir, malbec and pinot blanc.

As a general rule the M.I.A. produces what is known as 'flagon' wine but it has been shown that special plots can produce particularly high quality wines and many of the wines in the area have won gold medals in the various wine shows of Australia. The great difficulty in the making of fine table wines in the M.I.A. is the tremendous heat at time of vintage. All great table wines are fermented at low temperatures. The larger wineries, therefore, year after year are putting in more refrigeration. It is this refrigeration that has enabled them to produce the first class cabernets and rieslings which have won the gold medals.

Wynn's have acquired in recent years 179 acres of irrigated land which they have planted with shiraz, cabernet sauvignon, semillon and a little grenache, pedro, touriga and white hermitage. They plan to extend their plantings in the next few years but, of course, almost all the grapes processed by the wineries are purchased from small growers.

Hunter Valley

This area lies between the tablelands of New England and the Southern Tableland. The valley itself extends about 150 miles from the drainage divide to the sea and for the most part is about seventy miles wide.

From a grape growing point of view, the valley is divided into two areas. The newer area situated west of the town of Muswellbrook at the date of publication of this book has not produced sufficient wine for anyone to determine whether or not it will be of a similar type and quality as the old area (Pokolbin). Slight differences of climate, soil, wind and frost patterns and so on will possibly be the causes of a distinction between the wines of the two areas and, therefore, I have treated them both separately.

POKOLBIN

Generally, the soils of this part of the valley are not very fertile. In the vineyard areas the deeply incised valleys of the sandstone plateau have sandy creek flats poor in plant foods. The country around Pokolbin is plateau structure capped with sandstone and with outcrops of basalt. On the river flats there is rich alluvial soil over an area five miles wide.

The majority of vineyards are clustered around the township of Pokolbin a few miles out of Cessnock and about seventeen miles from the Hunter River itself. In this area there are about 2,000 acres of vines, but new plantings are being made all the time.

Temperatures are moderate, ranging from the fifties in the winter to the seventies in the summer. Rainfall is about twenty-five inches a year.

Grape varieties used are shiraz for the reds and semillon, white hermitage, verdelho and blanquette for the whites. New plantings include Rhine riesling, cabernet, traminer and malbec.

In general, Pokolbin reds have a deep red colour with no blue or purple even in their first year. Sometimes the colour can be very light. They are soft and round but with a curious lightness of body which differentiates them sharply from the north-eastern Victorian reds. In this respect, they are similar to the Coonawarras, but they have much less acid and much more depth than the latter. As they grow older they become velvety and rich. Hunter reds mature very quickly and have reached a satisfactory stage after five years.

Pokolbin whites are pale golden in colour; have a soft, flowery bouquet which is slightly sweet; and a beautiful, soft, full and rich flavour. A poorly made white can be thin and flavourless to begin with but even this seems to gain something after a couple of years in bottle. A fully matured white has a great volume of aroma and flavour.

There are three large wine companies in the valley –
Penfold's, McWilliam's and Lindeman's. The other wineries
are or rather, were, owned by family concerns, the largest
of which is Tulloch's, who market their wines as 'Pokolbin
Red' and 'Pokolbin Riesling'. Tulloch's have sold their
interest to Reed's Paper Products of England. They have
25 acres of hermitage at Pokolbin grown on volcanic soil.
In addition they have 300 acres at Fordwich planted with
hermitage, semillon, white shiraz, verdelho and white pinot.
The soil here is very sandy with a sub-soil of basalt.

Tyrrell's Vineyards Pty Ltd, is under the control of Murray
Tyrrell. This family has 141 acres at Pokolbin of semillon,
blanquette and hermitage. The top soil is podzolic and
the sub-soil is volcanic. Tyrrell's are planting another 50
acres of hermitage and 50 acres of semillon.

Lindeman's make their 'prestige' wines at their Ben Ean
vineyard and winery in the valley although ageing and
blending is completed at their cellars at Marrickville in
Sydney. 'Straight' Lindeman Hunter Valley whites and
reds are marketed usually under bin numbers. Such a label
will give quite a lot of detail, more often than not describing
the vineyard where the grapes are grown, the type of grape
used, the year of vintage and the time spent in wood.

This company is skilled in blending Hunter wines successfully with wines from other areas. The character of the
Hunters is so great that they add something to, say, a
Goulburn Valley or a Clare wine and many of these blends
have appeared, once again, under bin numbers.

McWilliam's are the proprietors of Mt Pleasant vineyard.
The wine is made at the winery here and transported to
the company's cellars at Pyrmont, Sydney for finishing and
blending. 'Straight' Hunters appear under the labels of
'Mt Pleasant' Hermitage and Riesling. McWilliam's also
market quite a number of straight wines and blends under
the bin number descriptive label.

Besides Dalwood, Penfold's have several plantations near
Pokolbin with its volcanic sandy loam and at Sparkling
Vale with its sandy soil. All vintaging is done at Wybong

and after a certain amount of ageing in wood, all wines are sent to their cellars at Tempe, Sydney.

Dr Max Lake who calls his property 'Lake's Folly' has 20 acres of vineyards consisting of cabernet sauvignon, hermitage and merlot and he has set aside another 20 acres for development. Although Lake is such a small grower he has produced outstanding wines in his few vintages, having begun the project only recently.

Hungerford Hill Vineyards Pty Ltd, has just recently planted 650 acres of land at Pokolbin and still has 314 acres which it is planting out gradually. Among these there are 580 acres of shiraz and 35 acres of cabernet sauvignon. All this vineyard is on red volcanic soil. Hungerford Hill also have a winery at Buronga in New South Wales near Mildura.

Rothbury Vineyards Pty Ltd, has purchased 1,000 acres of land suitable for vineyards at Rothbury near Pokolbin. It is anticipated that all plantings will be completed by 1974. The syndicate comprises Edward Gowing, John McDowell, Dr John Burgess, Dr Frank Mills, Alan Grainger, Allan Burgess,. Robert Sanders, Rudy Komon, Murray Tyrrell, Peter Davidson and Len Evans. Tyrrell is the vineyard consultant and Evans is the chairman and general co-ordinator. The winery will be completed by 1971 at a cost of approximately $300,000 and it is the intention of the syndicate to buy further properties and grapes from associated syndicates. Grape varieties planted are semillon, hermitage, blanquette, cabernet sauvignon, pinot noir, Rhine riesling, merlot and traminer.

Frank Margan, journalist, has begun a vineyard of several acres on part of Tyrrell's property.

UPPER HUNTER VALLEY
Penfold's began the development early in the 1960s and have been quickly followed by a number of other companies and private individuals.

Penfold's will soon have planted near Wybong the largest single vineyard in Australia. Already 400 acres of the 1,000 acres planned have been put under vine. In addition to the traditional (to Australia) varieties of shiraz, semillon and Rhine riesling they are experimenting with a number of new varieties such as merlot and pinot. They have erected a modern winery sufficiently large to handle not only their own crops but those of other vineyard owners in the area both existing and potential who may not wish to make wine themselves. The soil types change from a heavy black alluvial soil by the creeks to a sandy loam on the higher slopes.

Hamilton's Wines in association with the Adelaide Steamship Company have begun planting 600 acres of vines at Sandy Hollow. The new company will be known as Mount Dangar Vineyards (Hunter Valley) Pty Ltd. It has acquired 1,000 acres of land adjoining the Goulburn River about twenty miles from Muswellbrook. It is planting cabernet sauvignon, hermitage, Rhine riesling and semillon and it is expected that the first vintage should be made in 1972.

This company has introduced a new system of irrigation. It is called the 'drip' system. Plastic pipes run underground along each row of vines. At the foot of each vine a six inch long, half inch diameter plastic pipe extends above the soil allowing the water to be pumped along the main line at a pre-set pressure and to feed the quantity of water from the small plastic pipe on to each individual vine. This system has the advantage over flood irrigation or overhead sprinklers in that it enables small quantities of water to be added as a supplement to natural rainfall. As the water is applied under the vine, problems such as washing off the various sprays and pesticides applied to the foliage do not occur.

Another large property is that of Hollydeen owned by K. Cummins. He has purchased 500 acres, 300 of which are intended to be planted with vines. This property will also use drip-type irrigation.

David Horden has 20 acres under vine, R. Laws 30 acres, and C. Woodford 20 acres.

Air and water are indispensable: nothing else is. There is, of course, much else that is highly desirable, but not indispensable: wine and milk, for instance.

Andre Simon

13 VARIOUS OTHER VINEYARDS

Swan Valley   THIS INCLUDES an area around Perth along the banks of the Swan and Canning Rivers. The latitude is thirty-two degrees south; the height above sea level less than a hundred feet and the rainfall about thirty-five inches per annum. Temperature ranges well into the high nineties during the summer. The soil is a deep alluvial sandy loam.

The grapes are tokay, shiraz, grenache, pedro, muscat and frontignan for sweet fortified wines; shiraz and malbec for dry reds and semillon and Rhine riesling for dry whites.

The combination of rich soil, plentiful moisture and tremendous heat develops grapes that are very high in sugar content. Swan Valley tokays, ports, muscats and frontignans are of a very high standard, having a liqueur-like quality and are much sought after by the local Western Australians.

The dry table wines are difficult to make because of the excessive sugar in the grapes. The reds are inclined to be heavy and sweetish with a pronounced berry flavour. The whites tend to be flat and a little bit too full. However, they are not to be criticized because of this. This type of table wine is much appreciated by people who like wine that is not acid or astringent.

A wine made by Houghton's called White Burgundy is usually a big, soft white with a flowery nose and a pleasant flavour and is in fact a high quality wine.

There are about sixty wineries in the district, most of them are fairly small. The largest are Sandalford, Houghton's and Valencia, the latter two being the property of the Emu Wine Company of England. These three names are occasionally seen on bottles throughout Australia, but the product of the smaller wineries is sold in their own State.

The Benedictine Monastery at New Norcia, about eighty miles out of Perth, grow their own grapes and process them at their own winery.

The Valencia Vineyards are at Caversham. They comprise 68 acres of semillon, tokay, malbec, shiraz, pedro, grenache and doradillo.

Houghton's Vineyard is at Middle Swan and comprises 244 acres of semillon, tokay, malbec, shiraz, pedro, grenache, madeline, verdelho, Rhine riesling, frontignan and cabernet. The companies involved have purchased 2,000 acres at Gin Gin about fifty miles north of Perth and plan to plant these at the rate of approximately 100 acres per year. Irrigation is used on these vineyards from bores on the properties.

Another large vineyard is that of Noack and Sons who have 54 acres at Upper Swan and 100 acres at Bullsbrook. Both properties have shiraz, grenache, Rhine riesling, pedro, gordo, frontignan and hermitage. As opposed to most of the other vineyards which are on sandy soil, these are on a deep red loam. They do not use irrigation.

N. K. Waldeck has a small property of 12 acres in the Swan Valley and 41 acres at Bindoon. This maker has cabernet, grenache, semillon, shiraz and tokay. He uses spray irrigation. Waldeck's have about 100 acres at Bindoon suitable for planting vines as the soil is mostly a deep loam, but the project is subject to their obtaining sufficient water for irrigation.

The above makers, besides having sizeable properties themselves, are extremely large purchasers of grapes grown by the hundreds of property owners in the Swan and Canning Valleys which they process at their individual wineries.

New plantings have been made at Mt Barker and Frankland River. If these prove successful a winery will be established and many local farmers will plant wine grapes.

A Few Smaller Districts

Several vineyards are so scattered and are so small that none of them of itself could form a district.

There is the interesting winery of Penfold's at Rooty Hill just out of Sydney where Minchinbury Champagne is made as well as being made at Auldana in South Australia. It has recently been replanted with vines.

Lindeman's have a very important vineyard and winery at Corowa on the banks of the Murray River. The area can produce remarkably fine fortified and non-fortified wines. The winery, no doubt, is used as well for processing grapes grown in the irrigated areas.

Elsewhere in New South Wales there are well established wineries in the ranges.

Near Mudgee, for example, Craigmoor Winery has 110 acres at Eurunderee of black shiraz, white shiraz, cabernet, pedro, grenache, white muscat, black muscat, frontignan and semillon. The soil here is of a red loam and the vineyards are not irrigated. Craigmoor have set aside another 75 acres for future development.

At Forbes, Mr J. Genet of Sandhill Vineyards has 30 acres mostly of shiraz. Here the soil is mainly sand but irrigation is not used.

In Queensland, at the town of Roma, long before oil was discovered here, a vineyard was planted on the sandy loam banks of the Bungil Creek in 1866.

The Romavilla Vineyard has 210 acres of riesling, solverino, syrian, portugal, red muscat, white muscat, black muscat, black cluster, red hermitage and mataro. Romavilla have set aside 374 acres for future development and plan to plant these at the rate of 30 acres per year.

Also in this district, Mr A. Barbagallo has 17 acres of vines, most of them being muscats. The soil here is mostly sand or sandy loam and irrigation is not used.

Roseworthy Agricultural and Oenological College

This college is on the road to Clare, about thirty-five miles north of Adelaide. 'Oenology' is the study of wine and the course in oenology was added to the curriculum of the agricultural course in 1936. A student must do two years of agriculture and one year of wine.

Vines are grown on the property and a pilot winery is part of the equipment. This processes a fairly large quantity of grapes every year and well equipped cellars with beautiful oak storage casks are used to age the wine. The college boasts an extremely well set up laboratory since the study of chemistry is part of the course. The students are obliged in addition, to do some practical work in the local wineries.

The Australian Wine Research Institute

This was formed in 1955 to carry on the functions formerly performed by the Waite Research Institute and the C.S.I.R.O. in wine research. Funds were supplied by the Australian government from a special Wine Industry Assistance account to provide a Wine Research Trust Fund of $1,000,000. Part of the Fund was used to establish the Institute and the balance was invested to provide it with income. Income is also derived from the Australian Wine Board and the C.S.I.R.O.

The objects of the Institute are to carry out research into both viticulture and winemaking. An important function is to provide a technical advisory service to members of the Australian wine industry on oenological problems.

The Institute is controlled by a Council consisting of three members nominated by the Australian Wine Board, one representative each from C.S.I.R.O., Commonwealth Government, and the University of Adelaide, plus three other members. The chairman is elected by members of the Council. The work of the Institute is carried out by the Director of Research, Senior Research Officer, a Viticultural Research Officer and staff working under these officers.

Both the Director of Research and the Senior Research Officer are highly qualified. The latter (Mr B. C. Rankine) has had numerous works published on many aspects of wine research. His publications are eagerly sought after by oenologists throughout the world. The research officers are greatly in demand as wine judges at the various wine shows.

The laboratories of the Research Institute are in a modern attractive building situated at Glen Osmond on the outskirts of Adelaide.

The C.S.I.R.O. has established Horticultural Research Laboratories next door to the Wine Research Institute at Glen Osmond and is mainly occupied with the grape vine in the initial stages.

Viticultural Stations

In addition to the Wine Research Institute which was set up at the instigation of the wine industry, each wine growing State – that is South Australia, Western Australia, Victoria and New South Wales – has its own Viticultural Research Station. These Viticultural Stations are sections within the State Agricultural Departments, each under the control of a special officer trained in horticulture, especially viticulture, and research.

The Victorian station is in north-east Victoria at Rutherglen. It was originally intended to be a viticultural college for wine grower's sons but because of the decline in viticulture it never really fulfilled this function.

Today there are several acres under vines and the property

acts as a distribution centre for grafted phylloxera-resistant stocks. Experiments of various types are conducted especially as regards the suitability or otherwise of various vine stocks.

Viticultural research stations are actively engaged also in experimenting with pruning, bench grafting, and testing fumigations and sprays.

> A man cannot make him laugh; but that's
> no marvel, he drinks no wine.
> 2 'Henry IV', iv. iii

14 THE STORY OF AUSTRALIAN WINEMAKING

THE MOST extraordinary feature of Australia's colonization was that a non-wine producing country like England should be so intensely interested in turning Australia into a winemaking country right from the very start.

It probably illustrates very clearly that England, although not a producing country, was very much a wine drinking country. It shows that colonizing Englishmen yearned to have a land which was theirs alone in which vast vineyards could be developed and which would supply them for the needs of their country without having to depend on the precarious supply in times of war from France and Spain.

British governments, in addition, wished to see successful primary industries established in their new settlements and no doubt considered that wine growing would, because of the country's sunny climate, be a comparatively easy industry to begin in Australia. They too, would have confidence that if vineyards could be well established there would be no difficulty in disposing of the resultant wine in England.

This concept was carried on for very many years. Even a century after the first landing, Hubert de Castella wrote a book called *John Bull's Vineyard* in which he reiterates this popular conception that Australia could be almost the sole supplier of wine to England. The Victorian government at about this time offered a bonus per acre to every farmer who planted vines on his land.

As England was a large consumer and buyer of wine and as Australia, right from the very beginning, produced wine that was good and palatable, the concept of Australia being England's vineyard was not far fetched. It had every chance of succeeding just as the wool industry was successful because of the large demand from English mills even in the earliest days of the industry.

What the early, and even later, colonists did not allow for, however, was the ingrained bias of Englishmen towards the table wines of France, the sherries of Spain and the ports of Portugal.

Australian wines were never really accepted in England as comparing favourably with Continental wines.

True enough, every early vineyard could show medals and certificates indicating that they had won prizes in competitions and exhibitions in England and all over Europe. These prizes, in effect, then as even today, did not mean much.

During the 1800s there were dozens of these 'Great Exhibitions' which were showrooms for all kinds of products and manufactures. We even had one in Melbourne in 1890 and built the present Exhibition building to hold it. The organizers of the exhibitions naturally wanted as large a number of exhibits as they could possibly get and offered all sorts of lures to get winemakers from all over the world to show their products.

Just as there are in the 'Wine Fairs' of today in France and Yugoslavia, there were many divisions in each wine competition. We were placed in the 'Empire Wines' division in England and perhaps the 'Colony Wines' division in European exhibitions. Any awards made, therefore, conveyed very little merit to the wines in the eyes of Englishmen.

In the minds of the new Australian wine growers, however, these were proof of the merits of their wines and their acceptability in England. Urged also by administrators and governments it happened eventually that we hopelessly overproduced.

In the second half of the nineteenth century the amount of wine produced was not sufficient because new settlers, both free and ex-convict soon consumed any alcoholic beverage that was made in a country acutely short of liquor.

The dreaded disease, phylloxera, which spread through Australia in the eighties and nineties, wiping out vineyards by the thousands of acres, contributed to the general shortage and it was not until after the First World War when many vineyards had been replanted that vignerons realized that they were making wine which they could never hope to sell. By this time there were vineyards all over Victoria and in the districts around and north of Sydney. South Australia had begun to plant thousands of acres in the Barossa Valley and Mount Lofty Ranges. The Swan Valley in Western Australia was full of vineyards.

Exporters to England had found that the Australian product was not regarded in the same light as European wines and were forced to offer it on the market at a lower price. The British government, most anxious to promote the sale of its Empire's products in 1925 granted a preferential duty on the importation of 'colonial' wine.

Australian wine was marketed by English merchants, therefore, very cheaply and the sweet fortified reds or 'Australian port types' sold comparatively well against the more expensive 'genuine' Portuguese port.

Australian heavy, fruity and not too dry red table wines

were sold as 'Australian burgundy' by firms such as Burgoynes, The Emu Wine Company and Stephen Smith and Company.

The selling point with this style of wine was its 'tonic' qualities. It was supposed to contain more iron and was, therefore, very good for invalids and anaemic persons. It also acquired the name of 'boarding-house burgundy' obviously because of its price.

No wonder, then, sales did not improve at too great a rate. Australian vignerons in the 1920s soon became tired of selling wine at a low unprofitable price. Many of them pulled out their vines and engaged in other farming pursuits which at least gave them a living.

The depression of the 1930s made things even worse. Exports to England fell off and the local market, instead of gradually improving, faded away.

Sheep and cattle were not a very attractive alternative to winemaking but at least they offered a living and the process of tearing out vines continued.

Hence Victoria lost thousands of acres of vines around Ararat and Stawell. It lost all of them in the Yarra Valley and most of them in central Victoria. Even as late as the 1950s the policy of pulling out vines and replacing them with grazing continued in the north-eastern part of Victoria, not so much because of lack of demand for the wines but because sheep were more profitable than wine.

By this time New South Wales had lost all her vineyards around Sydney and had only a few hundred acres left to the north in Hunter Valley.

The 1950s, however, saw a remarkable halt in this depressing ripping out of vines. Vignerons in dry areas who had despaired of competing against the new irrigation areas established in the Murray Valley at Mildura, Renmark and Berri and near Griffith in New South Wales suddenly found the demand for their product had been renewed.

The Second World War gave a tremendous fillip to the wine industry. Although exports had fallen from 3¾ million gallons in 1939 to 1½ million gallons in 1945, home consumption had increased from about 3½ million gallons to nearly

9 million gallons in the same period. This was nearly all fortified wine, but the overall trend in consumption on the home market continued with the difference that table or unfortified wines became more popular and took up an increasing proportion of the amount of wine sold until in 1964 it was about 40 per cent of the total beverage wine produced.

This is a natural progression. Fortified wine was popular in Australia from the time the technique of adding wine spirit to sweet natural wine was introduced about the middle of last century. It was cheap and strong. This was exactly what new colonists needed. They were short of alcohol and the money with which to buy it. The local fortified sweet wines suited their palates, their taste for alcohol and their pockets. The 'depression' assisted this tendency. Shortage of money more or less maintained a demand for cheap fortified wine while the sale of imported spirits fell considerably.

In the early days of the Commonwealth, of course, the wine was unfortified and was drunk with as much enthusiasm as was the fortified wine later. Early in this century François de Castella deplored the almost universal drinking of fortified wine and forecast that the Australian wine industry would never be put on its feet unless it had as a basis the drinking, as a normal everyday beverage, of inexpensive unfortified wine and this by a large section of our population.

He would have been delighted to see how his desire is on the way to being realized. The increasing demand for table wine has been spectacular in the last ten years and the upward trend in demand is continuing.

The Second World War also created a striking change in the marketing of wine. Prior to this, wine had been sold almost entirely as an unlabelled product. Only a few of the 'giants' of today were well known names.

Hotels, licensed grocers and wine 'cafes' purchased almost all their requirements in cask and sold it either by the glass directly out of the cask or in containers they or their customers supplied. Usually the retailer filled his own bottles and placed his own labels on them. This enabled him to market wine very cheaply. Even the 'big name' wine companies such as Penfold's and Seppelt's were forced to sell a large proportion of their product in bulk.

After the war, the large wine companies took advantage of temporary shortages in supply to place their wine on the market under their own labels. This pre-packaging of goods as opposed to 'bulk' supplies revolutionized the whole food and beverage industry. It resulted in an overall increase in quality of the goods but probably contributed greatly to the increase in the price of wine.

This post-war era, nevertheless, saw a great difference in the personal prosperity of Australians. The poverty stricken era of the thirties when even necessities were done without gave way to a period of great affluence. Desiring to enjoy this affluence to the full, people began to enquire into 'gracious living' and finding that wine was a great contribution to this form of life, began to drink unfortified beverage wine in preference to beer. The pre-war fortified wine drinker who drank more for the effect than the flavour became a 'spirits' drinker. He was now able to afford something that was more to his liking.

The 'affluent society', therefore, is the main reason why table wine has come into its own and the day that François de Castella longed to see is on the way.

Early History in New South Wales and Victoria
The grape is not natural to Australia. It was brought into Australia by settlers and although it has flourished extremely well, no sign of any native variety has been found.

Captain Arthur Phillip, commander of the fleet that established the first settlement in the colony was, in addition to being our first Governor, our first vigneron. For it was he who brought grapes from the Cape of Good Hope and planted them at Farm Cove in 1788.

This was a remarkable feat for an Englishman, and a sailor at that, to attempt. Behind him he had no tradition of viticulture or winemaking. All he had to support his enthusiasm was the knowledge that this was a big land with plenty of sunshine and therefore, like South Africa, should be able to produce wines.

The contentious and turbulent Captain John Macarthur was the first man to establish a vineyard as a commercial enterprise. In his period of exile after being banished from Australia because of his quarrel with Governor Bligh he visited the vineyards of France and Switzerland and brought back cuttings to his property at Camden in New South Wales in 1817. He removed this vineyard to a 20 acre property at Penrith on the Nepean River in 1820 and by 1827 was making some thousands of gallons every year.

Plantings continued to be made by other settlers, particularly in the Hunter River Valley. Into this district in 1824 came a young Scot, named James Busby, a remarkable character who in fact became the father of the wine industry in Australia. He had come to Australia to teach orphans, one of the subjects in the syllabus being viticulture as the object of the exercise was that the orphans be taught subjects that would help them support themselves in later life.

Busby became extremely interested in this subject and wrote a text book on winemaking. In 1830 he returned to England and travelled through the wine producing countries of Europe. The British government requested him to purchase vines and on his return to New South Wales in 1832 he brought 20,000 cuttings which he established himself in the Hunter Valley. The influence of these new plantings was soon felt and it is likely that most Australian vineyards can claim these vines as their progenitors.

By 1852 the Hunter River district had 461 acres of vines from which 59,000 gallons of wine were made.

Victoria's Debacle
John Batman founded the settlement of Melbourne in 1834. Almost immediately settlers flocked into the surrounding districts from New South Wales. Vines were introduced from the mother State and by 1881 there were 4,923 acres under vines. In the ten years from 1881 to 1891 the plantings increased to 24,483 acres. Yet in 1954 there were less than 6,000 acres being used for winemaking purposes.

The Story of Australian Winemaking   183

Rutherglen in the north-east of Victoria was originally a gold mining area. The first vineyard was planted by a Lindsay Brown in 1851 and many of the gold miners, disappointed in their efforts at mining, followed his example. Most of the vineyards which still exist today were founded in the period 1851 to 1860 – the Sutherland Smiths at Wahgunyah, the Chambers and the Campbells, the Morrises and the Gehrigs at Rutherglen. Brown Brothers at Milawa were established about 1880 by the father of the present John Brown. The Baileys began vines at Taminick about 1875.

In 1863, an experienced French vigneron Jean Pierre Trouette planted half an acre of vines at Great Western. Seeing his success, two years later, Joseph Best had him and his partner Blampied, plant grapes on his property which he had called 'Great Western'. Joseph Best sold to Hans Irvine in 1888. Irvine was a man of tremendous energy. He brought out champagne makers from the Epernay cellars in France and after many experiments succeeded in making a first class sparkling wine.

He tunnelled into the friable subsoil at Great Western and excavated 3½ miles of subterranean cellars in which to store his champagne. Having built up a huge business with his locally made sparkling wine he sold to Seppelt's in 1918. Seppelt's in turn have built upon Irvine's foundations and at Great Western possess one of the show places of the Australian wine industry. The long underground tunnels of Hans Irvine still remain and are used extensively.

Henry Best, the brother of Joseph, in 1866 planted vines along the banks of the Concongella Creek which flowed through the hamlet of Great Western. He named his vineyard 'Concongella'. This is now the property of Best's Wines Pty Ltd, which is a company name used by the Thomson family.

In central Victoria the vineyards at Tabilk were planted in 1860. At this time this magnificent property was owned by an Englishman called John Pinney Bear. It was purchased by Reginald Purbrick in 1925 and is still under the control of the Purbrick family.

Almost everywhere you go in Victoria you will find that vineyards existed at some time or other. Either phylloxera or economic conditions forced them out. The fact that some remained when all the others were given up is due to a variety of circumstances. The main reason is that the vineyard and winery was a paying proposition when others because of poor management were not. If a winery survived the economic severity of over supply in the early part of the century and the lack of money in the depression it was either because the wine was so good and well marketed that there was a big demand for it as, for example, Great Western Champagne, or there were supporting primary industries such as at Chateau Tahbilk.

The vineyards and winery at Mildura were in a different category. Here irrigation made the growing of vine a much more economic proposition than in the non-irrigated areas and more and more in the post-war era the wine made in these areas took sales away from the less fortunate (so it seemed) districts.

Irrigation was begun at Mildura by the Chaffey brothers from Canada about 1890. The vine was first planted here in 1888 with the vision of a flourishing wine industry in mind. When a lack of appreciation of fine wines by our forebears became apparent the table wine varieties were converted into types more suitable for drying and distillation. It was not until after the Second World War that 'Mildara Wines' became a name of any consequence.

South Australia's Wine Families

South Australia is the wine state of Australia since approximately 75 per cent of all wine made in the Commonwealth is made here.

The first vineyard was planted by John Reynell in 1838 about fourteen miles from Adelaide with cuttings brought from New South Wales. He was quickly followed by Dr Rawson Penfold from England at Magill, and Dr Kelly south of Adelaide.

The history of wine in South Australia is the history of a few families. In our first century great emphasis was

placed on the export of wines to England. Several of the
English wine companies, Burgoynes, Stephen Smith & Co.
and the Emu Wine Co. set up their own vineyards and
wineries at Rutherglen, Noarlunga and Morphett Vale
respectively. Other winemakers interested in export were
forced either to sell to these companies or to endeavour
to interest English merchants in London and other English
cities to buy their products.

In the early years of the twentieth century many of the
South Australian wine families realized that if they were
to remain in business, they would have to find markets
in New South Wales and Victoria. Fortunately for them,
phylloxera had exterminated many of the vineyards in the
eastern States but had not attacked South Australia.

Dr Rawson Penfold and his son-in-law Thomas Hyland,
a remarkable character with intense drive and initiative,
decided to push the Penfold name in the eastern States.
Intense advertising campaigns were begun. All over New
South Wales and Victoria 'Penfold' signs were displayed
on hoardings, buildings, fences and railway lines. Efficient
marketing organizations were set up in the capital cities.
To keep pace with the now considerable demand for their
products, Penfold's spread from Magill to Nuriootpa in
the Barossa Valley where about 1912 they built an immense
winery and storage sheds. This was followed by the building
of wineries at McLaren Vale, Kalimna and Eden Valley
and the planting of vineyards in several parts of South
Australia – Modbury, Barossa Valley and Southern Vales.

Hyland's sons, Frank and Leslie, came into the business
early after the First World War and, following the lead
of their father, kept on their advertising campaigns and
opening further markets in England and New Zealand.
The champagne making winery of Captain Minchin at
Rooty Hill in New South Wales was purchased and the
Dalwood Winery in the Hunter Valley. This enormous
organization now has eighteen vineyards and wineries and
at Tempe five miles from Sydney have built what they
claim to be the most modern wine cellars in the world.

Joseph Ernst Seppelt came to Australia from Germany

in 1849 and settled in the Barossa Valley in 1851 with the intention of growing tobacco. He found that this venture was unsuccessful but he had planted some vines in addition to his tobacco plants and as these proved more successful he planted further vines, built new storage sheds and excavated new cellars. In 1868 Joseph Seppelt died and his son Benno, then twenty-one years of age, took control. He was a man of vision and enormous energy and, like the Penfold family, realized that marketing his product was as important as making it. In 1916 Chateau Tanunda, a brandy distillery in the Barossa Valley was purchased and in 1918 the Great Western winery. Vineyards and wineries at Rutherglen in Victoria followed. In the meantime the cellars at Seppeltsfield continued to expand and today it is one of the most beautiful and romantic wineries in the world.

A young Devon farmer, Thomas Hardy, landed at Port Adelaide in 1850. He applied to John Reynell for a position and worked for him at Reynella for twelve months before going to a cattle property at Normanville.

In 1853 he purchased a property at Thebarton, which he cleared and planted with vines and fruit trees twelve months later. In that year there were only 377 acres of vines in the whole State. By 1862 there were 4,000 acres. He found that it was necessary for him to purchase grapes from the southern districts in order to keep his presses and fermenting vats producing enough wine. He formed a close association with P. B. Burgoyne & Co., the London wine merchants, and in spite of the fact that Victoria and New South Wales had imposed stiff tariffs against South Australia to protect their own makers, managed to keep his markets.

In 1876 Thomas Hardy purchased the Tintara vineyard near McLaren Vale and in 1881 erected a substantial bluestone building in Currie Street, Adelaide for his head office and bottling cellars.

By 1889 in South Australia there were more than 7,300 acres under vines and the vintage was a million gallons. Overseas exports in 1890 were 221,000 gallons but this still fell short of production and winemakers were looking for outlets.

In 1887 Thomas Hardy took his three sons into partnership and the business continued to expand. By 1894 the firm had become the South Australian colony's largest winemakers with a vintage of 315,000 gallons. Almost all of this was claret or white table wine.

In 1901 a cellar and branch office were established in Sydney and in 1912 the firm erected one of the first electric bulb advertising signs in Australia. It became a landmark. A Melbourne office was set up soon afterwards.

So it goes on, this history of families building up the wine trade in South Australia. The German family of Gramp's set up the huge Orlando winery at Rowland Flat in 1850; the old English family of Samuel Smith began its vineyard, 'Yalumba' at Angaston in 1849; Henry Martin later on in the nineteenth century established himself at Burnside. All these early pioneers worked hard at founding family traditions and family names. Richard Hamilton planted 5 acres of vines at Glenelg in 1840. The Buring and Sobels families began 'Quelltaler' about 1889.

The Co-operatives came in the thirties when depression hit the wine companies hard and they could not afford to buy the grapes of the growers.

Today South Australia has over 70,000 acres of vines most of the produce of which is made into wines.

Western Australia

The first vines were planted in 1831 by a Mr McFaull but progress was so slow that even by 1881 there were still only 527 acres. A retired army officer named Houghton had planted 163 acres in the Swan Valley near Perth. In 1859 this was purchased by the Ferguson family and developed with great success until 1950 when it was sold to the Emu Wine Co. This latter company also purchased in 1945 the Valencia vineyards which had been planted in 1890 with about 90 acres of vines. Sandalford vineyard was established in 1840 by John Septimus Roe, first Surveyor-General of Western Australia. It was not until 1946 that his great grandsons, David and John, developed it as an important winemaking centre.

As in other States, the Second World War increased local demand enormously and the wine growers prospered. In 1964, about one million gallons of wine were produced.

The title of connoisseur and epicure are by no means synonymous. An epicure seeks pleasure for its own sake, not knowledge. A connoisseur is a scholar and a specialist.
Evelyn Waugh

15 THE CORRECT USE OF WINES

WINES, by their nature, are designed to be drunk in conjunction with food; but, of all beverages, except water, wine is the simplest. It asks for no special rules. It asks only that you enjoy it, whenever you have it or with whatever you have it.

For the most part and for everyday purposes, I am content to begin with claret and to end with claret even if this extends from the pre-prandial to the night cap drink. There are special occasions, however, when a closer attention to the selection of kinds of wine is necessary.

Lichine says, 'Wine and food go together, with or without

interesting effects on the liver, and it is impossible for the French to think of one without the other.'

Australian practice, quite rightly, is bound to be slightly different from the practices of other countries. Certainly, the practice of having wine with breakfast, lunch and dinner will never become regular. Experience has taught us Australians what are the most suitable drinks for our country and climate.

No matter what we have had during the day, let us have our glass of sherry before the evening meal. Let it be dry and let it be light. It will relax and soothe us and make us ready to approach our meal with zest.

On weekdays of no special consequence, share a bottle of dry white or red – whichever may appeal to you at the time – something taken without much thought from your storage rack. If it is a cold winter's night enjoy a glass or two of port in front of the fire before you go to bed.

The Special Occasion

APPETIZER WINE

If it is going to be a dinner party, champagne of the 'brut' variety is best. This is not sweet: it cleanses the palate and puts your guests in the right frame of mind for conviviality and for food and conversation very quickly.

Champagne, however, is expensive and, if you have frequent dinner parties or if the party is a small one or consists of intimate friends, give them dry sherry or dry vermouth.

Chill all these drinks.

TABLE WINE

Now for the meal itself. Our palates and our personalities have been put in the right condition by the 'aperitive' wine and if we wish to use wine during the meal the question will be 'do some wines go better with some foods than others?'

Well, some combinations and incompatibilities are obvious. Nearly everyone would agree that a rich red wine would go well with a juicy barbecued steak: most people would consider that the delicate white flesh of whiting would lose all its flavour if it was accompanied by a dark and astringent claret.

A chef will go to enormous trouble to ensure that the ingredients he uses all blend together harmoniously to produce a perfect dish. He is not a great chef unless he calls on tradition and the experience of his tutors to help him with his masterpieces. He may experiment and try new ideas, but, fundamentally, he adheres strictly to proved recipes.

It is something the same in the use of wines. For the great dinner party in your home, you will probably choose a white wine to go with some dishes and a red to go with others.

I am going to make a few suggestions. Do not take them as absolute rules. They are combinations of food and wine which I like and which I think suit the Australian way of life, but they may not be to everyone's taste.

The suggestions are as follows:

With SEAFOOD HORS-D'OEUVRES: Light dry acid style wines such as South Australian Riesling.

With MEAT AND VEGETABLE HORS-D'OEUVRES: Dry or Sweet Rosé wines.

With OYSTERS NATURAL: A very crisp dry white-Rhine riesling or semillon.

With CONSOMMÉ: Light dry sherry. This can be the continuation of the aperitive wine.

With CREAM SOUP: Brown sherry.

With FINNY FISH: A full rich white wine, dry but not too dry, or a fuller moselle.

With ENTREES: Say meat balls, kidneys, chicken's livers, paté or pastas. A light young red wine, say from South Australia.

With POULTRY – CHICKEN, TURKEY, PHEASANT: A full rich white wine or a light red with some age.

GOOSE, DUCK: A full bodied red wine, perhaps a magnificent old Hunter Valley or a first class north-eastern Victorian.

With MEAT: Say, tournedos steak, grilled steak of various sorts, roast lamb, beef or pork – a light red wine of some age and quality perhaps a very old Coonawarra, Reynella, Tahbilk or Hunter Valley.

With say, corned beef, ox tongue, shasslick, boiled beef or mutton, casserole beef with strong sauces, beef stew, liver, game such as rabbit, hare, venison, wild duck and other game birds, goulash, beef stroganoff – a full bodied red wine, perhaps a big Southern Vales of some quality or an old Milawa.

With CHEESE: Any red wine including port.

With SALADS: Iced water.

With SWEETS: Sauternes or late picked riesling, a not too dry champagne.

With FRUIT (excluding citrus fruits): Sauternes.

Before COFFEE: Port or muscat.

As a contrary opinion to the above, I am giving a fairly lengthy quotation from the Marquis de Lur Saluce, the proprietor of Chateau d' Yquem which is the place of origin of the best and most famous sweet white wine in the world. Take this fact into consideration when you are deciding on what policy you are to follow when serving wine, because he, no doubt, is looking to his markets as well as expressing a genuine opinion:

'Sauternes must be served very cold, after resting in the ice bucket, but it should never be completely iced. Which are the foods which complement them best? Everyone must decide according to his taste. But, contrary to the widely held opinion, it certainly seems that sauternes is not the best wine to drink with the sweet course. The art of combining wines and food consists of seeking among them suitable contrasts so as to heighten the flavour of each, within the frame of general harmony. All the sauternes present an

Australian hardwood storage tanks.

Stainless steel storage tanks used by McWilliam's.

(Top) Storage casks at McWilliam's Mt Pleasant vineyard. *(Bottom)* Old oak casks for table wine storage at Stanley Wine Co., Clare. *(Right)* Bottles of wine at Penfold's Auldana winery.

essential individuality, and some very fine flavours. What happens to these fine flavours in the presence of the vanilla or curacao of a souffle, or the chocolate of a pastry, or the sugar of this and that? Its individuality is, in my opinion, killed.

Sauternes' true place, in my opinion, is with the delicate fish – turbot, sauce mousseline, or salmon, lobster, fillets of sole of all recipes, with foie gras (here it is superb), with fruit; and finally, when one has just come home, it is perfect served very cold with a dry biscuit.'

The attitude implied in the above quotation, is that food should be served only to offset a fine wine; that various dishes should be chosen to show off a collection of beautiful wines to advantage. At times, this is perhaps what we should wish to do. As Lichine says, 'Great wines are not drunk with everyday food.'

However, the suggestions I have given you envisage your planning a dinner and, having chosen your dishes, you now set about choosing the wines that go best with them. Your object will be first to stimulate the appetite of your guests. You will do this by serving wines that are dry and slightly astringent, that cleanse the palate, brighten up the taste buds and set the gastric juices running. Your aperitive wines should begin to do this. Throughout the main part of the meal you will endeavour to maintain this stimulation of appetite and zest for food. You will blend flavours in your foods and combine the taste of food and wine as the chef does when preparing the various ingredients of a great dish, sometimes a parity here, sometimes a contrast there, but all in the general plan of making the meal interesting and delicious.

In the end you want your guests to feel satisfied without being replete, so you cover their palates with sugar by means of a sweet dish and a sweet wine. Sugar sates the palate, stops the gastric juices running and removes appetite. Your guests, at this stage, are then ready perhaps to sip a port or muscat, but in any case are feeling very happy and content with the meal you have given them without any sense of plethora.

Now, it may happen that you are having a dinner party at which you wish to serve a collection of rather good wines. Should this be so, your dishes must be chosen with an eye on the wines. A wine of great quality should not be served with a highly flavoured dish (say a hot curry) which would make it impossible to appreciate the wine. Any dish with vinegar must be excluded. Avoid caviar. Salads must be hidden away until the end.

Begin with a dry white wine which is an excellent accompaniment to raw oysters, but do not drink your best white here since the oyster's penetration will destroy the fine flavour of the wine.

Wines, at a dinner like this, are served in an order of ascendency; the lighter, not so great wines being followed by the richer and more powerful types and those with higher quality. If your object is to show off reds, the 'wine of the evening' is your last wine.

Cheese is an excellent foil for first class red wines but keep them away from 'mouldy' or 'ammonia' cheese like blue vein or gorgonzola.

At the cheese course, leave all your wines on the table so that your guests can study them more at leisure, comparing the first with the last and discussing their comparative qualities for as long as they (or you) wish.

Coffee follows the dessert wine (port or muscat) and brandy (if you wish) follows coffee.

When I am putting on a dinner party I always allow my wife the final choice of dishes. This puts me in the happy position of being able to choose my wines to match the dish, which is very much simpler than to choose the wine first and then to find a dish which can be served with it. I approach the problem by considering that wine is an adjunct to the food. My first job is to stimulate the palate and appetite of my guests so that I can bolster up their ability to distinguish flavours and to help obtain the mouth-watering effect which I hope the delicious odours from the kitchen have already begun.

Throughout all the courses I endeavour to use wine to maintain this stimulation of appetite and zest for food while at the same time having my guests exclaim with delight at the beauty of the wine I am presenting.

Obviously there are two methods of matching food and wine. Sometimes I look for a bland synthesis of flavour of wine, food and sauces. At others I seek a stimulating contrast, but not so great a contrast as to destroy the flavour of either wine or food. With the appetizer or with the fish course I usually select a light, crisp wine without any trace of sugar whatsoever. A good first wine of this kind would be labelled *Riesling*. I like the more acid style from the Barossa Ranges such as Gramp's Orlando, Yalumba Carte D'Or, Leo Buring's, Hamilton's Springton, Kaiser Stuhl, Stanley or Henschke. Similar to these but from other areas are Seaview, Hardy's Old Castle, Wynn's Modbury Estate or Coonawarra Estate, Seppelt's Arawatta and Chateau Tahbilk.

This wine goes particularly well with all fish entrées (if we may call fish an entrée) such as the various kinds of seafood cocktails, soused herrings, fish in aspic, crab meat, fish mornay, fish meuniere. They are delicate and beautifully flavoured and do not lose their flavour in the presence of these dishes.

Highly acid South Australian semillon and white hermitage produced by the above companies would be an alternative choice. If an appetizer was served as well as a fish course I should serve one of these latter with this and riesling with the fish.

Hunter Valley rieslings are softer and less crisp than the South Australian. They are most often made from the semillon grape which heightens this effect. Their flavour is magnificent and in a dinner where there are many courses, I should present one after the South Australian, particularly with an entrée such as a quiche, fondue, pizza, risotto, pasta or an egg dish. The best Hunter Rieslings are the special binnings of Lindeman's and Penfold's, Tulloch's, Tyrrell's, Elliott's, Drayton and Mt Pleasant.

Paté calls for a blander wine. Even a sauternes goes well with this, although the sugar of the sauternes tends to dampen the appetite. It is a matter of the number of courses. A paté served as the only dish before the main course means you would serve only one wine before the reds. In this case the combination is a happy one.

We are faced with a problem with first dishes consisting of melon filled with grapes, grapefruit cocktail, paw paw or similar fruit appetizer dishes. The acid of these fruits does not blend at all well with that of riesling style wines. An overpowering sensation of sourness is the only result.

Non-acid whites are the answer here. I think the perfect combination with these are the late picked rieslings of Orlando, Buring's, Kaiser Stuhl and Yalumba, or Wynn's Modbury Estate Semillon. The slight sweetness in these wines panders to the dish. I like these wines too with hearts of artichoke or palm.

Assuming that we have had at least one course with which we have had a crisp white wine to act as a palate teaser we could serve a more full bodied white with ensuing entrée dishes such as cheese savoury or fondues, wieners, brains, kidneys, chicken livers or rabbit.

The big soft white wines we call chablis or white burgundy go well with these. Houghton's, Hamilton's, Buring's, Lindeman's Hunter Valley and Seaview are my favourites. This type of wine goes remarkably well too with shell fish such as oysters, mussells and scallops. They are full flavoured enough to counteract the powerful and penetrating flavour of these crustaceans.

Provided we have had at least one crisp white wine, I should like to serve a light dry red with the course before the main dish provided it has some meat content such as cannelloni. This serves as a good introduction to the first class reds we shall see with the main course. Any average Hunter Valley red would suit me here very well.

The main course must be accompanied by a red wine which is of great quality and which ideally suits the dish.

Plain roast beef or lamb without seasoning or larding and unadorned grilled steak require a fully flavoured but light red wine such as a Mt Pleasant Hunter Valley Red or a Reynella Claret. I prefer the South Australian for the purpose because the penetrating taste and the pleasant astringency seems to provide a tactual buffer for the meat. In either case the wine must not be heavy or fulsome.

Chicken, turkey and pheasant have similar flesh and when simply roasted call for a full rich wine such as a Houghton's or Modbury Estate white burgundy or for a light red wine. My choice here is a Tyrrell's Hunter Valley red, a Best's Great Western claret or a lighter red of Leo Buring's.

Beefsteak served with strongly flavoured sauces such as Steak *à la Bordelaise, à la Bearnaise, Rossini* and *Chateaubriant;* beef casserole dishes; chicken, turkey or pheasant cooked casserole-style such as *coq au vin* and *chicken en cocotte;* veal dishes such as *escalope Viscayenne* or *côte de veau Normande;* lamb dishes like kebabs, lamb provençal and marinated lamb chops – all of them require a strongly flavoured wine as an accompaniment.

These dishes have sauces which contain one or more of the following ingredients: highly flavoured herbs and seasoning, garlic, onions, chives, black pepper, green peppers, mushrooms, olive oil, butter, celery, cognac, calvados, wine. These are high flavour elements which must be matched with a similar flavour level in the wine that goes with the dish.

Fortunately, Australia has many quality wines which fulfil this requirement: Coonawarra reds, whether they are made from cabernet or shiraz grapes or by Wynn's, Mildara, Lindeman's or any of the other firms which make wine from grapes grown in this area; Seaview Cabernet; McLaren Vale reds made by Ingoldby, Kay, Osborn and Johnston; Gramp's Orlando Cabernet; Hunter Valley reds of Lindeman's and McWilliam's and the rare bottlings of Seppelt's unblended Great Western wines.

They are wines of great character and are ripe for drinking after three years although I should prefer to present them when they are ten years old.

Duck is a strongly flavoured meat. The best way to cook it is with wine, brandy, herbs, truffles or salt pork or stuffed with rice, wheat, pine nuts and herbs and then roasted. Goose is even more strongly flavoured and in addition contains a great amount of natural fat. Both these birds create dangerous competition for the wine in the flavour sphere. In this respect they compare with jugged hare, venison, wild duck and other Australian game birds.

The host should accompany them with a heavy wine which has strong berry overtones and great vinous character. The older it is the better. Any of the heavier Hunter Valley reds of Lindeman's, Elliott's, Drayton's or Tulloch's; an old Tahbilk or John Brown from north-eastern Victoria or a well aged Chalambar will suit the purpose. Personally I prefer the Southern Vale reds: any of Ingoldby's heavier Cabernets, Reynell's Vintage Reserve Burgundy and Darrenberg Burgundy.

Corned beef, beef stews (including ox tail), boiled beef or mutton and roast pork do not call for great wines. Ham is different. Hot or cold ham steak is delicious; one wine only goes with this dish – champagne; but then, champagne is a celebration wine and under special circumstances goes well with any dish. Bottle-fermented Seppelt's, Hardy's, McWilliam's, Penfold's, Romalo or Lindeman's are my choice.

Champagne, particularly one that is slightly sweet, is a good accompaniment to fruit compotes, sorbets, cream custards, chantilly, mousses, parfaits, marshmallows, sponges, pavlova or meringues and chocolate flavoured sweets like Pear Helene. If a still wine is preferred with these I can think of none better than sauternes. The special binnings of Lindeman's Porphyry, Mt Pleasant, Seppelt's, Quelltaler, Hardy's Golden Nectar and Hamilton's Special Reserve are entirely satisfactory.

With fresh fruits such as peaches, nectarines, apricots, pears, plums, cherries and strawberries, I like the late-picked riesling style of wines such as those made by Orlando, Yalumba, Kaiser Stuhl, Buring's and Lindeman's. Wynn's Modbury Estate Semillon and Seaview Sauvignon Blanc are of a similar type and go just as well with these fruits.

Raspberries, loganberries and pineapple are inclined to be too tart for most wines. A very sweet wine like that of Houghton's West Australian Sauternes or one of McWilliam's Riverina Sauternes is the answer.

For most apples which also tend to be fairly tart, an Olorosa type of sherry such as that of Seppelt's or Mildara Chestnut Teal is a good foil. I think you could have these and enjoy them thoroughly with English Apple Pie.

Ice cream sweets do not go well with wines. It is best to wait for the sultanas and walnuts to have a good port or other dessert wine if ice cream is your final dish. Morris', Chamber's or Orlando Tokay, Lindeman's Special Bin Madeira, Hardy's Sauvignon Blanc, Seppelt's Frontignac or Houghton's Liqueur Hermitage are good wines at this stage.

After all this a large cup of strong coffee and a good Australian brandy is enough to extract a sigh of complete contentment from even the most blasé of trenchermen.

Temperature

When you are deciding as to what temperature you should serve your wine remember that the criterion to be followed is the answer to the question, 'At what temperature does it give the most pleasure?' Nothing else matters. Wines, however, are not like beer. They have different perfumes and nuances of flavour which must be brought out if we are to get maximum pleasure from them. Each different type of wine has its own 'best' temperature to enable this to happen.

There is one factor that we have to take into consideration. In summer our temperatures in Australia can well rise up into the nineties. Even at the time of the evening meal we sometimes find that the thermometer is still around eighty degrees. We have to adjust, therefore, our thinking on wine temperatures. We shall keep in mind that a bottle of wine placed on the table at the correct temperature might, unless we have an air-conditioned home, quickly take on a much higher temperature. Measures must be taken, in consequence, to ensure that this does not happen. In an air-conditioned house, where the temperature is set at about sixty-five degrees, there is no need to take any special precautions, but otherwise make certain that all wines are served at about ten degrees lower on a hot summer's day than at any other time of the year.

DRY SHERRY, VERMOUTH: Chilled. One hour in the refrigerator is enough.

WHITE TABLE WINES AND SPARKLING WINES, VIN ROSÉ: Very cold. Between 40 and 45 degrees. Leave in the refrigerator for two hours. In summer turn the refrigerator down about 10 degrees.

RED TABLE WINES AND DESSERT WINES: About 65 degrees.

There is not much difficulty in arriving at the correct temperature for red wines during the most part of the year. Australian homes mostly are comfortably heated in cold weather and in the winter the reds can be placed in the warm kitchen away from heating appliances on the day you intend to serve them. In an air-conditioned home there are no problems at all. Leave the bottles in the dining room all day and allow them to take on the temperature of the house either in winter or summer. On a hot summer's day in a home that is not air-conditioned, keep the wines in as cool a place as possible all day, but do not put them in the refrigerator. If it is a very hot day, do not serve red wines at all.

Decanting

Decanting is the act of pouring wine from a bottle into a decanter. There are two reasons for doing this: firstly, to enable the wine to 'breathe'; secondly, to eliminate sediment. The wines that need decanting are table wines and vintage port. All other wines can be served immediately from the bottle as soon as the cork is removed. Young wines, white or red, unless they have sediment, are quite well prepared if the cork is pulled about an hour before they are served.

Whatever may be said about French or other European wines in the matter of decanting, one thing is certain, Australian wines over five years in bottle, need it even if, sometimes, they do not deserve it. When first opened, an Australian wine does not show its true worth. For a time its perfume seems to be locked away and we have difficulty in finding it. Exposed to the air for an hour or so and it, as it were, opens itself and gives. Gradually, the bouquet is revealed and the flavour develops. Decanting the bottle about an hour before you are ready to serve it to your guests has the result of eliminating 'bottle stink' which is some peculiar odour that sometimes stays with the wine for a little while after the cork is pulled, and of enabling your wine to blossom out with its perfume, its esters and its ethers which have been locked away.

Any old wine you intend to serve should be allowed to rest quietly after it has been removed from its bin, for at least twelve hours. Resting it upright will allow the sediment to settle to the base of the bottle. If you are going to present a bottle of old wine which you have purchased from your wine merchant, have it in your home at least a week before the dinner.

Prepare a table on which you can rest a lamp, your bottle and a decanter. If you have several wines and only one decanter, use clean empty and dry bottles for your task. A funnel will be necessary for this purpose. Draw the cork with a corkscrew having a double action principle so that the bottle remains resting on the table and receives no sudden jerk which will upset the sediment. Raise the opened bottle very carefully and tilt it slowly over the funnel so that your eye can look through the neck of the bottle at the lamp. Continue pouring until the sediment begins to show in the neck of the bottle; then stop.

Do not fall into the error of decanting in the morning and leaving the wine exposed all day. This process will allow all the lovely perfumes, all the beautiful esters and the ethereal flavours to evaporate and disappear. Your wine, though quite sound, will no longer taste like a great wine.

Glassware

Drinking wine is part of the art of living. It is necessary, not only to cook beautiful food and to serve lovely wine, but to present the food and wine attractively. The arrangement of the table setting comes in for special care. The choice of glassware is, therefore, important.

The winemaker asks you only one thing: that you should appreciate his wine in a glass that is pure white and crystal clear.

For your everyday drinking, use your favourite tulip or thistle shaped glass for everything; but for your dinner party you will need a different glass for every type of wine – sherry, white table wine, red table wine, dessert wine and sparkling wine.

I am giving an illustration of shapes which I like *(see plates)*. Yet the only rules I can give you, in additon to the one above are: let your glass be graceful and let them be thin around the lips. As for the rest, taste in glassware is like taste in wine – let there be no dispute.

Cooking with Wine

Wine is a flavouring element in cooking in the same way as salt, saffron or paprika. The difference is that, whereas these other additions merely complete a dish, wine takes it into another sphere.

There is something different and exciting in the smell of food cooked with wine. Walk into a kitchen where a *coq au vin* is simmering on the stove and you will find the aromas that fill the air stimulating and somehow disturbing.

The addition of wine to say a ragôut made up of cheap cuts of meat transforms it into a delicious and tasty dish altogether different to the ordinary, savourless and uninteresting meal it was going to be without wine.

Do not imagine that wine can be used 'ad lib' in every recipe. There are certain dishes to which wine can be added and which are greatly improved accordingly; certain others cannot take it.

In general any meat cooked in a casserole or saucepan welcomes the addition of wine; so does any soup, any sauce or any sauté dish. Fish dishes cooked in the continental way in a pan with such ingredients as butter, milk, onions and oil nearly always call for wine to add the 'heavenly' touch.

Very few dishes that do not follow the recipe to the

letter are successful. You cannot add wine, for example, in any way but the prescribed quantity to a chicken cacciatore.

There is no harm done, however, if you are a little heavy handed in pouring your red wine into a beef stew.

Remember that it is not important to use a high class wine in cooking. The alcohol evaporates and the wine changes in nature so much that any fine differences of quality are entirely lost. A cheap red wine or a wine left over from a bottle you opened a week ago is quite good for cooking.

Finally, obtain a good wine recipe book. There are dozens of them available suitable for Australian cooking. Even if cookery books do not actually set out to give you *wine* recipes, you will find that most continental style books include dishes that call for wine as an ingredient.

A wine merchant combines the qualities of the business man, the trusted adviser and the tutor. His job is to sell wine; but, if he is to inspire his clients with confidence. he must do so with a difference. The good wine merchant must prescribe for each of his customers according to their tastes, but at the same time be ready to advance their knowledge and deepen their appreciation. The best wine merchants are those who will, on occasion, tell you not to buy from their lists.
'The New Statesman and Nation',
20 November 1954

16 AUSTRALIAN WINE MERCHANTS

IN THE simple meaning of the words, any person who sells wine is a wine merchant. In Australia you will find quite a number of different people who sell wine; hotel keepers, restaurateurs, licensed grocers, whole-salers and retailers.

Some of them, like the licensed grocers in Melbourne and Sydney, will have good and representative stocks of all the commercial wines. Others will have fairly good stocks of their own bottlings and their own selection.

The Australian wine merchant is not the same as his London counterpart. He can be a simple man who knows only a little of what he is selling. He probably does not

have a great knowledge of wine but he is usually a likeable
fellow who will go out of his way to try to get you what
you want.

To comply with the definition given in the heading, we
would expect 'the complete Australian wine merchant' to

1. have large stocks of Australian wines;
2. have wines from all major Australian wine companies;
3. have wines from the better small vineyards of Australia;
4. have wines from every notable wine producing country
   in Europe;
5. be a foremost wine man himself;
6. have a well trained staff who know and respect wine;
   and
7. have large stocks of red table wines and ports ageing.

The wine merchant must know wine. This is his job in
life. He is drinking, tasting, comparing and assessing wines
all the time. He will be able to tell you at any particular
time what are the best names, the best vintages and the
best binnings available.

Your wine merchant's task is to protect you as far as
possible from disappointments in wine. It is his burden,
pleasant though it may be, to watch all Australian wines,
to study the ageing of his own precious vintages, to watch
the progress of new areas and the advent of new winemakers. He should be the first to tell his clients of the
arrival in the world of beautiful new wines.

Of necessity, this type of wine merchant is rare. He will
need large underground areas for storage, large bottling
areas and large display sections. He will need to have many
thousands of dollars tied up in wine from which he expects
no return for many years. He must have many more
thousands laid out for the large range of commercial wines.
To maintain his staff of trained men he must have a
permanent staff training scheme in wine.

The wine merchant must, above all, be an enthusiast.
Avoid the man who knows only labels. The true vintner
is a wine lover. He devotes all his spare time to investigating
wines so that he will know his subject thoroughly both

for his own satisfaction and in order to be able to advise his clients for their satisfaction. The true merchant is a cheerful, urbane fellow, for his is a pleasant life.

It is important to find a merchant who is not tied to any particular brand or maker. A good wine merchant is convinced by his palate and his experience of drinking wines. He likes to feel completely independent of outside influences.

Should he stock only commercially labelled wine of current vintages he is not a wine merchant in the true sense. On the other hand, if he has a range merely of his own bottled wines and very little else, he is a poor wine merchant.

Penfold's, Seppelt's, and Lindeman's have adopted a policy of selling some of their better wines under Bin numbers. These special bottlings are the prestige lines of these companies. They are always of outstanding quality, at least at time of bottling. There is always the chance, of course, that they could be complete failures later on. Your wine merchant is there to advise you on these wines.

There is not enough of a wine like this to be sold in large quantities in every store. In any event, none of them can be a continuous line. It is better to signify this by giving each one a recognizable Bin number which will, of itself, convey the idea that the bottling will run out and not be available any longer.

Many other companies issue even smaller binnings from time to time, and it is the task of the wine merchant to seek them out and to discover if they are worth drinking or keeping.

This question of the 'special binnings' is often raised among the large companies. Geared, as they are, to turning out hundreds of thousands of bottles of any one particular line, it imposes a severe strain on their efficiency to put out a few hundred bottles of some special line. In addition, by the mere fact of doing so, they create a demand for a product which they have no hope of satisfying.

Some companies try to find the answer to this difficulty by issuing special binnings which are blends of various areas and are therefore available in larger quantities. For example one firm issues a wine under a bin number which is practically a continuous line being a blend of Hunter River, Goulburn Valley and Clare districts. The wine merchant's task is to follow these from year to year to determine whether he should recommend them or not.

The Vintners of the Capital Cities

In *Melbourne* the wine merchants can be listed as follows:

'The Cellar'. Staff at this establishment have a magnificent knowledge of Australian wine. The Cellar aims to carry a complete range of all wines from every vineyard and winemaker in Australia, a vast stock of maturing wines and a representative range of imported wines.

W. J. Seabrook & Son. This is a very old family concern at present presided over by Douglas Seabrook, an excellent judge of wine and a devoted wine man. The firm specializes in several sherries of their own blending and a range of wines under their own label together with a selection of the better wines from the the large makers.

Rhine Castle Wines, under management of Peter Walker, specializes in a variety of wines under its own label. This firm knows its wines and has built up a reputation with some of the dry reds it has put down over the years.

The largest and most outstanding of the licensed grocers is O. R. Crittenden Pty Ltd, who stock an enormous range of all types of wine, both local and imported. A feature of Crittenden's also is their large selection of specialist foods and imported delicacies.

In *Sydney* the better wine merchants are:

Len Evans, a vigorous personality with a good palate and an intimate knowledge of wines.

Douglas Lamb who acts as an agent for some of the smaller winemakers and carries a good variety of excellent wines under the title of St Patrice. He has a good appreciation of wine and imports a carefully selected variety of vintages from Germany, France and Spain.

Leo Buring's 'Ye Olde Crusty Cellar', which has a limited

range of extremely high quality Australian wines under its own label.

Rhine Castle Wines, is under the direction of 'Johnny' Walker, a man of enormous personality and wine reputation. Like the Melbourne branch, this firm has a variety of good sherries, ports and table wines under the Rhine Castle label.

Brittany Cellars, has excellent Australian wines under its own label and a good range of imported wines.

The Italian wine merchant, who features largely on the scene in Melbourne and Sydney, is not to be ignored. His part is not that of the wine connoisseur. His business is to sell good common wine in quantity at a fairly low price. His customers, are undoubtedly, mostly Italians or of Italian descent but he has a following among all other types of Australians. In Melbourne the best of these are F. Agostini and Co., Chiodo and Santamaria. In Sydney you have Fiorelli and Cantarella Bros.

In *Adelaide*, the wine merchant is somewhat daunted by the practice of wine lovers of applying direct to the makers for their supplies. In spite of this, several good wine merchants exist. Among them are:

The 'Vintage Cellar' conducted by Jack Edwards who keeps a big stock of his own selected bottlings and a reasonable range of commercial Australian wines.

'408' Drive In, which has a wide range of local and imported wines.

Derek Jolly of Derek Jolly Pty Ltd is a man of vast experience, initiative and drive. He carries a large range of his own selections under his firm's label and a representative collection of commercial wines.

Adelaide is a 'wine conscious' city and even the hotel keepers are enthusiastic about the product of the grape. The bottle departments of the largest of them carry large supplies of table wine. That of the South Australian Hotel has a comprehensive selection of both Australian and imported vintages.

A pot still used for making brandy.

Glasses for wine (from left to right): port, white table wine, champagne, red table wine, sherry.

Brisbane is a poor city for wine. Beer and rum are drunk enthusiastically by the local people and any interest in wine is likely to be stifled by the lack of knowledge and enthusiasm of the vendors. The difficulty of the licensing laws makes it necessary for the holder of a spirit merchant's licence to sell two gallons and not less to his customer.

However, Rhine Castle Wines keep a comprehensive range of both dessert and table wines.

17 WINE AND FOOD SOCIETIES

WITH the tremendous increase in the interest in wine shown in the last two decades, there has appeared on the scene the 'Wine and Food Society'. The sole purpose of this group is to enjoy food and wine and the good company they engender.

Dining groups, of course, have been with us always. These little groups which had their origins in England and Europe, placed more accent, perhaps, on food than wine and in fact did not necessarily call for the use of wine. Other beverages were quite popular.

The 1930s saw the institution of the English Wine and Food Society and later of the Victorian and New South

Wales branches. The Bacchus Club of South Australia was formed with similar objects to the Wine and Food Society, wine appreciation being the *raison d'être* of them all, particularly as it was the wine trade that initiated their formation.

After the Second World War, quite a number of smaller Wine and Food Societies were formed, some affiliated with the London society and some just existing without caring about ties with the parent body.

In the fifties, the Adelaide Beefsteak and Burgundy Club was formed and from this foundation, B & B Clubs multiplied all over Australia, each receiving their 'charter' from the original institution.

In Australia today, there are several hundred groups of a similar nature, each of which meets monthly to enjoy food and wine.

The working principle of each society is similar. There are usually, though not always, a president and committee which will include a Foodmaster and Winemaster. Meetings are on a fixed day every month. Meetings are more often held in a restaurant or private dining room so that discussion can be held without interference from the other diners. Sometimes meetings are held in private homes.

The main object is to show off the wines, of which there will be several of each different type, aperitive, white table wine, red table wine and dessert wine. Food will be chosen to fit in well with these wines.

The chairman of the evening will call for comments on the wines from various members and sometimes for comment on the food. The foodmaster, or even the chef, called in for the purpose, will explain the recipes and the methods used in cooking the various dishes. The winemaster will give a brief story about each wine.

Conviviality is the essence of the meeting but the chairman will see that the procedure of meetings is more or less carried out and that order is maintained. He will endeavour to 'bring out' all members present so that each may express his opinion about the wines.

More often than not, the wine is 'masked', that is, a wrapper is placed around the label of the bottle so that members do not know what wine they are drinking. This enables them to make comments much more freely and without any pre-conceived ideas.

The Wines

The most important point regarding these is that there is no good reason to call a party of wine lovers together to enjoy wine unless first class wines are served. After all, the ordinary beverage wines can be bought anywhere off the shelves. The bottle of claret we picked up from a vineyard a week ago can be consumed with pleasure any night at home.

The winemaster's task is to collect high quality wines from various sources which are not normally available from a restaurant; to prepare them carefully, and to ensure that they are correctly served at the dinner. The restaurant will charge 'corkage' on each bottle for this purpose.

No wine and food group will be successful unless care is taken on this point. No member whose wife is a good cook and who has a reasonable collection of good wines is going to leave the comfort of his home every month unless he expects wines and food of above average quality.

To make a wine and food society a success a restaurant which serves good food, therefore, must be chosen and better than ordinary wines must be sought out by the winemaster. To assist the winemaster in his choice of wines for the night, I am making the following suggestions:

First, the wines must be identifiable.
You can buy wines which have back labels reading something like this:

> 'This wine was made from cabernet sauvignon, shiraz and grenache grapes grown at McLaren Vale, Hunter Valley, Goulburn Valley and Clare, especially blended by our winemaker.'

Now this may be very pleasant wine and I have met with wines which have labels identical to this which are very drinkable. You cannot, however, put on this bottle with the label masked for two reasons:

1. it is impossible to identify the grapes;
2. it is impossible to identify the area.

One of the benefits of these dinners is the chance to learn the merits of the wines from the different areas. What chance have you of learning anything from such a wine?

Another error of inexperienced winemasters is to put on a wine, the label of which conveys nothing. For example, he might present a masked bottle of wine. When the label is revealed, it reads 'Flintstone's Gold Label Claret'. Flintstone's might be a company which grows vines in ten different areas, buys wine from everywhere and blends everything. When the label is revealed nobody gains anything in knowledge.

Secondly, there must be a progression in the order of excellence.

To put a second rate Barossa Valley red of only twelve months old after a first class Hunter Valley of twelve years would be a great mistake. Serve the lesser wines first so that the qualities of the greater may be appreciated.

Thirdly, serve extraordinarily good wines unmasked.

There is nothing more devastating to a winemaster than to hear a wine for which he has paid a small fortune and which he knows is extremely good consigned to oblivion as 'not bad'. Unless you have a remarkably experienced group who know their wines, let them have the benefit of knowing they are drinking a very good wine so that they can study it a little more closely.

Picking the Wines

Every wine and food club likes to play the game of 'picking the wines'. The good wine man knows wines and can comment excellently on their good points. He may not, necessarily, be able to identify them exactly as regards area. Others again, while they may not be particularly good judges of wine, have fine 'palate memories'. They will be able to say very often where the wine comes from and sometimes who made it. Occasionally, they will nominate the wine exactly, e.g. 'Grange Hermitage 1959'.

Some men have remarkable palate memories. They will be able to recall with complete clarity a wine they tasted perhaps one week, one month or one year ago. This enables them to identify with accuracy individual bottlings of wine. It is a very interesting phenomenon somewhat akin to an actor's ability to recite some intricate piece of poetry. But it does not necessarily indicate any sound knowledge of wine, just as the actor need not necessarily have a sound knowledge of or even appreciate poetry.

As a man nears his sixties, his powers of memory tend to deteriorate and with it his palate memory. But that is not important. The best judges of wine think about the good qualities of a wine. Sometimes they recognize it as being a particular bottling. That is only incidental. More often than not, they will recognize the locality. But first quality localities produce wines very similar in many respects to each other, provided they are grown on a similar soil. So it is not surprising that good wine men will sometimes err in picking the locality. What is important is that they do not call an average wine a quality wine or vice versa.

At these wine and food dinners it is sometimes irritating and a cause of wrath to a knowledgeable wine man to have a winemaster bring out a wine purporting to come from a certain area when it does not. As I have explained, it is easier to pick areas than to pick individual wines.

In an example given above, a winemaster has presented a wine simply called 'Flintstone's Gold Label Claret'. It was impossible to pick the area because it was a blend of different areas. Members will be annoyed because there is nothing on the label to identify the area. Some will have called it a 'Hunter Valley'; others 'McLaren Vale'. They cannot be expected to pick it as Flintstone's Claret especially as Flintstone's Claret might have a different blend for every bottling.

To give another example of bad presentation by a winemaster, we shall take the case of a wine labelled 'Rockvale Claret'. On the label is a line which reads 'Rubble's Hunter Valley Vineyards'. Now Rubble's do not say that their 'Rockvale' claret comes from the Hunter

Valley but they are implying it by this line on the label. The knowledgeable man in the club knows that 'Rockvale' claret is made up of a blend of Hunter Valley, Coonawarra and McLaren Vale wines. There is much irritation and controversy, therefore, when the winemaster unwraps the bottle and presents it unequivocally as a 'Hunter Valley'.

You will have the same kind of trouble with grape varieties. The inexperienced winemaster will present a wine as made from a 'riesling' grape when it could in fact have been made from any kind of grape but is only named 'riesling' because the maker or merchant thinks it is in the 'riesling' style.

'Cabernet' is another difficult grape variety. This is a fashionable grape and, therefore, practically every company markets a 'Cabernet'. Most often, if you turn the bottle around you will find that there is a back label which states that the wine is made from a mixture of 'cabernet' and 'shiraz' grapes. One maker might have 90 per cent cabernet grapes in the mixture; another might have only 5 per cent. Can you blame anybody for not being able to pick the 'cabernet' grape? I am not criticizing the winemakers for these practices, but, if the exercise of the evening is 'grape varieties' then the winemaster must get varietal wines that are beyond question.

Wine and Food Societies, as a rule, serve wine from Australia, France, Italy, Germany and Spain. After a while members become adept at picking wine from these countries and it gives them great pleasure when they are right. To put in a wine from South Africa or Bulgaria, adds nothing to the evening if it is picking wines that the members want. No one will pick it and it is better to serve it unmasked.

How to get the best out of Club nights

Very much depends on the winemaster and the chairman; the winemaster, first of all, because unless he chooses interesting wines, the evenings will be flat; and the chairman, for he has to know how to keep the flow of comment lively and how to keep in check the longwindedness of the member who loves an audience.

A winemaster may go for 'exercises'. For example, he might say, 'The exercise tonight is to pick the grape varieties in the four red wines. They are cabernet, shiraz, malbec and grenache. Which is which?' Or he might say, 'In the reds tonight, two wines are of one age and two of another. Bracket these wines and state the age of each bracket.'

Other exercises are wines grown in the hills on scanty soil and wines grown on the flats; French wines and Australian wines; wines with progressive ages; blended wines and 'straight' wines; 'out of four wines pick two grown in the same district.'

For all these exercises, absolutely dependable labelling is required. Avoid the firms or wine merchants, the labels of which you suspect do not always tell the truth about the wine. If you suspect a label or merchant, do not put the wine on the table masked. The wine may be excellent drinking but it has no place in an exercise of this nature.

After a few years, clubs will grow out of exercises and they will have sophisticated evenings where members will simply talk knowledgeably about the wines with no particular desire to discuss a bracketing devised by the winemaster.

Sometimes, on an evening like this, the winemaster will say, 'I have chosen four whites and four reds which I think are pretty good. I have masked them. Tell me what you think of them.'

Each member can get the best out of these nights if he comes along completely at ease and looking for relaxation. The night provides him with an opportunity to enjoy good food and wine and good company. He can express himself without any embarrassment or fear of making a fool of himself because the man who can pick the district of every wine put before him does not exist. He does not have to impress anybody with what he has to say. Those who try to impress usually have a miserable time. Wine and Food Societies, at least in Australia, are great levellers. There is no distinction between the small and the great, the wise and the foolish, except, perhaps, that members are willing to suffer fools gladly only for a certain time.

18 WINE SHOWS AND WINE JUDGING

T HE 'Wine Shows' take place in Australia as part of the Annual 'Royal Agricultural Shows' held in Brisbane, Sydney, Melbourne and Adelaide. As those who are unfamiliar with an Australian pageant of this nature might be interested to learn, the 'Show' is a kind of tremendous fair where primary producers of all types exhibit their products and subject them to judging by qualified people. Engraved silver cups, gold medals and colourful ribbons are awarded to prize winners.

Every year, therefore, there is an enormous presentation of sheep, pigs, cows, bulls, dogs, horses and hens. There are competitions for horse riding, horse turnouts, sheep trials, dog contests, wood chopping competitions, exhibitions of agricultural machinery, transport and fertilizers. All told there is a great and picturesque display of everything relating to animal husbandry, agriculture and horticulture.

There are competitions for fruit and vegetables, for cake making, for jam making and fruit pie making, for honey and for butter, for milk and for cream.

Among all this the competitions for the making of wine have featured largely from the beginning. At first vignerons within the State exhibited their ports, madeiras, sherries, muscats, clarets, burgundies and chablis. These are the names they remembered from the days when they were farmers in England and Scotland.

As time went by vignerons from other States entered their wines in neighbouring State agricultural shows and, with larger entries, the number of sections for judging increased. Ultimately, the number of judges had to be increased.

Today, the various sections for judging in Melbourne, for example, are as follows:

MOST RECENT VINTAGE:
  Light White wine, Hock or Chablis type
  Claret type
  Burgundy type

ONE YEAR OLD:
  Light White, Hock type
  Chablis type
  Claret type
  Burgundy type

OPEN CLASS, ANY VINTAGE:
  Light White, Hock type
  Chablis type
  Sauternes type
  Burgundy type
  Claret type

EXPORT CLASS. ANY AGE, BUT WINE EXHIBITED
MUST BE AVAILABLE FOR SALE:
  Dry Red
  Dry White, Hock, Moselle and Riesling types
  Sauternes

In addition there are classes for sweet whites, sweet reds, muscats and sherries.

All these wines are further divided into different sections merely for the sake of judging. For example, one set of judges may be allocated the task of judging red table wines, another for judging white table wines and so on. Each of these sections is examined by a panel of three judges and there is, in addition, a presiding judge who has the final decision over the results of all classes.

Awards are made in each section according to the number of points allotted. The possible score is twenty and any wines which score eighteen and a half or over receive a gold award. Those which receive seventeen or over, but less than eighteen and a half receive a silver, and those which receive fifteen' and a half, but less than seventeen receive a bronze.

The wine judges of today are usually men in the 'trade'. Mostly, they are winemakers either with their own small wineries or are employed by the larger firms as winemakers. There is a smattering of wine merchants from the capital cities and one or two persons who, although they are not directly engaged in making or selling wine, are recognized for their ability to be discerning about wine.

Shows today are comparatively 'big business'. All the large makers enter. They devote entire sections of their organizations to developing wines for show purposes. Skilled winemakers spend weeks of valuable time making, ageing and caring for wines simply for this. As there are four major shows every year, the amount of money and time spent by each firm in preparing the entries is enormous.

Add to this the fact that reserves of each wine entered must be kept to qualify for each section; that executives

must make special trips to each show; that top winemakers
are called from their wineries and normal work to attend
the shows in order to taste wines which have been given
awards, so that they may in turn produce similar wines.
All this must make you realize how much money is spent
by these firms on the 'shows'.

The award winning wines are examined very carefully,
the judges are questioned, their preference for styles
watched, their opinions as to what wines should be exhibited
sought.

This tremendous effort and amount of money is expended
because success in the wine shows has an enormous capital
value. For months after awards are announced, full page
advertisements will appear in the papers by award winners
announcing their trophies and medals.

A large wine company would be very unfortunate indeed
if it could not, after all its endeavours, announce something
it had won in the papers.

There are special trophies for:
  The most successful exhibitor in all wine classes.
  The most successful exhibitor in all light table wine
    classes.
  The best hock or chablis.
  The best pale dry fino sherry.
  The most successful exhibitor in the 'open' table wine
    classes.
  The most successful exhibitor in the one year old wine
    classes.
  The best sherry in any class.
  The best young, white table wine.
  The most successful exhibitor in the 'open' white table
    wine classes.
  The best port.
  The best dry white table wine.
  The best red table wine.
and for several other successes depending on the venue
of the Show.

The Judging of Wine

Fundamentally, the judging of wine is based on answers to these three questions:

Has it a good colour?
Has it a good bouquet?
Has it a good flavour?

The answers are not at all simple. If we are to judge between the colour of several red wines, all of which seem to be fairly good, what criterion are we to use to decide which is the best colour? One wine might be a light red; another a dark crimson. Which is the better colour?

In the matter of flavour the answer is even more difficult. Each wine district has a distinctive taste. If a judge has a great admiration for north-eastern Victorian reds, he may be tempted to award more points to a wine from this district rather than to a Coonawarra. With a change of judge, the award could possibly go the other way. This, naturally, would be ridiculous. There must be some way of making awards which takes into account district variations.

The perfect answer to the problem, of course, would be to divide the competition into various areas and to award a prize to the winner of each area.

This is unsatisfactory from a national point of view and would not take into account wines blended from different areas. The public wants to know what are the best wines in Australia. Any wine competition must make provision for awards to the best dry reds and the best dry whites available from anywhere in the Commonwealth.

In the early days of the Agricultural Shows, wine judges decided that it was no use trying to judge light red wines against heavy reds or highly acid whites against non-acid whites. So they divided the show into classes, each class representing a 'style' of wine.

The system, no doubt, was very fair. A winemaker from north-eastern Victoria could submit an exhibit which was rich and full bodied in the 'burgundy' section knowing that he would have a chance of winning a prize against wines of similar body. He knew his chance would not be damned from the start because a wine from Great Western might have more appeal to the judges because of its much lighter body.

Similarly, a winemaker who made a full, non-acid white wine in his district, would not have to compete against a wine which was light and crisp.

The difficulty with this Victorian era 'style' system of judging was that it forced the winemaker to exhibit under four table wine headings: claret, burgundy, hock, chablis. These names and styles in the early days of Australian winemaking and exhibiting were derived from the fact that the first winemakers and, of course, the wine merchants, were preponderantly British. They called their wines after the names of wines that were popular in Victorian England.

The system, therefore, compelled judges to look back at the original wines and hence to judge table wines according to these four basic European standards.

All the red wines of Australia do not fall into two types, light and heavy, claret and burgundy or whatever you like to call them. There are districts which produce medium wines. There are certainly others by the hundred which do not produce either of the European types 'claret' or 'burgundy'.

The authority which organizes the wine competition lays down very detailed guide lines which the judges must follow for each class of wine.

Let us say, for instance, that there is a class defined as follows: White Wine, unfortified, varietal wine made from Rhine riesling grapes – light, crisp style, less than one year old. The authority lays down the following guide lines for this class:

Judges will allot points for
Colour: Must be pale golden or golden tinged with green, must be brilliantly clear with no opacity.
Bouquet: The aroma must be strong and distinctive; clearly referring to the Rhine riesling grape; there must be no odours other than those of the grape or wine;

it must be pleasant, not unduly sharp or smelling of yeast or skins.

Taste: Must have a crisp and fresh acidity with plentiful flavour of the grape; must be clean to the palate; must have no undesirable non-wine flavours; must have intense fruitiness on the palate but very little sugar content; must have lightness of body.

General: The most successful wines should impress with their volume of aroma and their fineness of flavour. There should be a richness of olfactory and taste sensations but, at the same time, a lack of heaviness or fullness. No importance is to be placed on characteristics attributed to area or origin, other things being equal. As with other classes, if judges are unable to separate wines of what they consider to be of equal excellence, a medal of equal value is to be awarded to each. If no wine is considered to be worthy of a gold medal, silver or bronze medals only are to be awarded, or if the wines are poor, no medals at all.

Wine Judges

Wine judging is a different science from the judging of other exhibits at Agricultural Shows. The judge of horses has certain definite rules or precedences to go by. He can see the horse. He knows that a certain depth of chest is an asset or that a certain shape of the head calls for marking down.

The judging of wine, however, involves much more indefinite judging processes. It is akin to judging works of art. Nothing is very clear cut. Experience is a great help but it does not make a good judge. The ability to be able to paint enables a critic to appreciate another painter's work but it still does not make him a good judge of painting. Certainly, the ability to make wine does not make a good wine judge.

The good wine judge must have a sound mental balance. He must have an even tranquil temperament. He must have an ordered mind and be at least of average intelligence.

Some training in logical thinking such as a university course or experience in an executive capacity is a great help in order that he may make assessments quickly. Sensitive organs of taste and smell and a good memory are essential. He must love wine and drink it constantly in preference to any other beverage. He must have drunk a great deal of wine of all kinds and from all parts of Australia. He should have had at least a little experience of the best overseas wines.

Winemakers should because of their profession, make good judges, and we have had many winemakers who have been so. The winemaker who prefers a glass of beer to anything else and does not drink wine constantly with his meals is not the man we are looking for. If he lives in some remote area and has not the opportunity, daily, to drink wines from different areas, he is not our man.

The man we are seeking is not difficult to find. Usually, he will be a city dweller, successful in his occupation in life, who has many friends with the same interest in food and wine as himself. He, therefore, is in constant touch with different wines and is forming detached judgements about them every day.

The industry should pay the wine judge for the time and effort he gives to his task. In addition, all expenses incurred in travelling, finding accommodation and in meals should be paid for him. The wine judge must be, to a certain extent, a man of leisure in order that he can afford the time off to perform his arduous task.

> Our lighter wines do not receive fair treatment
> from those who ought to know better . . .
> Nature puts her own hallmark of origin on
> each locality's product; one wine may be as
> good as another, but not identical; a quite
> good wine can, for example, be a very bad
> chablis.
>
> Francois de Castella

19 AUSTRALIAN WINE NOMENCLATURE

Perhaps just as apt a quotation
would be that from Shakespeare, 'a rose by any other name
would smell as sweet'. The cynic might add, 'but it might
not sell as well'.

The selling motive is behind all the names we see on
consumer products.

The wine trade in Australia is no more concerned about
names that sell than the Germans who have had the almost
insuperable task of selling on the English-speaking market
wines under unpronounceable titles like, 'Schloss Boeckel-
heimer Kupfergrube'. The Alsatians have had to overcome
the difficulties of tongue twisters like 'Riquewihr' and

'Voegtlinschappen'. The French, also, realize that the English-speaking world baulks at asking for wines under names of say 'Gevrey Chambertin' or 'Grand Echézeaux'.

In a world that is becoming more and more naïve and gullible in its blind obedience to the dictates of advertisements, it has become important for the merchandisers of nationally advertised products to dig deeply into the sub-liminal approaches to selling.

Mr Louis Cheskin, the head of a Chicago research firm that conducts psychoanalytically oriented studies for merchandisers says '. . . preferences generally are determined by factors of which the individual is not conscious . . . actually in the buying situation the consumer generally acts emotionally and compulsively, unconsciously reacting to the images and designs which in the subconscious are associated with the product.' *

The importance of choosing the right names for wines, therefore, is rooted in the fact that it is not only a matter of being geographically and etymologically correct but is a matter of how they psychologically affect potential consumers. It is not only what we can reasonably and consciously explain that influences us to buy one product rather than another but, very often, we are motivated by a cause which we could not explain if we were asked.

If Australia had been colonized by the Spaniards, as it might easily have been, we should probably be calling our wines 'riojas' or 'vina de pasta'. If we had had a few more Italian migrants in the early days of our winemaking, we should probably be calling some of our wines 'chianti' or 'orvieto'.

It is only natural that a colonizing nation should use terms with which it is familiar when it is faced in a new country with the problem of finding names for new articles and products. We have the problem of names in many fields. Our birds carry quite a variety of English titles (e.g. magpie, kingfisher); so do our trees (mountain ash, Queensland maple).

---

*Vance Packard: *The Hidden Persuaders.*

For centuries, England had used generic names for wines – 'hock' for white wines from Germany, 'claret' for red wines from Bordeaux; generally 'burgundy' was used for practically any heavy red wine from elsewhere in France.

The problem of choosing names for wines is not only one for oenologists. As it is also a matter of good English, it is one for grammarians, university dons and journalists. As it is a matter of good merchandising it is a problem for public relations experts and advertising researchers.

In formulating principles to determine what names should be used in the wine trade, it is not a bad suggestion to follow the advice given in Fowler's *The King's English*:

Prefer the familiar word to the far fetched.

Prefer the concrete word to the abstract.

Prefer the single word to the circumlocution.

Prefer the short word to the long.

Prefer the Saxon word to the Romance (Latin).

There is a certain amount of hostility from the French towards 'new' wine growing countries like America, Australia and South Africa because of their adoption of French district names to indicate their wines . . . Burgundy, Chablis, Sauternes, Graves, Champagne.

The English have prohibited, because of a trade agreement with Portugal, the use of the word 'Port' used on its own without a qualifying prefix, as a description of any wine not made in Portugal.

While there is a great deal of justification in the objections of the French and the prohibitions of the English, they are of little importance as regards Australian wine sold in Australia.

The wine industry in Australia is concerned with selling its products in Australia to Australians under names that are easy to read, easy to pronounce, easy to remember; that are short, simple and descriptive and, above all, merchandisable.

Some names that are being employed at present are apt, descriptive and saleable. Others suffer from one or two serious defects.

Let us examine these titles.

Group 1: TRADITIONAL NAMES
Sherry, Port, White Port, Champagne, Sauternes, Vermouth, Pearl, Claret, Hock.

These are all good names. They have become deeply ingrained in the minds of consumers. They are familiar, clear cut, descriptive, succinct. There is nothing confusing about them. The titles convey the following meaning to an Australian consumer:

Sherry – a highly alcoholic wine, lightish in colour, usually used as a before dinner drink; either sweet or dry.

Port – a highly alcoholic wine, red in colour, sweet to taste, used generally apart from meals or after dinner.

White Port – same as for 'Port' except that the colour is amber.

Champagne – a sparkling wine, light in colour and made by some process of fermenting inside the bottle.

Sauternes – a light, sweet and not highly alcoholic wine most often used with meals.

Vermouth – a highly alcoholic wine with a herbal flavour; sweet or dry; light or dark coloured.

Pearl – a sparkling wine, white or pink in colour, sweetish in taste and made by some process of fermenting in a tank.

Claret – a fairly light bodied unfortified wine, red in colour, sometimes astringent.

Hock – a light coloured, fairly dry white wine, unfortified, usually fairly tart.

As you can see, these 'popular' definitions are broad. Whatever arguments can be used against these names out of Australia, they are completely acceptable and understood in Australia.

Group 2: NAMES DERIVED FROM GRAPE VARIETIES
Muscat, Frontignac, Tokay, Riesling, Semillon, Pinot, Hermitage, Shiraz, Cabernet, Cabernet-Shiraz.

These are all good names. They describe wines made from the grapes whose names they carry. There is nothing confusing about them, but the consumer may need a little more explanation before he finds them familiar.

The first three describe amber coloured wines, highly fortified and sweet. The remainder describe light table wines which are not sweet.

There are several unsatisfactory features about the present use of these names. Let us take them individually:

Riesling – this is used by most makers as a title for a wine made from the Rhine riesling grape. The style is that of a wine with fairly high acid, with little sugar although it may also be fruity. In this sense, the title is exchangeable with 'Hock'. A 'late picked' riesling would be so called when the fruitiness was greater and a certain amount of sugar was present.

Some makers, unfortunately, use the word 'riesling' only as a style of wine irrespective of whether the wine was made from the riesling grape or not. Wines made from the semillon grape are very often called 'Riesling' on the grounds that the semillon is also called 'Hunter River riesling'. These practices confuse the minds of the consumer and more accurate terminology should be used. Ampelographers, that is , people who study grape variety, agree that the grape called 'Hunter River riesling' is probably the French grape 'semillon' and not related to the Rhine Valley 'riesling' grape at all. Is it not about time, therefore, that we began calling it 'scmillon' and end the absurd type of labelling currently being seen on a South Australian wine:

BAROSSA VALLEY
SEMILLON
Also known as
HUNTER RIVER
RIESLING

If a wine is not made from the Rhine riesling grape and is of the same style as the wine named 'Riesling', it should be called 'Hock' or should use the name of the grape from which it is made, for example, 'white hermitage'.

Semillon – this is most often used as a description of a dry wine with little sugar content made from the grape of the same name. One or two makers use the name to describe a sweet unfortified wine. It is not successful

under this, title and the makers would help uniformity
if they changed the title to 'Sauternes'.

Pinot – a dry white wine made from the pinot grape.

Hermitage or *Shiraz* – are clear enough, usually signifying
a dry red wine made from this grape. In Western Australia there is a sweet fortified wine called 'Liqueur
Hermitage'. The word 'hermitage' as distinct from
'shiraz' is used by most makers to describe a distinctive
type of wine of a heavier type.

Cabernet – a dry red wine made from the grape 'cabernet
sauvignon'. Quite often a proportion of 'shiraz' grape
is mixed in at the crushing and the fact is noted on
the label by the more conscientious makers. It should
not be so called unless the proportion is at least 80 per
cent of cabernet.

Cabernet-Shiraz – a dry red wine made from the two grapes,
cabernet sauvignon and shiraz mixed together in the
crushing.

Group 3: NAMES DERIVED FROM
EUROPEAN DISTRICTS

Burgundy, White Burgundy, Chablis, Madeira, Moselle.
These are poor names. They confuse the consumer.
Confusing names should have no part in the nomenclature
of any range of products. Moreover, they are psychologically
bad from a selling point of view. The difficulty is that
the more they are used, the more confusing they become.

Burgundy – in the early days of the Australian wine industry,
'burgundy' was thought of as a round, soft, full bodied,
deep coloured wine, very popular on the English market
where it was sold as 'Emu' or 'Harvest' Burgundy.

In these days of greater wine consciousness, many
Australians have come to realize that 'Burgundy' from
the 'Bourgogne' area of France is not always dark and
heavy. On the contrary, it is usually much lighter red
coloured and lighter bodied than 'clarets' of Bordeaux.

The winemaker who is endeavouring to keep up with
the latest wine developments is marketing his Australian

burgundy in this lighter style – light in colour, fairly light in body, but round and smooth.

Since the majority of wine drinkers still think of 'Burgundy' as heavy and dark coloured, there is sometimes considerable astonishment when a wine lover opens his bottle of 'Burgundy' and finds it quite the opposite to what he had expected.

To call light coloured, light textured wines 'Burgundy' adds nothing to our nomenclature. This type of wine can amply be covered by the general name of 'claret'.

Now that a quite definite difference of opinion has been created among Australian wine men, this title is an ill omened name. It has always been questionable and has caused quite unpleasant arguments among wine lovers. This should never be so where wine is drunk. Since, today, the name 'burgundy' can be said to describe a large range of diverse types it is no longer useful and should be scrapped.

Chablis or *White Burgundy* – these are interchangeable names. At one time, wine drinkers thought of an Australian 'Chablis' as being a soft, full white wine usually without the tartness of a 'Hock'. As time went by the word 'Chablis' fell out of popular favour and the title of 'White Burgundy' was introduced to describe the same type of wine.

Just as with 'Burgundy', the more discerning discovered that white wine from the 'Burgundy' district of France was a tart, crisp style of wine quite different from the flat 'Chablis' with which they had been familiar.

The modern winemaker distinguishes 'chablis' from 'white burgundy' if he detects in the former a flavour which reminds him of wine from the Chablis area of France – the so-called 'flinty' flavour.

Hence, once again there is confusion.

Moselle – we are inclined to think of this as a slightly sweet white wine similar to a riesling. Those who know German Moselles take serious objection to this word.

What we are lacking in our catalogue of names are words

which describe unequivocally the big, soft, fruity and round red wines which we make so well in Australia and in such large quantities – in the Hunter Valley, north-eastern Victoria, Southern Vales area and in the Swan and Barossa Valleys; and which describe the soft, flowery and fruity white wines made in the Hunter, Barossa and Swan Valleys.

The words 'Burgundy' and 'White Burgundy' are not good enough because somebody will always come along and say, 'You know the *real* burgundy is much lighter in colour and of lighter weight than this,' or 'white burgundy has a much greater bouquet than this and a very much different flavour.' And so the controversy and confusion will go on.

The name that appeals to me for the red wine is 'Hermitage'. Most of this heavier and rounder type of wine is made from the 'hermitage' grape. The name 'hermitage' has no overseas connotations which would detract from its merit and it is a good, easy-to-remember and euphonic word. It is true that there is a vineyard in the Rhone Valley called 'l'hermitage'. This can hardly be used as a serious objection to the name, since in the first place, 'hermitage' is the name of one of our grapes and, secondly, a small vineyard does not command the same entitlement to the sole use of a name as does a large and top grade area of France such as Burgundy.

Again the name 'Hermitage' is already being used by quite a number of our large winemakers in the sense I have described.

For the name of the white wine, I like the title 'Semillon'. This is the grape variety most used to make the lovely soft white wines we have been discussing.

What is needed, of course, is a commission appointed by the trade to make rules regarding the naming and labelling of wines. The State governments would, necessarily, have to make laws to enforce these rules.

The system of labelling wines after the grape variety used would bring us into line with several other countries faced with the same problems as ourselves, for example, U.S.A. and Alsace (France). This type of labelling, as it is well known, is already used extensively and we have some excellent examples of clear distinctive labelling in practically every large company. The system, however, lacks consistency, universality and completeness.

Ugly, meaningless names should be abolished forever from our nomenclature. Names that are copied from European districts of origin should be excluded except where they are so steeped in our tradition and so exact in description that we could not find other names to replace them. Let us consign words like Burgundy, White Burgundy, Graves, Chablis, Moselle, Madeira, Liebfraumilch and Berncastle into the limbo of forgotten things.

20 SPELLING, PRONUNCIATION & MEANING OF WINE TERMS

How frustrating it is to write an article on wine and to find that you are not sure whether you should use a capital C or a small c for claret! The question of the use of capitals or lower case for wines and grape varieties is not a simple one. It literally drives editors 'up the wall' when they come to correcting copy. Sub-editors are at their wits' ends to know what rules to use.

It is perfectly true that the scientific world follows the precepts as set down by the Swedish botanist Linnaeus. In spite of these principles, I am propounding the following theory of spelling of grape varieties. Dictionary spellings very often ignore Linnaean principles in order to accord more with common usage.

In all humility I dare to lay down a few rules. I do not intend to be arbitrary. I am following old established norms and practices.

The names of wines are not proper names. Therefore, they should not have a capital first letter.

For example, the word 'claret' is similar to 'tea', 'coffee', 'lemonade', 'beer' or 'cider'. Hence we would not use a capital first letter for any of the following words – claret, burgundy, riesling, sauternes, champagne, port, frontignac and so on.

On the other hand if we are talking about the specific product of a certain maker to which he has given a proper name we should use the capital initial. For example, 'Penfold's Royal Reserve Port' or 'Henschke's 1968 Riesling'.

In the matter of grape varieties the rule is similar. Where the grape variety does not signify a proper name it is not entitled to a capital initial letter. For example, the word 'shiraz' is similar in this respect to 'currant' or 'sultana' for which we do not use capital initials. It is a member of a species, namely 'grape' and is no more entitled to a capital than the name of the species. In the same way under the name of the species 'dog' we have greyhounds, terriers and poodles. In certain cases we might attach a proper name to a grape variety and so we use the capital letter for the proper name and the lower case for the variety. Thus, for example, we write 'Rhine riesling' in the same way as 'French poodle'.

Correct English, therefore, is obtained when we write shiraz, cabernet sauvignon, semillon, white hermitage and so on, all without capital prefixes.

Difficulty may arise with wines or grapes which have adopted their names from proper names of districts. For example we have the districts of Chablis, Sauternes, Barsac, Champagne, Frontignan and Moselle (or Mosel) and we have the country of Madeira, the town of Marsala and the man called Pedro Ximenes (Peter Simon).

These really present no problems. Once a proper name becomes a word for a common article it loses its right to a capital letter. The product once made exclusively by Martini Rossi and by now by every home barman, is simply 'martini' and brandy from the district of Cognac is correctly written today as 'cognac'. In England they 'hoover' a carpet with an Electrolux. This is a wonderful advertisement for the Hoover Electric Company but still does not give the word 'hoover' any more entitlement to a capital initial than the words 'vacuum clean'.

In consequence we can write, chablis, sauternes, barsac, champagne, frontignan, moselle, madeira, marsala, burgundy, white burgundy, tokay, port, white port, semillon, verdelho, cabernet-shiraz, hermitage, claret, marsanne.

Pronunciation of Wine Terms

Pronunciation of wine industry names is controversial only in the matter of a few words. The principal matter to be decided is – are we to use the pronunciation of the nation of origin or are we to anglicize?

Probably the word 'riesling' is the one which causes most trouble. Is it – *rihzling* (with the i as in mite)? Or *reezling* (with the e as in mete)? Riesling is a German word and in German is pronounced *reezling*. If we anglicize it we are faced with the same choice as with the word 'either'. Is it *eether* or *ihther*? Either pronunciation is correct; and so is either reezling or rihzling. In Australia the wine trade prefers reezling.

Shiraz is the name of a grape variety which is said to have been grown originally in Persia, was taken to France and became the syrah or petit syrah. When it was brought to Australia it quickly became known under the Persian name of shiraz. There are two schools of pronunciation – the South Australian which calls it *shirrahz* with the accent on the final syllable, and and the north-east Victorian which calls it *shihruz* with the accent on the first syllable and the final syllable slurred as in 'Sarah's'. Heaven knows how the Persians pronounced it. I favour the north-east Victorians since the practice in anglicizing is to take a long i and to pronounce it as 'eye' and to slur the final syllable of a two syllable word with the accent on the first.

'Cabernet' is a tantalizing word. If we are to anglicize it we should probably have to follow the example of words like 'godet', 'ballet' or 'valet'. The a becomes a as in 'cat' and the 'et' becomes a as in 'mate'. The accent would be thrown on the first syllable and the 'er' would become slurred. Hence we have *cabunay.* Sauvignon by the process of anglicizing becomes *sovinyon* with the accent on the middle syllable. Amontillado anglicized is *amontillaydo.* Cognac becomes *cohnyac.* Chablis is *shablee* with the accent on the final syllable. Chianti is *keeantee* – accent on middle syllable. Hermitage is *hermitage* with the 'age' slurred.

Take some of the well-known grapes that are used consistently in the industry. We are at a loss to know how to anglicize, for example, the Spanish word *albillo.* The Spaniard pronounce this as *ahl bee yo.* The obvious English interpretation would be to pronounce it as it is spelt; thus *al bill o,* although I regret to say that I have never heard it pronounced this way in Australia, where you more often hear for some strange reason *al bill io. Blanquette* is simple enough, although I suppose we could hardly describe it in the same way as we would describe a sumptuous meal or banquet. In Australia it is pronounced as *blan kett* with accent on the final syllable. *Frontignan:* as this term comes from France, the correct French pronunciation would be *front een yan* and this is the way it is usually pronounced here. *Malaga,* a Spanish term from the well-known city should have the accent on the first syllable. *Palomino:* the Spanish pronunciation is *pal o meen oh* with the accent on the second-last syllable. It is not usually anglicized. *Pedro Ximenes:* I think it is better to ignore the Spanish pronunciation since it is so remote from the way we pronounce it that we would be wasting our time trying to imitate it. Australian vignerons prefer the pronunciation *peedro zim n eez* with the accent on the first syllable of the second word. Incidentally, the word vigneron is usually pronounced as *vin yer on. Semillon:* most people love to show off their knowledge of overseas languages. It is said that the wine

Nuits St Georges is one of the largest-selling French wines in England because people love to say the words; thus giving an illusion that they speak French very well. *Semillon* occupies a similar role in Australian wine terminology. The French student calls it *sem ee yon.* I prefer the anglicized *sem ill on,* with the accent on the first syllable. Is it *tram ee ner* with accent on the central syllable, or *tram n er* with accent on the first syllable? I prefer the anglicization of the second pronunciation. *Verdelho,* also spelt verdelhao, should be pronounced as it is spelt with the accent on the second syllable. *Grenache,* is nicely anglicized to *gren ash* with the accent on the first syllable. *Mataro* is pronounced *mat ah roh* with the accent on the central syllable. This grape is also known as *esparte* and as there is no accent (grave or acute) on the final e, it should not be pronounced as espartay.

Oeillade: an attempt has been made to anglicize this to *ool ee ahd* with the accent on the first syllable, and very often you see a bastard attempt at anglicizing the spelling – *oulliade.* The spelling, of course, is incorrect and so is the pronunciation. The French pronunciation is hard to get away from – *o wee yahd* – with equal accenting on every syllable. There are variations on this name too. It is sometimes called *cinsaut* (pronounced *san soh,* accent on the first syllable)and *blue imperial. Pinot meuniere:* I find it hard to arrive at any anglicized pronunciation differing much from the French, hence it is pronounced *peen oh mern ee air,* with the accent on the final syllable of the second word. *Pinot noir:* it is hard again to do anything about the French word for black except to say that it should be pronounced *nwah.*

Touriga is a Portuguese word and is usually pronounced in Australia simply as *too reeg ah* with accent on the middle syllable. *Ugni blanc:* one can hardly imagine a more ugly word for a wine grape and it presents almost insuperable difficulties in arriving at a suitable pronunciation. I presume we should use the original, which is *oon yee blong,* a peculiar combination of the Latin and Gallic languages. This grape is also known as *white hermitage* and *trebbiano (treb ee ah no). Chasselas* can be anglicized like *chateau* to *shass el ah. Chenin* is too French to change and so is *she nan* with accent on the second syllable. For the same reason, *folle blanche* is *fol blahnsh; marsanne* is *mar san* with final accenting; *alicante bouchet* is *al ee cahnt boo shay. Merlot* is *mer lo; mondeuse* is *mon ders* and *chardonnay* is *shar donn ay* with equal accent on every syllable.

Meaning of Wine Terms

All of us are terrified when we have to describe our reactions to an experience in the technical terms of an industry with which we are not familiar. I remember seeing a most articulate and fast talking radio announcer, reduced almost to incoherence when he was asked to describe a fashion parade. He tried desperately for a few minutes to get away with fatuous descriptions likc 'this is a pretty frock' or 'what a nice jacket' but before long he was lapsing into language more familiar to one of his calling, such as 'isn't she a fabulous girl?' which of course cut no ice with the matrons who had come along to get the most out of the mannequin parade. An experienced fashion saleswoman took over from him and immediately swung into the smooth patter of modern *haut couture.*

Unless we have had a good basic education in elementary chemistry we might find the terminology at a wine dinner a trifle esoteric. However, with a little study you, too, can be a wine expert. Moreover, there is intense satisfaction to be gained from being able to describe exactly what you detect in a wine.

Obviously there are many thousands of wine terms which are taken from everyday language. I have tried to explain only those which are particularly relevant and those which perhaps are not altogether clear to the newcomer to the subject of wine.

Acetic: An acetic wine is one which contains acetic acid. This is readily distinguishable by the nose. Acetic acid is the main component of what we call vinegar. It does not mean that the presence of acetic acid is the only occasion when a wine could be called vinegary. It is largely due to the fact that the wine has become 'pricked', which means that it has been attacked by bacteria called acetobacter which has converted some of the alcohol into acetic acid. If sufficient conversion has taken place the wine will be completely spoiled and become undrinkable. Small quantities, on the other hand, can add to the attractiveness of the wine.

Acidity: This is detected by the tongue. A considerable amount of acid in a wine creates a sharp tingling sensation on the first part of the tongue and on the lips. If you relate the sucking of a lemon to acidity you will know exactly what it is in wine. There are four main acids in a newly made wine, the chief one being tartaric and the others being citric, malic and sulphuric. These are called 'fixed' acids because they are not affected by the application of heat. 'Volatile' acid, on the other hand, is an acid which will evaporate in the presence of heat. Acetic acid is the main volatile acid but other ones are succinic and propionic. Wines containing these are known as volatile.

Aroma: This is the peculiar odour of the grape as detected in the wine. Aroma is distinguished from such words as bouquet, smell, or odour. Aroma is a distinctive smell which is usually found in young wines. For example, we might talk about the aroma of the Rhine riesling grape. We might also talk about the aroma of a certain brand of tobacco. It is the particular smell of something individual and is usually pleasant. We have, for example, the aroma of a rose or of a pine tree or of kerosene. As a wine ages, the various aromas with which it began are blended into a unity of smells which is more correctly called a bouquet.

Astringency: This is the tightening of the skin surfaces and mucous membrane of the lips, tongue and palate caused by the presence of tannin. It creates a drawing sensation, tending to roughen the surfaces of the mouth and tongue and to create also an impression of dryness in the mouth.

Auslese: A German word meaning specially selected. Auslese wines are similar to spaetlese wines in so far as they contain more sugar because they are picked later in the season, but they are of higher quality than a wine simply termed 'spaetlese' because the bunches of berries have been selected so as to include only those that have arrived at the desired degree of ripeness and which contain no bad berries or mould.

Austere: A term which is used to describe a wine containing a considerable amount of acid and tannin and without much sensation of fruit on the middle palate.

Balance: This specifically relates to the acid, sugar and tannin content of a wine. A wine that is out of balance is one in which any of these components is too prominent. A wine that is in balance conveys the impression to the taster that there is just the right amount of each in proportion to the whole. To use the term 'wine in balance' means that you have a wine with very good flavour as well and therefore it would indicate that the wine was of unusually good quality.

Baumé: The Baumé Scale or hydrometer is used universally in Australian wineries to measure the sugar content of the must or finished wine. A reading of zero indicates that there is no sugar in the wine at all and each degree of Baumé indicates that there is sufficient sugar which when fermented will yield one per cent by volume of alcohol.

Big: A *big* wine is one which tastes *big* in the mouth. That is, one gets the impression that it is more solid than, say, a *thin* wine. We might describe a wine as being *big bodied* or also as being *full bodied* or *generous* or even *fat* or *weighty*. It is related to the viscosity of a wine. The more viscous a wine is the greater its body. One might say that it is the rate of flow over the palate which determines whether a wine is *big* or not. The viscosity is due to the presence of glycerol (glycerine) which is a by-product of fermentation. As a white wine ages it grows bigger in body.

Binning: To bin means to put bottles of wine intended for ageing on their sides in some selected cool place. If any particular designation is allotted to this bottle, such as a number or code, all of the bottles in the section are described as Bin such and such.

Bitterness: The tongue is capable of detecting four sensations, one of which is bitterness, the others being sweetness, acidity and saltiness. Bitterness in wine is usually attributed to tannin and this is derived usually from the stalks or seeds of the grapes. Bitterness is never good in a wine although there are many tannin effects apart from bitterness which are pleasant.

Blend: This means that two or more wines are mixed together so that the separate elements so mixed cannot be distinguished. Australian wines are blended for several purposes. The main reason is to ensure that a certain product, for example, So and So's Gold Medal Sherry, will always be the same from year to year. The winemaker *blends* together different quantities of sherry material he has on hand and so performs an operation which he calls 'blending to a standard'. The second reason is to bring up the quality of a poor wine to a standard at which it could be sold. For example, a wine lacking in colour, acidity or character can be improved by blending it with a wine with high colour, bigger body and great flavour.

Body: Body is the texture or consistency of a wine. A wine may be thin or big bodied according to the amount of viscosity it appears to have. See also *Big* and *Thin*.

Bottle Stink: There is no other word which so accurately describes this smell as 'stink'. Stink is defined by the dictionary as a strong, offensive smell. Sometimes when the cork is drawn from the bottle of a very old red wine the concentrated odours that have been building up over the years are suddenly released en masse. Such intense impact on the sense of smell creates the sensation of unpleasantness. After the wine has been in glasses for a while, it absorbs some of the oxygen from the air and the concentration of odours is lessened. Then the wine, so to speak, 'breathes'. Sometimes this takes up to two hours. After this the stink is gone and the wine reveals itself as a pleasant-smelling and fully developed, bottle-aged red.

Bouquet: This is to be distinguished from odour, smell or aroma. It is the combination of several odours, some of which may be good and some which may be bad. We may have a *good* bouquet, a *full* bouquet, a *rich* bouquet or a *poor* bouquet, depending upon the pleasantness, the absence of smell or the intensity of impression it creates on our olfactory nerves. Bouquet by its definition cannot be the smell of one single article. We may have the *smell* of the Rhine riesling grape or its aroma, but we cannot have the *bouquet* of the Rhine riesling grape. We may have the *bouquet* of a wine made from the Rhine riesling grape, but this bouquet is a combination of all the odours from the wine including the smell of the grape. Hence in a bouquet we may detect a *vinous* odour, a *grape variety* odour, the smell of oak, a distinctive *regional* smell, the development of odours created by age and a host of other smells perhaps which will not even relate to the grape such as, for example, tar or rope or metal. The bouquet embraces also the different chemicals that have developed in the wine . . . the volatile acids, the aldehydes, the amino acids the esters and the ethers.

Brut: This is pronounced in Australia in a manner similar to 'put'. It is a French expression which means that the wine is *natural* in the sense that no sweetening has been added to it. It is only applied to champagnes and therefore brut champagne should taste completely dry, that is, without sugar. In practice, however, champagne makers do add a little sugar because completely unsweetened champagne is not pleasant.

Carbonated: Carbonated means that carbon dioxide gas has been injected directly into the wine in the same way as with lemonade or beer. Naturally, champagne is a wine which contains carbon dioxide gas but in this case the gas has been produced within the wine itself. Carbonated wines have the gas added.

Chambrer: A French term which means to bring a wine up to room temperature – it is rarely used today.

Character: A wine with character has a distinctive flavour which is strong and reminiscent both of the grape from which it was made and the district from which it came. A wine without character is lacking in flavour and creates a feeling of disappointment in the taster.

Clone: A selected strain of a variety of grape. Wine-growers observe that particular plants in their vineyard thrive better and yield more profusely than others. In addition they are more resistant to disease and are able to withstand better adversities of drought and excessive rain. If these special plants are used as mother vines for cuttings, a whole vineyard can be developed from them which results in stronger, healthier plants and a far better overall yield. The selected cuttings or vines are called clones and the process is known as clonal selection.

Cloudy: Cloudiness in wine can be caused by two factors. The first is that the sediment that has dropped to the bottom of the bottle during its ageing has been upset and has been mixed through the wine in the form of a fine powder. This does not mean to say that the wine is not as good as it ever was. All that is necessary is to allow it to settle down again so that the sediment will fall out. The second reason is disease. This could be a bacterial fermentation such as one known as 'malo-lactic', or it reveals the presence of some spoilage bacteria such as casse. A wine in this condition must be treated or thrown out.

Corkiness: This is the flavour of a mouldy cork. Sound cork has no flavour whatsoever. However, should there be some seeds of the cork bark still remaining in a stopper it could be subject to the cork mould and impart this flavour to the wine. Corkiness is not caused by a cork which happens to have disintegrated because of age. It is not caused by a poor cork which has allowed air to enter because of cracks which have appeared. It is not the flavour of anything but mouldy cork.

Crust: This usually occurs in a vintage port bottle and is purposely induced by the bottler sometimes by scratching the inside surface of the bottle so as to encourage its formation. As a wine grows older in bottle it will precipitate solids consisting of tannins, tartrates and pigments. Normally if a bottle is lying on its side there would be a layer of this deposit in one position along the side of the bottle. If the bottle were turned slightly during the bottle-ageing process, eventually the whole of the inside would be coated with this deposit. Hence the expression 'old crusty port'.

Dry: This has several meanings in the liquor trade. As applied to wine it means lack of sugar. Therefore, an absolutely dry wine has no sugar whatsoever or, more correctly, no sugar that can be measured by a hydrometer. One that is scarcely dry, on the other hand, may give a reading of 1.5 on the Baumé hydrometer.

Sweetness may be concealed by the presence of tannin, the astringency of which takes away the sensation of sweetness. The term, therefore, tends to be complicated.

Champagne has its own rules in this matter. The French use the term *sec* in exactly the same way as the English *dry* and a champagne labelled *extra sec* is not, as one would expect, completely without sugar, for this would be a *brut* champagne. It may indeed taste quite sweet and would be what we would describe in other language as *medium dry*.

When applied to spirits the word takes even another meaning. A *dry* martini is one which is composed of vermouth and gin in various degrees and when we say that we have a *very* dry martini. we mean that the amount of gin is greater than usual. This does not mean, of course, that there is necessarily less sugar in the mixture.

Astringency is sometimes confused with dryness because it creates a dry or non-moist feeling in the mouth and very often people describe a sherry as very dry when all they mean is that it is very astringent.

Earthy: Some wines smell exactly the same as freshly turned soil in the garden. This is very often due to the district from which they come and it is usually the bigger and fruitier wines which have this characteristic.

Ester: An ester may be regarded as an organic salt of an acid. It is produced by the direct interaction of an acid and an alcohol. The esters are known by the names of the alcohols and acids from which they are derived. Thus ethyl alcohol and acetic acid give ethyl acetate. Propyl alcohol and butyric acid give propyl butyrate.

Ether: Chemically speaking, an ether is derived from an organic acid by a process whereby the hydrogen of this acid is replaced by an alcohol radical. An alcohol radical is that component in the alcohol molecule common to all alcohols. It is a very light, volatile and inflammable fluid and it has a strong, sweet smell.

The difference between an ester and an ether is that an ester retains its radical, that is, its basic component which distinguishes it from other acids, and takes on the basic component of the alcohol which distinguishes it from other alcohols. Whereas an ether is an alcohol which retains its basic component, that is, that which distinguishes it from other alcohols, and it takes part of an acid after throwing out the H_2O, or the water. In both cases we have a similar result and from the combination of various alcohols and acids the wine builds up a series of esters and ethers and this results in a combination of aromas and taste ingredients.

Fining: To 'fine' means to add some glutinous material to the wine in order that it may gather together all the little specks and pieces of grape pulp and other fine solids which are not heavy enough to fall to the bottom, and by gathering them together creates enough weight for this to happen. The result is that the wine becomes bright and clear. Fining materials are gelatin, white of eggs, fish glue, casein and certain clays among which bentonite is by far the most efficacious.

Finish: A finish is the end impression received from tasting a wine. See page 257.

Flat: This simply means that the wine tastes as though it had no life or interest to the palate. It is due to the lack of acid.

Flinty: Wine men have a habit of twisting the original meaning of words to mean something entirely different. Like many other words in this glossary, the dictionary meaning is the correct one. Wine language is not a language on its own. It is only the language that we use in everyday life with particular application to wine. The words we use describing wine should be just as valid as in any other sphere. The word *flinty* means simply, having the odour and taste of flint. It is usually ascribed to the chablis wine of France and Australian writers sometimes think of it as relating to chablis-style wines made in Australia. This, of course, is incorrect because it is the district or vineyard area which imparts characteristics of smell and taste to a wine. If French chablis has a flinty taste, it is peculiar to wines from the Chablis area of France. It will not be observed in Australian wines. If a wine labelled 'chablis' came from the Hunter Valley it would have Hunter Valley aroma and taste characteristics.

Foxy: This is an American term which is used to describe the aroma of natural or native American vines. American wine experts are not quite sure where the term originated but they are universal in stating that wines made from these grapes have the smell of a caged animal.

Fruity: Fruitiness is the aroma and taste of the grape which have undergone changes because of fermentation but which are still there in the wine, making it pleasant and satisfying. A fruity wine does not necessarily have sugar. It may be completely dry but still fruity.

Gout de Terroire: The exact equivalent to this in English is 'raciness'. This means that the wine has a strong flavour indicating its origin. For example, we might say that some Hunter Valley reds are highly *racy* or have strong *gout de terroire,* because the Hunter flavour is very pronounced.

Hard: Some wines taste hard. That is, we feel as though they do not yield or give anything to the palate. This is due to the lack of fruitiness and full flavour and to the presence of high acidity and bitter tannin. Nevertheless, a wine of this nature may have good character and eventually soften into something really good.

Heat Summation: As used here it means the sum of the mean daily temperature above 50°F for the period concerned. The base line is set at 50°F because there is almost no shoot growth below this temperature. The summation is expressed as degree-days. For example, if the mean for a day is 70°F the summation is 20 degree-days, and, if the mean for June is 65°F the summation is 450 degree-days (15 degrees × 30 days).

Lees: This is the deposit at the bottom of a cask of

wine which is formed by the falling out of the wine all types of solids including precipitates which were once held in suspension. A cask of newly made wine will deposit a lees which consists of dead yeast cells and flakes of cream of tartar. A wine is usually pumped off its lees into a clean cask because the disintegration of yeast cells imparts a flavour to the wine which may not always be desirable.

Light: Lightness is lack of body in the same way as bigness or fullness denotes a wine with plenty of body.

Maderization: This is a French term and hence the difference in spelling to the English 'madeira'. It comes from the French word 'madérisé'. This is similar to oxidation. In fact it is caused by oxidation but it does not necessarily mean that the wine is inferior. Undoubtedly, some people like a *maderized* wine. The term obviously refers to thé wines of the island of Madeira which of all wines are the most maderized. In the case of these latter wines, oxidation is purposely induced by leaving the wines for very many years in casks where they are subject to the rather high temperatures that occur on the island.

Nose: This is identical with the word 'bouquet'. The wine has a good nose, or a good bouquet, or a bad nose, or a strong nose, or a very poor nose. We may, if we wish, talk about a kerosene nose and in this case it is similar to the word 'odour'.

Nuttiness: Nuttiness is the flavour of nuts. It is a word often used recklessly but as with the word 'flint' it has a specific meaning. If we eat a hazel or Brazil nut we notice how it crunches in the teeth and imparts a sensation of cleanliness to the mouth. We notice that it is faintly oily and yet astringent. It is this characteristic which we describe as *nuttiness* in wine. It is usually applied to dry madeira or sherry and very often the odour and flavour of nuts in these wines come through very strongly.

Over the Hill: This is an expression which is subject to various nuances of meaning. Wine, like man, grows perceptively older every year and gradually disintegrates. Man's progression over the hill may be observed only in a slight failing in one or two of his faculties. He may perhaps show clear signs of shortsightedness in his late forties, being eminently vigorous in other respects. An old wine may show signs of brown colouring matter while not exhibiting the slightest taste of acetic acid. Age, both in men and in wine, is purely relative. It is not tied unrelentingly to the passing of the years. Perhaps it has a lot to do with what went into their make-up in the first place.

Oxidation: This is a chemical change brought about by the action of oxygen on the various components in the wine, for example, on alcohols, acids, pigments. An oxidized wine is one where the colour has changed from dark red to brown in a red wine and from pale amber to deep gold or brown in a white. An oxidized wine has the typical smell associated with oxidation and the tarnished, worn and unpleasant flavour which is also a characteristic.

Palate: This is another complex term which has several meanings. In the first place our palate is that part of the mouth comprising, in very wide terms, the roof, the tongue, the lips and the inside of the cheeks which we use in savouring and assessing a wine when we taste it. It also means the actual taste of the wine because of a transference of meaning. Thus we might say that a man has a fine palate or that a wine has a good palate.

Rancio: Old Spanish sherries often have this term applied to them. Undoubtedly the word has a similar meaning to the English word 'rank' and describes the typically strong, pungent and oxidized smell and flavour of this type of wine.

Sec: See *dry*.

Sour: Strictly speaking any acid wine could be called sour. However, we should not describe a wine as sour simply because it is tart and acidic. In wine terminology sourness acquires the meaning of being unpleasantly acid. More of a lactic sourness or the sourness of milk which has turned.

Spaetlese: Literally, late-picked. It is the description of a white table wine which tastes sweet because of sugar left in it after fermentation has been completed. Usually this is because the grapes have been left on the vine.

Thin: The opposite to *big*. A thin wine tastes thin in

the mouth. It has no body. It lacks viscosity and might be described sometimes as 'watery'.

Vinegary: Refer to *volatility* and *acidity*.

Vinosity: This is the wine flavour as distinguished from any other flavour in wine such as the grape flavour. As with words like *flinty* and *nutty*, the word 'vinous' has a meaning in the wine language no different from its dictionary meaning. It simply means, 'having the characteristic of wine'. In recent years red wines have been made in such a way as to acquire a flavour of oak. The wine judge, therefore, has to distinguish between the various flavours. He must not be confused with the idea that an oaky flavour is the typical flavour of red wine because he has not had experience of any other type of red wine. He should be able to distinguish between a wine's vinosity and the other characteristics which it has acquired from either the grape, or from outside sources such as from the cask, metal, or any contaminating container or machinery. As a wine grows older its vinosity becomes more pronounced. A wine with vinous character fills the mouth, throat and nasal regions with a full fragrance and aroma.

Volatility: A volatile wine is one which contains volatile acid, the chief of which is acetic acid. Volatile acids are sometimes called fatty acids because they are derived from animals, for example, lactic acid. Usually when the term volatile is used we mean that it is offensively volatile and that it is well on the way to becoming undrinkable. Volatility will eventually occur in every wine. It is a symptom of old age. It is caused by the oxidation of alcohol. Acetic bacteria can also attack a wine and produce the same effect. Hence, if an unfortified table wine is exposed to the air it will certainly be attacked by the aceto-bacter micro-organism which will convert it into vinegar and thus it will become completely volatile.

Woody: Because of the practice of exposing newly made red wines to the influence of virgin oak, today a woody wine simply means wine which tastes of oak. The stronger the flavour of the oak the more woody the wine.

> Many people with restricted experience of
> wine are nervous of buying it ... The real
> problem – and art – lies, I maintain, not so
> much in the selection of the wine as in the
> choice of wine merchant.
> Edmund Penning-Rowsell

21 HOW TO BUY AND STORE WINE

WHEN we go to a wine merchant
to buy a bottle of wine, we will have one or more of several
objects in view.

First, we might want to buy something for ordinary
everyday drinking and for immediate drinking.

Or, secondly, we might wish to entertain guests and desire
to have something that is quite good, quite mature, but
quite moderate in price.

Again, we can conceivably desire something that is out-
standingly good, thoroughly mature and fit for a special
occasion at which we expect to be present a number of
discerning people who know a good wine and, what is

more to the point, very much appreciate it. Price is not so important in this case.

Finally, we might intend asking our wine merchant to find something for us that is good for putting down, is quite low in price and will be really good after several years' ageing.

We shall at one time or another ask our wine adviser for a selection of wines which will serve for a meal of varied dishes.

One thing is certain, you do not want your wine merchant or licensed grocer to recommend wines that, irrespective of quality, show him a greater margin of profit; or wines that have impressed him because they are widely advertised. You hope that he will recommend wines to you because he knows his wines and wishes to have you back as a customer.

If you are to fully appreciate what he has done, you will have to learn what to look for in the wines yourself. This will give you the power to assess his astuteness, his gullibility or his integrity.

Wine is judged according to different circumstances. We cannot expect a young wine to display the qualities of a mature wine, nor would we wish it. We can look for the qualities of a young wine and enjoy them for what they are.

Therefore, examine your wines by dividing them into the following categories and looking for the qualities appropriate to each.

What to Look for in a Young Red Table Wine

This is the type of wine you will look for when buying stock for everyday drinking. You will not want to put it down for ageing. You will wish to buy it much more cheaply than any other red table wine.

Australia makes sufficient of this type of wine to cover the needs of us all in the irrigation areas of the Murray and Murrumbidgee rivers. You will probably want to purchase it by the half gallon flagon or in glass gallon jars or even in larger quantities.

The main quality you will look for is 'soundness'. The detection of unsoundness or acetic acid is a matter of experience. If you wish to know what it smells like, nose the remnants of a bottle of red wine you have left in your backyard for a couple of months.

Your wine may be very light red in colour or it may be very dark. It may even be purple. It does not matter. This is only a matter of choice; but it must taste pleasantly on your palate.

It will cost you half the price of or less than that of any bottle of ordinary commercially labelled claret.

What to Look for in a Young White Table Wine

Young white wine to be used for the purpose of everyday drinking like the red wine mentioned above is available in vast quantities in our irrigation areas.

We would wish this to be very pale in colour, almost water white, but it is likely to be golden or slightly brownish. It could be flat in nature and have a flavour that reminds one of fruit, not necessarily grapes. Yet it will be pleasant enough. The presence of acetic acid is to be watched for. Any sign of turbidity or unsightly discolouring is an indication that the wine is unsound. However, the mere presence of cloudiness caused by the disturbance of a deposit on the bottom of the container is nothing to worry about. This type of wine should cost you the same as a young red wine as described above.

Not all young white wines are cheap, nor are they intended for everyday drinking.

It has become the practice for winemakers to bottle their first class whites young and to recommend that they be drunk within two years of making.

This latter type of wine will be made from a first class grape such as a Rhine riesling or a semillon. Its colour will be

> watery white, that is, almost colourless like water, or greenish white, or
> very pale straw coloured, or
> pale straw coloured with green tinges.

In judging the appearance of this better style of wine, avoid wines that are reddish brown, brown or dark in colour. Place the wine between the eye and a weak electric light bulb. Although they do not damage the wine, the appearance of small floating particles detracts from the perfect clarity of the liquid and hence its perfection. At home these particles can be eliminated by allowing them to settle and then by slowly pouring the wine off into another bottle until the sediment begins to show in the neck.

In a young wine one speaks of aroma or smell rather than bouquet, since the characteristics of the grape from which it was made are still obvious. Bouquet refers to other odours besides the aroma of the grape. The fresh, fragrant perfume of the grape is, of course, one of the attractions of a first class young white wine.

The quality young white wine should have a crispness, something like the freshness created in the mouth by eating a freshly picked but ripe apple. It should, however, taste of the grape. The feeling of its being clean to the palate should be accompanied by a sensation of fruitiness in the centre of the palate. It must have no 'off' flavours which are those not usually associated with wine.

When the wine has passed from the palate it should leave it fresh and clean. These first class young white wines should cost anything between $1.00 and $2.00, depending on their perfection.

What to Look for in a Mature Red Wine

Australian red wines need at least two years in wood and three in bottle before they are mature. Many of them, such as those made in southern South Australia and western Victoria, need much more than this.

The appearance of a mature Australian red is brick red in colour if it is of the lighter variety or deep red with brownish tinges if it is heavier. As reds grow old, they become more and more brown in colour until there is no sign of red left. At this stage they are well past their prime and far too old.

This 'breaking' of colour does not necessarily mean that

they are old in years but it indicates that the ageing process, largely created by the action of oxygen, has reached the stage where the wine has already deteriorated beyond the stage of drinkability. However, a fully mature red wine will show no signs of the purplish or bluish tones of youth. The presence of gold or brown is a proof of its maturity.

The combination of all the olfactory sensations of wine is called the 'bouquet'. As a wine grows older it loses the aroma of the grape, but the perfume of the wine (apart from this aroma) becomes stronger, first in the cask and then in the bottle.

In a good mature red wine the bouquet must be strong and pleasant. It may be perfumed or have the faint scent of pine trees, cedar wood or of other trees. Australian wines are sometimes accused of having a eucalyptus flavour. If this is so, certainly no Australian can detect it while drinking in Australia. It is possible that people in other countries, not so conditioned to the eucalypt as we, can find its presence.

The perfume of some Australian red wines reminds us of Australian trees such as a freshly cut red gum or the musty, baggy smell of wet stringy-bark or mountain ash. These smells or perfumes are revealed, of course in a much more subtle and distant way and are very pleasant. Sometimes we can detect the odours of the kitchen like vanilla, or chocolate, bran or salt and pepper.

The flavour of these mature reds should be rich. They should give the impression of 'sinking' into the palate. There should be some sharpness at the beginning and a definite feeling of astringency on the inner surfaces of the mouth and tongue.

In the centre of the palate there should be some sensation of the wine 'giving' to the palate, an as-it-were sensation of sweetness which makes acceptable the otherwise harshness of the wine with its rough grip.

This taste sensation leaves a satisfaction and a contentment with the wine.

Nevertheless, the mature red must be completely dry; there must be no real presence of sugar. It must leave the palate as though it had been slightly roughened and refreshed.

Summarily, a mature, good quality red table wine has the following characteristics:

1. good nose
2. good colour
3. balanced fruitiness
4. good flavour
5. balanced astringency
6. good acidity
7. good finish
8. pleasant vinosity

It is entirely without flabbiness, sugariness, foulness, heaviness, strongly scented aromas, after-taste or satiety. It approaches the palate almost with severity; it embraces it with a gentle clinging and departs with a lingering perfume. It is highly interesting and exciting.

Fruitiness is the aroma and taste of the grape metamorphized into a vinous flavour by fermentation. In a good wine it is full but refined; distinctive, pleasant, satisfying, deep, positive, soft, without harshness or too great a richness; not sour nor sickly nor strongly berry tainted. It must be a delight that passes quickly as the wine moves on to the latter part of the palate.

Flavour embraces all the sensations of taste and smell that the palate and olfactory organs are able to perceive from the moment the wine enters the mouth. It, of course, includes fruitiness. In addition it is the sum total of astringency, acidity, prickling and the sensations of taste at the beginning and end of the palate. Flavour in a good wine must be distinctive, that is, outstanding among the flavours of a number of wines. It must be recognizable, that is having something that sets it above and apart. It must be thoroughly pleasing and satisfying, creating sensory enjoyment without any alloy of discontent.

A high degree of tannin makes the wine astringent. Tannin comes from the skin, seeds and stalks of the grapes but is mostly extracted from the skins during fermentation. There is good tannin and bad tannin. Bad tannin is bitter and puckers up the entire surface of the tongue without imparting any pleasant sensation. A red wine with a balanced astringency imparts a pleasant 'drying' effect to the inside of the lips, the front palate and the end palate. In such a wine the tannin has no taste of its own, is not obtrusive nor unduly rough and it leaves the palate cleansed and refreshed.

Acidity discussed thoroughly becomes too technical to be of any interest to the average wine lover. Good acidity in a wine is detected in the first approach. It creates a tingling on lips and palate. It livens up the wine and makes it interesting. It has chemical effects not detectable to the palate which improve the appearance and keeping qualities of the wine.

Good acidity freshens up the palate. It is not so powerful that it makes one screw up the face as though sucking a lemon. It carries the wine over the palate with an easy grace, allowing it to make its farewell lightly with a promise that the next mouthful will be as delightful as the last.

Good finish is allied to balanced astringency, to good acidity, to complete dryness and to good vinosity. It covers all these factors, or rather, it is the complex of them all and more.

A red wine with good finish has ruffled the surface of the tongue. It has sharpened the taste buds and left the palate without any cloying sweetness. Instead the palate is now full of a fragrant wine flavour but is fresh, clean and keen with anticipation of more.

A good bottle of ordinary quality but mature red wine will cost today about $1.25 a bottle. But beware! Not every bottle that has a well known label and costs about this price is a satisfactory wine. Very often, it will be no better than the immature young red mentioned earlier.

Indications to help you will be the mention on the label of the area or areas (if it is a blend) where the wine was made, and the presence of a vintage year. This will, at least, indicate the age of the wine. Yet many a good wine will not give the areas on the label because the marketing company has blended it to what it considers a satisfactory standard and does not wish to be tied down to particular areas.

At all events, having set your mind on what to look for in a good red wine, it is then a matter of experiment and experience.

What to Look for in an Outstandingly Good Red Wine

All the features that you would look for in a mature red wine as described above must be present. In addition, there must be several factors present which make the wine outstanding.

Great age, for instance, may be one of them, provided that it is a mere passage of time and not a stage that has been reached where the wine is undrinkable because it is over oxidized. Some reds will age for twenty or thirty years and still be in a very drinkable condition. Among these are well made Hunter Valley, Coonawarra, Great Western, Reynella, McLaren Vale and Tahbilk reds, but not, by any means, every bottling of these wines. Only a good wine merchant who knows his stock can help you here.

Another feature which makes a wine outstanding is its reputation, the fact that it has been hailed by connoisseurs as a great wine. For instance, we might say that the Grange Hermitage of 1962 or any of the Coonawarra prize winning red wines had tremendous reputations.

Still another factor contributing to an outstanding wine is the fact that it has won one or several awards in the Royal Agricultural Shows of Adelaide, Melbourne, Sydney or Brisbane.

Probably the one most powerful and convincing reason why you should believe a wine to be outstanding is that one of the large companies or merchants believes it to be so and proclaims to the whole world that it has a masterpiece. By this I do not mean by general advertising, but by singling out one particular bottling of a particular year and announcing it to be unusually good. Such a bottle is likely to cost very much more than an average commercial wine. Wynn's did this with their 'Michael' Hermitage of 1957 and were quite justified in their praise. Penfold's have so proclaimed with equal justification some of their 'St Henri' clarets.

There is, of course, always the foolish executive who will make a 'splash' with a wine fairly good but not outstanding simply to boost sales. This has happened occasionally and results in the 'shrug of the shoulder' attitude by knowledgeable wine men when next his company produces a so-called masterpiece.

An outstanding wine must have all the features of a good mature wine in a more remarkable way. With every nosing there must be a new pleasure. With every mouthful there will be an effusion of different and delightful sensations. It must be a wine which lives in the memory of experienced wine lovers and about which they will sigh from time to time.

What to Look for in an Older White Wine
In Australia, we look today for our good white wines among the young wines. The present fashion is for these and winemakers apply all their talents in this direction.

It would be quite erroneous to suppose on this account that white wines do not improve with age.

Whether a wine made for early drinking will do so is open to doubt; but a wine from an area noted for its older whites and with plentiful good acid to begin with will certainly age very well. Beautiful old white wines are coming from Great Western and the Hunter and Eden Valleys.

The grape aroma in a first class older white wine will have disappeared and will be replaced by a perfume which bears no relation to the grape. This bouquet in a good white will be extremely attractive and desirable.

The colour will have deepened slightly but not so as to be brown or even deep gold. The flavour will give the impression of richness with a myriad of transient sensations, not those with the taste of the grape, but fruity in another way. The acid will no longer be apparent and the wine will be soft. Overall there is the feeling that the wine holds together well. It is not flat, nor flabby nor worn. When it has left the palate, the feeling is one of satisfaction. A cloud of scents and pleasant odours clings to the internal sensing cavities, and an airy lightness is all that otherwise remains.

What to Look for in Wines Intended for Binning Away
There are two types of wine worth putting down in bottles for many years – red table wine and vintage port. There is no point in ageing any other Australian wine in bottles. Sherry is made for immediate drinking; white wine with some exceptions tend to over oxidize very quickly; tawny ports and fortified sweet white wines are aged in cask; further ageing in bottle does them little good.

Heredity is the most important thing to look for in seeking wines to put down. If you exclude the Murray Valley, most of South Australia produces red wine which shows a history of ageing well. Great Western, Tahbilk and some vineyards in north-east Victoria and some wines from the Murrumbidgee Valley and from the Hunter Valley of New South Wales are generally good wines for ageing.

Choosing your area is important because, in spite of their early promise, some wines never do any good. Even in areas that produce high quality table wines there are vineyards that never seem to make anything worth keeping. Heredity, therefore, is very important. Before choosing your wines for ageing for a long time, look for the history of previous wines made by the vineyards. The following vineyards can show histories of red wines that have aged well for many years:

Reynella and several other wineries in this area of the Southern Vales district; Penfold's Grange Vineyard and Auldana Vineyard near Magill; Martin's Langhorne Creek; Yalumba and Gramp's from Barossa Valley; Henschke from Keyneton; Birks and Stanley from Clare; Wynn's at Coonawarra; Seppelt's and Best's at Great Western; Tahbilk; Bailey and Brown from north-east Victoria; most of the wineries in the Hunter Valley.

There are certainly exceptions among all these. Before we can expect a red wine from any of these vineyards to age well, it must have all the qualities outlined below.

The list is obviously not exclusive. Those who experiment will occasionally be rewarded.

When we talk about red wines ageing well we mean ageing well over many years – anything between ten and twenty. Every Australian red will certainly show a great deal of improvement after two years in bottle. Beyond this, it may begin to decline very rapidly.

It is the long living wines that are interesting, exciting and usually of much higher quality.

Having chosen your wine from an area and a winery most likely to be successful, look for the qualities that are necessary in this wine when beginning its life in bottle to make it worthwhile putting down for a long time.

Firstly and obviously, it must be a good wine to begin with even at this early age. That is, it must have a pleasant, though perhaps grapey nose, and it must taste well, having good flavour and pleasant fruit.

Secondly, it must have sufficient acid. Acid is detected by the tingling present at the tip of the tongue. If a wine has little acid, its life will be a short one. Acid keeps it sound, pleasant and interesting.

Then it must have a good supply of grape tannin. This is the substance which gives a grape its 'grip', or astringency. No red wine has quality unless it has astringency. Since it loses tannin as it grows older, it must have plenty to begin with.

Colour is dependent on the areas. Coonawarra's, Great Western's and some Hunter Valley reds at bottling time can be quite light in colour and yet age successfully for many years. South Australian wines should be (apart from Coonawarra) fairly deep in colour.

Some of our red wines need more time in cask than others. They possess, perhaps, more hardness, a more bitter tannin and a higher acidity than others. Hunter Valley wine is soft and full. Even after twelve months in wood it could conceivably be ready for bottling. A Great Western or a Coonawarra needs at least three years, never less, and sometimes up to five years in cask. If bottled earlier they are apt to become acidulous and bitter.

Coonawarra's contain a large percentage of malic acid, particularly in a cold year. This is the acid of unripe fruit. Nature has its own remedy for eliminating this excess acid. It induces a fermentation which converts the malic into lactic acid. During the process the total acidity drops and the wine is much improved. But beware! This process must take place in cask. Should it occur in bottle, the carbon dioxide released during the fermentation will never escape and it will be one of several elements which will make the wine unpleasant and will prevent gracious ageing.

Experience and, once again, the history of wines from specific areas and vineyards will help you decide whether your wine has had long enough in cask or not.

Vintage port should definitely have a very dark red colour at bottling time. It should have a very high sugar content. Vintage port must be of extremely high quality to make it worthwhile putting down. It is going to spend most of its life in bottle without benefit of blending if weaknesses begin to show. This is so different from a port intended for cask ageing which need not be of superb quality to begin with. Its future will be only a part existence with a number of other wines with which it will become integrated.

Vintage port is a prince of wines. To begin its life in bottle it must have more of everything and have everything better than other wines intended for a less noble life.

Summary

As a final thought, buy your table wines or vintage port from a merchant or storekeeper who has more than the four walls of his shop to store his wine. Make sure he gets them for you from some cool recess, or if he has aged them himself for some time, from an underground cellar or thick-walled room where the temperature is always low. Never accept them from a shelf or from the window where they possibly have been exposed to heat and light or even have been allowed to stand upright.

Very often you will see in English books on wine the advice that you should go to a reliable wine merchant and seek his help when buying wine. You should be very cautious about doing this in Australia. There are very few trained wine men about. There are fewer experienced wine merchants. Those who set themselves up as wine merchants as opposed to wine-merchant-cum-grocer usually do not know their wines very well. This is not altogether their fault. The trouble goes deeper than the ignorance of the retailer.

Very few of the big name winemakers adhere strictly to the practice of selling 'straight' district wines. Today it is impossible for the average wine merchant or licensed grocer to know whether he is selling a straight Hunter Valley red or Eden Valley white. The art or artfulness of the blender is creeping in everywhere. The label does not always tell the truth. A company may blend wines from different areas and endeavour to convey the impression on the label that all the wine comes from one high quality area. Even if the wines themselves are not blended, there is no knowing if the grapes from which they were made were brought in from another district and processed at the winery; and so the wine passes to the public as the wine of a certain district because the winery is in that district.

One cannot even be sure that the wine was made from the grapes that the label claims as the material from which the wine was made. The 'cabernet' grape is now fashionable. From my experience, a wine labelled as such could have been made from a blend of cabernet and some other grapes or even from some other grapes altogether.

The practice of advertising the fact that the company was a great success with the number of medals it won with its wines at the wine shows of Sydney, Melbourne, Adelaide and Brisbane is another popular deceit. The advertisements, naturally, do not actually claim that these wines are available for purchase, but endeavour to convey the impression that wines available for purchase are prize wines.

All this is very discouraging. Yet the wine trade is no better or worse than any other. The main purpose is to present an object to the public which is attractive in appearance, pleasant to taste and, above all, saleable. After that one can afford to put a few details on the label which are representative of facts, as long as these details help sales. If they do not, they might have to be doctored slightly.

The main criterion to follow in buying wine is that of 'experience'. Get a reliable wine merchant if you can. He, at least, should be able to recommend wines that he has tried and liked. However, if you are a keen enthusiastic student of wine you will know as much about the subject as your average wine retailer.

What to Look for in Buying Dessert Wines and Sherry

Tawny ports, sweet sherries, muscats and other dessert wines are easier to buy than table wines. As a general rule, the more expensive they are the better they are, because the national advertiser has graded this type of wine very carefully. He has a range of labels for his younger, inferior wines; for his medium quality wines; and for his oldest and best wines. Usually he has one or two special master-pieces for which he demands an extraordinary price.

In dessert wines the main quality is softness. The wine must be 'liqueury', that is, it must adhere to the side of the glass as the glass is slightly rotated making the liquid caress the sides.

They must, of course, be fairly sweet. Though this may be fairly obvious, some dessert wines are presented which do not have enough sugar. The bouquet should be per-fumed, clean smelling and satisfyingly full.

Aperitive sherry is a different proposition. It must always be clean and crisp to the palate. Without any question, our best sherries are our 'flor' sherries. They must have several essential ingredients.

First, they must be completely dry, that is, there must be no trace of sugar.

Secondly, they must be elegant or refined, that is, they must be clean without any trace of odd flavours, sharp on the palate without any coarseness, astringent without being rough.

Thirdly, they must be soft without any fiery or hard spirit.

Fourthly, and most importantly, they must have plenty of flavour, giving something to the palate to find interesting.

You will find quite a number of these good sherries about. But avoid those so-called 'flor finos' and 'pale dry's' that are thin watery concoctions with no flavour and only acid to give some stimulation to the palate.

You need to buy sherry only when you require it for use. Never store it.

Wines for Everyday Use

As Australia is a wine producing country, and in spite of the recent imposition of a tax on all our wines, we would still expect to purchase wine at a lower price compared with say, England. While this, to a certain extent is so, we would not have the advantage of these prices if we purchased by the bottle. While it is advisable to purchase the better wines by the bottle, it is infinitely preferable to purchase wine for everyday use in larger quantities.

Most of the major wine companies market wine in what is called the 'flagon'. This contains the equivalent of three bottles and the price, of course, is less than if you purchased it in three bottles.

However, your wine merchant can do much better than this. He usually buys in bulk direct from the maker and will sell you flagons or gallon jars at prices much lower than those you pay for the commercial flagons.

The wine merchant will usually show you a range of sherries which he has either blended himself or has had blended for him by the maker. In many cases these sherries are better than those under the label of the national advertisers. The larger wine merchants will be able to offer you a range of sherries from a first class 'flor' to a fairly average quality 'dry' which might be one-third lower in price than that for the equivalent quality under a commercial label. The same thing will apply to tawny ports, sweet sherries, tokays, muscats and vermouths.

Ordinary quality red and white table wine can be purchased in this way by the gallon or half gallon containers. The question must arise as to whether table wine deteriorates in these containers after they are opened. Naturally, they will be exposed to air and, therefore, will eventually suffer from oxidation and acetification. They will not, however, deteriorate very much in a week except in the very hot weather. Keeping them in a refrigerator or ice box will further delay oxidation and infection from bacteria.

These table wines bought in bulk are hardy products designed to stand up to fairly rugged conditions. A bottle of first class riesling or claret on the other hand, will begin to deteriorate almost from the moment it is opened. It has more to lose than the 'bulk' wine and in twenty-four hours it is not the same wine as it was when the cork was first pulled.

Sherries, tawny ports, vermouths, and everyday table wines do not suffer very much from being exposed to the air for a week or so. Therefore, to buy them in bulk containers is wise.

A further refinement in bulk packaging is the plastic bag. This is enclosed in a box, outer plastic barrel or metal container as the wine is drawn from the bag through a tap at the bottom, the bag collapses. Thus no air is needed to fill a vacuum which would be created in a rigid container. The wine therefore is not affected either by oxidation or acetification.

CONCLUSION ON HOW TO BUY WINES

All the foregoing must by now have terrified the novice. How can he ever learn how to select wine?

The answer is simple. Ultimately, there is only one question to be asked in relation to wine. – It is 'does it give me pleasure?' Let the critics praise colour, bouquet, flavour, vinosity and so on, but if the wine does not give you pleasure, it is not the wine for you.

The Storage of Wines

TIME IN CASK

Good wine will age in cask, more or less rapidly, until

it reaches a stage where, instead of gaining qualities, it will begin to lose them.

It is wise, therefore, to bottle the wine once it has reached its optimum time in wood. What this optimum period is, only experience can tell you. In a Hunter Valley red, it could be a year; in a Coonawarra red it could well be five years. Leave the wine too long in cask and it will over oxidize; it will become brownish in colour and unpleasantly bitter in flavour. It is not worth bottling at all in this condition. Bottled too early, it will take too long to age from then on, if ever, and there will possibly be the occurrence of the malo-lactic fermentation whereby malic acid is converted to lactic acid and undesirable turbidity and unpleasant flavours are retained in the wine. Although this malo-lactic fermentation is not always undesirable, it is wise to get it over before the wine goes into bottle.

Experience takes into account the history of similar wines from the same vineyard. In judging the life of wines, this is the surest and most conclusive criterion. It is not the function of the amateur wine lover, nor even of the merchant, to age wine in cask. This is a perilous task which only the winemaker with all his knowledge and facilities should attempt. Bottle your own claret if you like, but do not try to keep it in cask.

HOW TO BOTTLE

The bottles must first of all be perfectly clean and free from mould or traces of yeast cells. For home bottling, it is advisable to rinse them thoroughly with hot water containing 10 per cent of carb soda. They are allowed to drain and must be completely dry before bottling begins.

Bottle only on a bright sunny day since any humidity will cause condensation inside the bottles. Moisture is a danger to any table wine. The cask or demijohn from which you are about to do your bottling should be resting in an elevated position for at least twenty-four hours before you commence. Place a rubber tube through the bung hole at the top in such a way that it does not rest on the bottom but leaves a space of an inch or so in order that no sediment is drawn up during the process of syphoning out through the tube. It is essential that the wine should come into contact with air as little as possible. Corks must be neither too hard nor too soft. Soak them in luke warm water immediately before bottling in order to soften them. Rubbing them with glycerine helps their insertion into the bottles.

Home bottling may be fun. It is well to know, however, that the most perfect table wine, will have been bottled at the vineyard where it was made. Any movement of wine from its place of birth in anything but an air tight container can result only in a slight deterioration. This factor is not important in wines meant to be drunk immediately or within a couple of years but it is a deciding factor when the wine is intended to be aged for, say, twelve years.

STORAGE

Table wines are stored on their sides so that the bottom of the cork is soaked with the wine. This keeps it expanded and thus prevents the passage of air into the wine which would result in over oxidation and eventual acetification.

An underground cellar is the ideal place in which to store wine for ageing. Control of temperature is the objective and underground cellars do not, as a rule, have wide variations of temperature. If possible, the cellar should be dry. Dampness induces mould on the corks and this, after a long period, will creep through to the wine.

If an underground position is not possible, any position where the temperature does not exceed seventy degrees is a good one. Heat hastens the ageing of wine. This is to its detriment. Excessive heat has the same effect as 'cooking' the wine creating chemical and physical changes which create non-vinous flavours.

Slow ageing in cool conditions produces the best results. Gentle oxidation under these circumstances produces volatile ethers and esters and a myriad of flavours which are all released when the bottle is ready for presentation to an appreciative company and the cork is pulled.

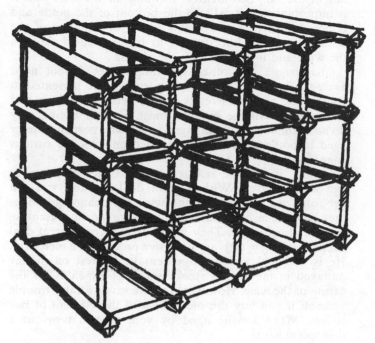

A good wine bottle storage rack.

Tawny port, dessert wines like muscat and tokay, sherry and table wines purchased for immediate drinking do not need this special treatment. They can be kept in a cool cupboard above ground or even in a refrigerator and presented as the occasion demands.

Table wines, sparkling wines and vintage port should be stored on their sides so that the corks are covered. All other wines may be stored standing up.

It is the table wines and vintage port worthy of keeping for a long time that concerns us. Not only is it important that these special vintages are aged away from heat, vibration and light, but that they are kept as still as possible throughout their life. Make sure that they cannot roll or fall in the bin. Sediment is forming all the time and it is important that it falls to the bottom of the bottle and is not disturbed. Any reckless tilting or handling of the bottle causes the fine deposit to be distributed through the wine and interferes with the ageing.

Champagne and other sparkling wines do not need ageing. Like sherry and tawny port they are presented to you by the maker as ready for immediate drinking and at this stage will be enjoyed most. Further ageing may do no harm but old champagne and tawny port and sherry aged in bottle are oddities intended only for the curious connoisseur.

Finally, it must be realized that it is not necessary to age wine yourself. With a great deal of effort you can get from one or other of the wine merchants old wines that have been aged carefully and are worth presenting on special occasions. They will probably cost a great deal because ageing wine is an expensive process for a merchant. He is involved with storage rentals, interest on money outlayed in the ageing stocks and staff expenses for the caring of the wine. However, you are saved all this trouble yourself if you buy the old wine and the element of risk is less. Many a wine aged by yourself will turn out a disappointment.

Yet there is something very satisfying in ageing your own wines. There is a sense of triumph and achievement something akin to that of having made the wine yourself. Since the art of winemaking involves ageing the wine, you are, in a sense, partly the maker.

In addition, there is the knowledge that you are probably the owner of a wine which very few others possess – a wine specially selected by yourself, watched over and cared for by you until the day you have pronounced it ready to drink. By this time it is probable that most other bottles from the same binning have passed to other hands and have already been consumed.

22 TECHNICALLY TALKING

THE AVERAGE reader of any book designed to cover a subject as factually as possible flicks through the pages and picks out the chapters which will interest him. As most wine drinkers are not interested in the technical points of winemaking I have endeavoured to exclude them from earlier chapters except where the technical processes must be described in order to explain why the wine type is what it is. For the sake of the enthusiastic student I am including the more esoteric points here.

A few simple technicalities in wine making
We have seen that fermentation is simply the transformation

of sugar to alcohol and carbon dioxide and the creation of several other minor constituents. The true wine yeast is called *saccharomyces cerevisiae ellipsoideus*. On the skins and stems of grapes there are hundreds of varieties of wild yeast which greatly outnumber the true yeast and seriously impede the fermentation produced by the true yeast. In addition grapes often carry on their skins moulds and bacteria which are a danger to a skin fermentation. Most winemakers, therefore, sterilize their musts by adding about 100 parts per million of sulphur dioxide to the crushed grapes at the crusher or to the must line.

A yeast 'starter' of the pure and true wine yeast is added and so fermentation begins and carries through to the end without any of the troubles which could be caused by these wild, unwanted plants.

However, the sulphur dioxide which kills the unwanted fungi is also likely to destroy the true yeast. The yeast starter, therefore must be 'educated' to sulphur dioxide. A tolerance to it is induced in the true yeast by exposing it over a period of time to a greater and greater concentration of SO_2 (sulphur dioxide).

Alcoholic Fermentation
Wine is the product of the grape. It is not, however, the end product. There is a very interesting series of cycles which take place from the moment that the budding of the vine begins and the grape commences its formation. Basically the vine is drawing its sustenance from the soil. Its roots absorb moisture, minerals, salts and a host of other elements but mostly it is water that passes through the root system up through the body of the vine and into the berry that eventually becomes a fully mature grape.

Nature begins a conversion of some of the water into other chemicals. This is of intense interest to the organic chemist. He can observe a chain of reactions with a fairly rapid exchange of atoms from one molecule to another. Mostly these atoms are carbon, hydrogen, oxygen and phosphorus. Gradually an atomic and molecular chain is formed which consists of six atoms of carbon, twelve of hydrogen and six of oxygen. The atoms are arranged in a certain fashion or form inside this molecule and we know it as glucose or sugar. A particular elaboration of this molecule becomes sucrose or, more particularly, grape sugar. This is the material with which the wine chemist is mostly concerned.

One series of cycles has been completed with the formation of the sugar and a second series is about to begin which will result in the formation of alcohol. Nature, however, has not yet completed its work.

The third series of cycles will break down the alcohol and in almost a reverse action, convert it back to the water from which it originally began and thus we have a complete turn of the wheel.

During the course of all this action a number of other compounds are formed and very many chemical elements have been drawn into the operation. By-products are inevitable in the series and the wine chemist is just as much interested in these as he is with the main conversion of sugar to ethyl alcohol, also known as *ethanol*.

Fermentation, however, is not only confined to wine making. Any sugar or, for that matter, any starch can be converted to enthanol through the chain of reactions known as fermentation provided that a certain natural aptitude to fermentation has been induced in the starch or sugar in the first place. Thus we have the conversion of grains to maltose or malt and thence by fermentation into beer. We have the conversion of cane sugar into rum and of honey into mead.

In latter days the term *fermentation* has been extended to chemical conversions which do not begin with sugar. For example, a bacterial chain of conversions where one of the products is carbon dioxide is also termed fermentation. This is a logical consequence because the term 'fermentation' comes from the Latin word *fervere* which means to boil and this appearance of boiling is given by the bubbling up caused by the passing of the carbon dioxide gas as it is created by the fermentation process.

Basically the fermentation we are interested in is the

conversion of sucrose to ethanol. A winemaker need only pick ripe grapes, crush them and leave them in any container and he will find that within a few hours fermentation will begin and will carry to the stage where wine is made and all the sugar in his crushed grapes has been used during fermentation to produce almost equal parts of carbon dioxide and ethyl alcohol. Ostensibly, this action was begun by the yeasts which appeared on the surface of the grape skin in the form of a bloom, looking very much like a very fine powder. Wherever grapes are grown this bloom will ultimately appear. It is simply a mass of yeast cells which have accumulated on the skins and have been attracted to the grapes from the surrounding atmosphere.

A yeast cell is a living plant. It belongs to the fungus family and in many ways is similar to mould which is another branch of this family. It is probably the simplest form of life. Each cell consists of a cellular sac containing a substance known as protoplasm. It is sustained and obtains its nourishment by consuming sugar. It multiplies by the very simple process of bulging out of the side of the sac until the bulge buds and separates and the separated bud then is a completely self-contained cell.

In the yeast family there are many thousand different species. The winemaker is most interested in one which is called *saccharomyces cerevisiae ellipsoideus,* which simply means that it is an elliptically-shaped cell depending for its existence upon sugar.

However, it is not the yeast cell which effects fermentation. It is a substance which chemists call *enzyme.* This is a non-living chemical which acts as a catalyst. That is, it is capable of causing a chemical change without suffering any change itself. To add to the complication, every enzyme has a partner which is called a coenzyme. It is necessary for these two to work together in order that the change can be effected. The yeast cell produces many thousands of enzymes, not only of the same type but of different types and it takes twelve enzymes and their partners to bring about the series of changes which we know as fermentation. An enzyme is strictly 'unionist'. It will not, or cannot, do more work than the purpose for which it was made and therefore every change requires these different enzymes.

The first change that takes place is achieved by pushing the arrangement of atoms in the sugar molecule around in such a way that a phosphorus tail is added to one of the oxygen molecules and a new chemical is formed which is known to scientists as fructose – 1,6-diphosphate. This is known as *hexose phosphate* because the form of the carbons in the unit is that of a six point chain.

The next reaction splits this six carbon chain into two three-carbon chains which are now called *triose phosphate*. Each of these chains is a different laboratory chemical which can be converted one into the other by the action of an enzyme called an *isomerase*. The isomerase is simply an enzyme which converts an isomer. (An isomer, incidentally, is simply a compound or molecule of a certain composition which is part of a group of molecules having the same percentage composition, that is, having the same number and type of atoms but which shows different properties from the other members of the group.)

Then a series of reaction steps take place, each being evolved by its own enzyme and eventually we find that there are two molecules of the substance known in a laboratory as *pyruvic acid*. Pyruvic acid is written chemically thus: $CH_3-CO-COOH$, which as you can see means that there are three carbon atoms, four hydrogen atoms and three oxygen atoms, all arranged in a particular pattern within each molecule.

The next conversion results in the loss of one molecule of carbon dioxide and we now arrive at a substance written as CH_3CHO. This is known as *acetaldehyde*. Carbon dioxide, of course is CO_2 which means that the pyruvic acid has lost one atom of carbon and two of oxygen. This escaping carbon dioxide is one of the major products of fermentation and as it escapes in the form of gas it bubbles through the fermenting liquid and gives that typical appearance so similar to boiling water.

During all these series of reactions there are a number

of side reactions taking place. For example, there is the formation of a complex chemical known as *adenosine triphosphate,* usually abbreviated A.T.P. During the series of reactions hydrogen is transferred to a coenzyme carrier and two new molecules of A.T.P. are formed for each three carbon unit. The hydrogen transferred to the coenzyme carrier is added to the acetaldehyde and this final reaction is written chemically thus: $CH_3CHO + H_2$ to CH_3CH_2OH. This is known as ethanol or, if you like, ethyl alcohol.

As we have seen in the making of flor sherry the process is reversible and we can produce acetaldehyde from ethanol.

Side Effects of Fermentation

All these reactions may seem a bit complicated but it does explain the origin of the major products of alcoholic fermentation. It also explains the presence of at least small amounts of many of the intermediate compounds in the sequence such as, for example, acetaldehyde and pyruvic acid. Acetaldehyde reacts with sulphur dioxide or rather the bisulphite ion in solution to form an addition product which cannot be reduced to ethanol by the coenzyme hydrogen carrier system. (An ion is only another type of compound. That is it is an atom charged with electricity, the compound being atom plus electricity.) Now if we have a solution of sulphur dioxide which has been subject to an electrical charge in the solution we will find these charged atoms and the solution is known then as an ionized solution. That is the charged atoms drift apart from the other atoms in their respective molecules.

The hydrogen is diverted under this condition to produce *glycerol.* Glycerol is a slightly sweet substance and may contribute to the viscosity and apparent body of some wines.

Higher alcohols (sometimes called fusel oils) occur in fermented beverages. A higher alcohol is simply one that has more than the two carbon atoms which we saw in ethyl alcohol. Thus we have the five-carbon amyl alcohol, the four-carbon butanol and the three-carbon propanol.

As we have seen, the grape berry contains sugars, acids, pigments, tannins and odorous compounds. When ethanol is formed it acts as a solvent and taps these elements from the skins and seeds when they might otherwise not have yielded them. Some yeast cells disintegrate and they contribute their soluble constituents to the newly made wine. 'Therefore the composition of wine may be effected by the grape, by the direct and indirect reactions of alcohol fermentation on grape must, by yeast cell breakdown products, by activity of other micro organisms and by reactions during processing.'*

---

*M. A. Amerine and V. L. Singlet, *Wine*.

23 BRANDY

BRANDY is a liquid distilled from wine in such a way that some of the flavour of the grape is retained.

Distillation
The distillation of any fermented beverage is accomplished by means of a 'still'. The objects of the 'distiller' are to separate the alcohol contained in the fermented material from other elements such as water and non-vaporous materials. He desires, nevertheless, to retain so much of the flavouring element as will enable one to recognize the distillate as having been derived from grapes, grain,

molasses or whatever was the original ferment.

If his final distillation is almost pure ethyl alcohol or about 95 per cent alcohol, which is as close to pure alcohol as he can arrive without the addition of certain chemicals which will deprive the distillate of water, he has arrived at a neutral spirit. This has no flavour or smell of any kind except the faint smell of ethanol (ethyl alcohol).

Distillation is accomplished by heating the original mixture of alcohol and water, by leading the vapours so created through a 'condensor' and by capturing the condensed liquid or 'distillate'.

Distillation is based on the chemical properties of alcohol to vaporize at 78°C and of water at 100°C. The principle is evolved that if a mixture of water and alcohol is boiled the resultant distillate will contain a higher percentage of alcohol than the original liquid.

During distillation various lower alcohols will vaporize at various temperatures. Not all of these are pleasant. Some are harsh and evil smelling. However, most of these undesirable elements are vaporized either during the first heating of the original liquid or are released when the main body of the alcohol has been extracted. They are called, therefore, heads (or foreshots) and tails. The object of the distiller is to obtain a clean flavoured spirit free from these unpleasant flavourings while still retaining a pleasant remembrance of the original ferment.

THE POT STILL
This is a 'kettle' or container, usually of copper into which the distiller places all the fermented material he wishes to distil at one time. It can be heated by a fire underneath or by steam coils placed inside. A 'spout' leads away to a condensor which consists of a series of coiled tubes cooled down by brine or some other liquid. The condensed liquid drips down the tubes into another container.

The brandy distiller is anxious to eliminate all of the harsher elements which 'come over' in distilling and will, therefore, separate the 'heads' and 'tails' from the 'heart' of the distillation.

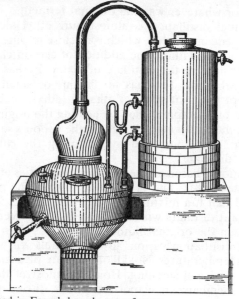

Pot still used in French brandy manufacture.

Applying the principle above that there is more alcohol in the distillate than in the original liquid he may distil twice in his pot still to get a cleaner and stronger brandy.

The quantity of volatile acids in the wine, the duration of the distillation and the total acidity of the wine affect the composition of the distillate. Brandies distilled slowly are found to be richer in esters than those distilled rapidly.

THE CONTINUOUS STILL

Applying this same principle again, it is obvious that if we could build a still whereby we could vaporize an alcoholic liquid, condense it and vaporize it again, and so on continuously, our vapours would be getting richer and richer in alcohol. Eventually, we should arrive at a vapour which was over 90 per cent alcohol.

The continuous still does just this. The wine is introduced low down in the still on to a plate. The plate is heated

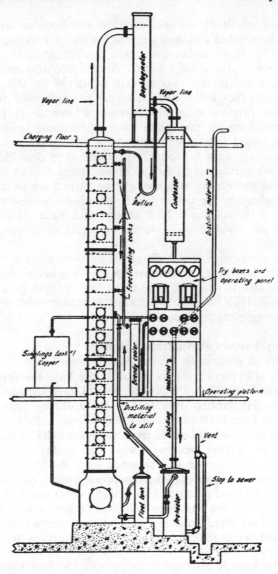

Diagram of a 'patent' or 'continuous' still.

and the resultant vapours pass up a column to another plate perforated with holes through which the vapours can pass. 'Bubbles' on the plate will enable liquid to collect on it while still allowing through the alcohol containing steam. Some of the vapours will condense on this plate. Naturally, they will contain a higher percentage of alcohol than the original wine introduced at a lower level. Liquid will build up on this plate until it overflows and some of the liquid falls downward. As it flows down it comes into contact with heated vapours and is re-distilled, this time, of course, at a higher alcoholic strength than before.

These re-distilled vapours will be carried up to a plate still higher up the column and the whole process begins again. If the column is high enough and there are enough plates the distiller will eventually arrive at almost pure alcohol.

The spirit with this high alcoholic content, will not be brandy. However, if the distiller can tap each plate, he will be able to draw off a liquid at any strength he desires and will thus be able to obtain a brandy with all the flavouring elements necessary.

Quality Factors of Australian Brandy

Quality in Australian brandy is determined by

1. THE MATERIAL USED. Wine is the base material for the brandy distiller. Obviously, he will have various types of material handed over to him for distilling. Some will be made from high quality grapes usually used for beverage wines; some will be made from grapes usually considered poor for making beverage wine but quite suitable for brandy; again, some will be made from the leached skins and pips after pressing or from pressed wine, or from the 'marc', the hard pressed skins and pips after every remaining drop of wine has been extracted; others again will be made from dried fruit rejected by the exporters or from acetified wine rejected by the winemakers as unfit for drinking.

Some brandy distillers consider that the best brandy is made from grapes grown in 'dry' areas, for example, the pedro or grenache. Others consider that grapes grown in the irrigation areas are satisfactory, for example, doradillo and sultana. Doradillo is a most suitable brandy grape in any case. It is used in France for high class brandies, and by the Nathan and Wyeth-Remy Martin group for making brandy at Avoca in Victoria.

Pomace, marc, acetified wine or leachings are not considered good materials from which to make brandy although, naturally, they are quite good for making neutral spirit. This latter liquid is distilled to such a high strength that no flavour remains and it is used for fortifying sweet wines or sherry.

As the bulk of Australia's brandy comes from the Murray Valley, there is no doubt that irrigated grapes such as doradillo are used extensively in our brandy making. Doradillo can be grown at the rate of sixteen tons to the acre as against about two tons to the acre of, say, pedro, in a dry area. It is only natural, too, that brandy distillers in a dry area bring the grapes from the irrigated areas to their plants.

2. THE SKILL OF THE DISTILLER. The composition of brandy, provided a good base material is used, is almost entirely the result of operation of the still. The distiller must be well trained; he must know his still thoroughly, he must know what he wants to achieve and how to achieve it.

It is easy to imagine all the variables in distilling – the temperature at which it is run, the rate at which the still is heated, the times at which heads and tails are cut out. If it is a continuous still, the imponderables are innumerable – the rate of supply of steam, the rate of feed of the wine, the plate at which the feed enters, the temperature of the incoming wine, the plate which is tapped and so many other factors that only a technician could comprehend.

3. THE TYPE OF STILL. This is perhaps only a matter of opinion, subsidiary to the question of a skilled operator. In Australia, most distillers consider that a pot still makes the best brandy. In addition there are numerous types of continuous or 'patent' stills each with its particular merits.

4. CORRECT TYPE OF OAK FOR AGEING. Not every oak is suitable timber for a brandy cask. Some oak casks impart an unpleasant flavour to the spirit. A good cask will age it gently and impart some of its colour and pleasant flavour to it.

5. TIME OF AGEING. Australian brandy must by law be aged for a minimum of two years in wood. Normally the longer it is in cask, the better it is.

6. BLENDING. Brandy must be blended to a pre-determined standard. A good blender will use brandies from different vats and of different ages to arrive at a spirit which is the most pleasant and aromatic and, just as important, is the same always, year in and year out.

Kinds of Australian Brandy

Australian brandy, without any additions, is a good clean spirit, smelling, after two years, of the fresh strong aroma of grapes.

As it grows older it acquires an odour which is peculiar to old brandy alone, but it is still clean and refreshing to the sensory organs of taste and smell.

It is unlike any other brandy in the world. There is no perfume that is not of the grape. Compared to French brandy, it lacks bouquet at first but on closer examination you may perceive that it has a clarity of aroma which is clear cut and appealing because of its very simplicity.

Its flavour is strong and clean.

Some of our makers add vanilla and other flavouring elements to their brandy to give it a 'liqueur-like' effect. This type of brandy to me is inferior.

The addition of sugar is a different thing. Not everybody likes a perfectly dry spirit. It cleanses the palate, but as a drink leaves little satisfaction. The amount of sugar a brandy contains depends on the maker. Only cane sugar is used in Australia.

Distilleries are operated by all the large companies and by most of the co-operatives, both for the purpose of obtaining neutral spirit for fortifying wines and for making brandy.

All distillation and ageing is under the supervision of the Commonwealth Excise Department and extraordinarily high standards of purity are maintained.

The titles of Australian brandy have little significance. A three star brandy could be anything; so could a 'hospital' brandy. Usually if a spirit is called 'liqueur brandy' it has a little sweetness and some flavouring.

CONCLUSION

ONE often hears the question, 'Are Australian wines as good as European?'

Having drunk hundreds of gallons of Australian and only tens of gallons of European wines, I suppose that I have become partial to Australian wines. On the other hand, the English writer who writes so glowingly of French wines has become just as partial to them for the same reason – he has drunk many times more French wines than those of any other country.

There is certainly a difference between the taste of European wines and Australian. Perhaps the occasional wine drinker would not notice it. Sometimes, when the labels are masked, it is difficult for the experienced drinker to pick the difference. Even the most skilled connoisseurs have sometimes been deceived when a great French wine of some age has been matched against a great Australian wine of similar age and the labels have been concealed.

The best red wines of Bordeaux with their enormous reputations certainly seem to the Australian drinker to have something that his own wines lack. This is, most often, a greater character or a more distinctive finesse. The method of making employed by the chateaux of Bordeaux must have something to do with it. They age their wines for the first three years in new oak casks. This imparts a very striking flavour to the wine. The palate trained to look for this in a first class wine will always appreciate it. To my mind it does not necessarily denote greatness. Wine is a natural product with its own innate tannin and it should not need tannin from the oak to make it better.

Whether it is parochial or not, I do not know, but to me the average Australian table wine is as good to drink as the average wine from any other country. The first class wines need some seeking out but the best of them is remarkably much the same as the best from any other country.

If I lived permanently in England, I am perfectly sure that I should drink French, Italian and Spanish wines. I say this because I know that, being so close to these countries, I would search around France, Italy and Spain and I should be able to find a large number of good and interesting wines. I am certain that I could not have the same success with Australian wines in England.

On the other hand, living in Australia, as I do, I certainly will not bother very much about European wines. In the first place the best are far too expensive and in the second place the wines we import at a reasonable price do not compare favourably with Australian wines at the same price. Being in Australia, I can search around for the very best and know I can get them at not too high a price. I cannot be at all confident that I can do this with European wines.

To put things on a universal basis, if I lived in Brazil, I fancy that I should drink neither European nor Australian wines but only Brazilian wines. Having tasted a few, I could live happily with them. This brings us to the point that, if the wines of a country are good, we grow used to them and have a distinct preference for them.

The English-speaking world, at least, recognizes Bordeaux and Bourgogne as being areas where the finest reds in the world are grown and made. France produces such enormous quantities of wine and it is consumed by so many millions of Frenchmen who take such an avid interest in wine, that it is only logical that over a period of centuries the French should have defined without question what are the best areas.

It is absurd for Australia to contend in the same field. We produce too little wine in comparison. We have so few people interested in first class wines that we cannot expect to have the same consistent flow of first class wine that is enjoyed by the French.

All Australian wines are characterized by a great overall similarity. When tasting a wine with the label masked, the first question we ask ourselves in the matter of origin is, 'Is it Australian or not?' We do not attempt to ask, 'Is this Hunter Valley or Bordeaux?' until later on in our analysis. This first question is usually the easiest to answer.

Except in the case of very old wines which tend all to become alike, Australian wines are very distinct from the wines of other countries.

This 'Australian' character or 'country of origin' similarity extends to all wines – clarets, hocks, ports and sherries. We are able to say first that a sherry or a port is Australian and perhaps only with difficulty discover its locality. Of course, this national similarity is not confined to Australian wines. We could say with equal truth that all French wines taste alike and that it is only with difficulty that we can pick out in what district they were made.

The consistent factor with Australian grapes is that in almost every district they ripen to a high sugar content. This is inclined to leave the wine with a certain amount of residual sugar after fermentation and with a slight lack of acid. To produce a perfect dry wine, grapes must ripen to a nice acidity. That is, the grape must be perfectly ripe without having excessive sugar. A winemaker could, of course, pick his grapes before they are completely ripe. This would give him a smaller amount of sugar but might produce a wine with too much acid. This state of affairs contrasts strongly with conditions in many parts of Europe. Here the difficulty is to get enough sun for the grapes to ripen. Sugar content is inclined to be lacking in the grapes. In the Rhine Valley vineyards it is a matter of 'the higher the sugar content in the grapes, the better the wine.'

Summarily, then, Australian table wines are identified by the fact that they are inclined by their very nature to be fruitier and heavier than most European wines.

Of their quality, it is universally agreed that the average quality wines are comparable with those from any part of the world. With respect to the best, I can say only that we do not produce enough of them.

It is easy to 'knock' current practices in the Wine Industry. Over the last one hundred and fifty years writers, including journalists in the daily papers, have attacked our nomenclature. We can find fault with the deceptions that are carried out in labelling wines, with the blending of wines purporting to come from certain areas. We may dislike the strict categorization by judges at wine shows of our wines into certain 'styles'. We can certainly criticize false labelling regarding grape variety and district of origin.

In spite of all this it is comforting to know that the men who run the industry from the top executives in the 'giant' companies to the smallest licensed grocer are, almost without exception, men of utmost integrity and sincerity.

The industry has progressed enormously, in the twenty-five years since the end of the Second World War and has incorporated many ideas in nomenclature and labelling that have been suggested even by men outside the trade.

Anomalies and unintelligent incongruities must exist in any industry and the wine industry suffers from these defects as much as the others.

I know there is nothing more irritating than the question, 'Why don't you call your wines after Australian districts rather than after European places?' Only those who have had this question thrown at them a thousand times know the difficulties that are involved in this problem.

And there are dozens of questions similar to this that the trade has hurled at it every day which are almost as irritating because they usually come from people who think they have hit on some brilliant new idea, not realizing that the problems have been passed around and discussed and various solutions proposed over many years. The policy the industry has adopted is 'hasten slowly'.

As compared with almost every other wine producing country, our wine industry is amazingly small.

The fact that it has progressed so far with so small a population is due to the energy, drive and intelligence of our leading wine men. I have every confidence that future progress will be as satisfactory.

The history of wine in Australia can be depicted graphically as a series of regular curves where the difference between the crest and the succeeding trough is incredibly great. We do not seem to have arrived at any state of equilibrium. We are forever planting vineyards in one generation and pulling them out in the next.

In the last five years enormous planting has gone on in the Hunter Valley, Victoria and South Australia. Increase in wine consumption in this period has been at the rate of .15 gallon per head per year. It would seem more than likely that we can look forward to a period of great prosperity and stability in the wine industry and I do dislike sounding any note of pessimism by expressing a hope that we do not have a similar catastrophe as we have had so often in the past where production has become far greater than consumption and that we have the same pitiful ripping out of vines as we have had before. Everything looks rosy for the future and I, for one, am utterly confident that nothing will go wrong. I feel that Australians will continue to drink more and more wine, both individually and as a group of civilized people. More and more of us, in other words, will give up drinking beer and spirits in order to enjoy the product of the grape.

INDEX

292

296